WAR AND S

When is it right to go to war? The most persuasive answer to this question has always been 'in self-defense'. In a penetrating new analysis, bringing together moral philosophy, political science, and law, David Rodin argues that this answer is not all it seems. The simple analogy between self-defense and national-defense—between the individual and the state—needs to be fundamentally rethought.

This book proposes a comprehensive new view of the right of self-defense which resolves many of the perplexing questions that have dogged both jurists and moral philosophers. By applying this theory to international relations, Rodin produces a far-reaching critique of the canonical Just War Theory.

Wars of national-defense cannot be justified reductively as 'collective self-defense'. Nor can they be explained in terms of a state-held right analogous to the right of personal self-defense. A line of argument that has dominated moral and legal thinking about war for over 1,500 years is shown to be bankrupt. This conclusion points the way to what must surely be one of the most significant challenges of the twenty-first century; the development of a new framework for the regulation of international violence, one which appropriately balances the rights and obligations of states, communities, and individuals.

War and Self-Defense

David Rodin

CLARENDON PRESS · OXFORD

OXFORD

UNIVERSITY PRESS

Great Clarendon Street, Oxford OX2 6DP

Oxford University Press is a department of the University of Oxford.
It furthers the University's objective of excellence in research, scholarship,
and education by publishing worldwide in

Oxford New York

Auckland Cape Town Dar es Salaam Hong Kong Karachi Kuala Lumpur
Madrid Melbourne Mexico City Nairobi New Delhi Shanghai Taipei Toronto

With offices in

Argentina Austria Brazil Chile Czech Republic France Greece
Guatemala Hungary Italy Japan South Korea Poland Portugal
Singapore Switzerland Thailand Turkey Ukraine Vietnam

Oxford is a registered trade mark of Oxford University Press
in the UK and in certain other countries

Published in the United States
by Oxford University Press Inc., New York

British Library Cataloguing in Publication Data

Data available

Library of Congress Cataloging in Publication Data
Rodin, David.
War and self-defense / David Rodin.
p. cm.
Includes bibliographical references.
1. Self-defense (International law) 2. War (International law) I. Title.
KZ4043 .R63 2002 341.6–dc21 2002070184

ISBN 0-19-925774-4
ISBN 0-19-927541-6 (pbk)

3 5 7 9 10 8 6 4 2

Typeset by Kolam Information Services Pvt. Ltd., Pondicherry, India
Printed in Great Britain on acid-free paper by
Biddles Ltd., King's Lynn, Norfolk

For Nina,
Always a source of peace.

Let everyone, then, who thinks with pain on the evils of war, so horrible, so ruthless, acknowledge that this is misery and if any one either endures or thinks of them without mental pain, this is a more miserable plight still, for he thinks himself happy because he has lost human feeling.

St Augustine of Hippo, *The City of God*, 19.7

The greatest challenge for the human race, which nature compels it to meet, is to attain a universal civic society based on the rule of law.

Immanuel Kant, *Idea for a Universal History from a Cosmopolitan Point of View*

Foreword

One of the few moral ideas about warfare that is generally agreed upon is that the use of armed force can be justified in the cause of national self-defense. This aspect of traditional 'Just War' doctrine is widely accepted by public opinion and is enshrined in international law, including the Charter of the United Nations. David Rodin's remarkable and original book mounts a powerful attack on this idea. His method is that of moral comparison. The tradition justifies a right to national self-defense as a parallel to the right of self-defense possessed by an individual person, a right which in certain circumstances can allow the use of lethal force. It is this supposed parallelism—'the domestic analogy', as it is called by Michael Walzer, a defender of the tradition—that Rodin criticizes.

In the first part of his book, he examines the basis of a personal right to self-defense, and carefully identifies conditions in which that right can justify the use of lethal force. In the second part, he argues that these conditions have no sufficient parallel in the national case. One question his argument takes up is whether it is the nation as such or its individual people that are supposed to figure in the analogy. Defenders of the tradition, Rodin points out, have notably disagreed with each other about this, and neither answer, he argues, will deliver what the supposed analogy requires. There is a further question of what is being defended—autonomy? a culture? a way of life? Again, what moral difference will it make if the government which is attacked is at war with some of its own people? There are further arguments based on general matters of fact. For instance, it is true of very many armed conflicts between states that each party can make a case that it is defending itself, or pre-empting aggressive action by the other.

Rodin builds a very powerful case against 'the domestic analogy'. He might be expected to end up with a pacifist conclusion, but he does not do so. Rather, he argues for the possible moral acceptability of armed force brought against states in police actions; though in his view this ultimately calls for the presently Utopian ideal of a universal state.

Although Rodin refers to international law and to historical examples, and he is fully aware of the brutal circumstances of actual life which 'realists' in these matters have in mind, his argument is entirely and professedly a moral one. His question throughout is: how, if at all, can the use of armed force by states be morally justified? And it is in terms of moral justification that the idea of self-defense fails as an answer.

Some readers may question Rodin's concentration on the moral. They (including no doubt the 'realists') will think that morality inevitably comes a distant second in these matters to violent and impassioned human reactions, and (consequently) to politics. 'Méchant animal', Clemenceau memorably said, 'quand on l'attaque, il se défend', and to the extent that people in a community react in anger to what they perceive as an assault 'on us', as they will put it—a reaction shaped, no doubt, by the media, but rarely created by them—moralists, whatever they think of it, should scarcely be surprised. Such reactions have political consequences: these people's government may well have to do something forceful, or it will be replaced, very probably, by one that will.

These very familiar facts do not really stand against Rodin's argument, but rather provide a dark background to it. In fact, the response in these situations is often one of retaliation rather than strictly one of self-defense, and it is often a good question, against whom the retaliation is directed; particularly when, as with the events of 11 September 2001, the actual perpetrators have blown themselves up and they were not the agents of any state. Moreover, the retaliation, however urgent the demand for it, may well have a negative effect on self-defense and security themselves, as with certain actions that Israel has taken against the Palestinian authority. The important points for Rodin's argument, however, are that such reactions are not understood by the people in question or by most sympathetic observers simply as natural responses, but as justified and legitimate; and that the prime form of legitimation, at least to the world at large, is in terms of self-defense. If his argument is correct, it is not merely that the plea of self-defense is, often, a cover for more primitive reactions, but that the plea itself is worthless and cannot cover anything.

It is a question that Rodin himself recognizes, whether things would be better if everyone came to agree with him. Bad moral arguments, after all, may well be replaced not by better moral arguments, but by impatience with any moral arguments at all. David Rodin's book demands serious and uncomfortable thought not only about the specific question of national self-defense and its morality, but about the role of moral ideas in international conflict altogether.

Bernard Williams

Preface

The book before you is perhaps unusual in that it hopes to say something of interest to a number of discrete audiences: moral and political philosophers, international relations theorists, criminal and international lawyers—as well the general reader interested in the problems of war and violence. In part this is a result of my own interest in these various fields. More fundamentally, however, it reflects my belief in the interconnectedness of the issues under consideration. War, aggression, and violence are at once moral, legal, and political problems. Indeed the interplay between these different features is one of their most striking and challenging characteristics. Treating a single aspect of these problems in isolation can be useful in some respects, but it can also lead to sterile and unrealistic results. I believe that the best approach is often one which engages actively with the distinctive characteristics and literature of each facet of these problems.

The connections between law, politics, and morality are evident wherever one begins to think about the problems of war. From the moral point of view, it is a commonplace that, as Immanuel Kant stressed: 'ought implies can'. In other words, what one has a moral obligation to do is limited by what is possible—and this must include what is politically possible—in the circumstances. It follows that the ambitions, structure, and content of an account of international morality must be sensitive to what we know of the political constraints on state behaviour (though this observation is subject to an important proviso that I shall discuss below). On the other hand, what is politically possible in a given circumstance is itself affected by moral considerations. This is particularly true within the western democracies where leaders must justify to, and seek approval from, the public for their foreign policy—a public which is increasingly concerned about issues of justice and morality. So the relationship between moral discourse and politics is complex: one of a dynamic mutual engagement rather than a simple or outright conflict.

In this engagement between politics and morality the position of law, and in particular of international law, is of great importance and interest. International law represents an attempt to implement principles of justice within the sphere of politics. The content of international law is derived from international treaties and from state practice and, furthermore, international law has no reliable independent enforcement mechanisms. It is therefore deeply imbued with the processes of international politics with all the compromise, horse-trading, and bully-tactics that this implies. And yet as an effective moral framework, international law has advanced, unsteadily but unmistakably, during the past century. Though it continues to have many failings, it has also registered many notable achievements. These have included codifying consensus norms on human rights, the use of force by states, the rights of combatants, and many other aspects of international relations, and establishing its organs and mechanisms as the preferred (though by no means exclusive) channels for international action by states.

What is most interesting in this process, for our purposes, is how international law has acted as a dynamic intermediary between the differing and often conflicting demands of morality and politics. The corpus of international law is a living example of the attempt to forge a working compromise between what is desirable and what is possible, and as such it is an indispensable source for anyone interested in the moral problems of international relations. The debt of international law to moral and legal philosophy, in turn, has been substantial and explicit. This was particularly true in the early stages of its development, when, as the Supreme Court of the United States put it, the works of jurists and commentators were resorted to by judicial tribunals 'not for the speculations of their authors concerning what the law ought to be, but for trustworthy evidence of what the law really is'.[1]

In the domestic sphere the relationship between law and philosophical analysis has also been fruitful. Philosophers provide theoretical accounts of legal constructs whose development, particularly in case law, is often piecemeal and fragmentary. Theoretical principles, once made explicit, can act as guides for further codification or even amendment of the law. In the first part of this book I will attempt precisely such a theoretical account of a prominent feature of criminal law: the right of self-defense.

The contribution of domestic law to moral philosophy is equally important, for law provides a rich repository of first-order moral

---

[1] *The Paquete Habana Case*, quoted in Dickinson, E. D., 'The Analogy between Natural Persons and International Persons in the Law of Nations', *Yale Law Journal*, 26 (1917), 564–91, at 565.

assessments or 'moral intuitions' which are the primary data of moral philosophy. As the jurist Sanford Kadish observes: '[In the law] we have a body of formulations that have evolved over time through reflective and tested examination of what we regard as of greater and lesser value and of what we regard as right and wrong'.[2] For all of these reasons criminal and international law will be important and fruitful interlocutors during the course of this investigation.

This being said, it is to the philosopher's tools that I have made greatest recourse in this text. Thus you will find critical analysis of key concepts, the development and assessment of general principles, the exploration of shared moral intuitions, and the attempt to find a satisfactory reflective equilibrium between the two. At all times, however, I have tried to keep firmly in sight the constraints, limitations, and implications entailed by law and by politics. I have also made liberal use of legal and political resources as sources of theory and argument and also as foils to more explicitly philosophical positions. In this way I have tried to produce a lively and provocative text which reflects and balances the insights of these different theoretical perspectives.

Connected with the relationship between morality, law, and politics is the distinction between realist and idealist theories of international relations. My argument will clearly be characterized as idealist, in the sense that it is committed to the existence of objective moral norms and to the possibility of their operation within international relations.[3] However, I believe the best and most resilient kind of idealism is one which grows out of a solid and realistic appreciation of the operation of international politics (see on this point discussion in Chapter 9).

At times, however, I have developed arguments which may appear to be so idealistic that they could have no possible application to the world as it really is. For example in Chapter 8 I give a sympathetic account of arguments for a minimal form of a universal or global state. Clearly such a proposal has almost no chance of implementa-

---

[2] Kadish, S. H., 'Respect for Life and Regard for Rights in the Criminal Law', *California Law Review*, 64/4 (1976), 871–901, at 872.

[3] The term 'idealism' has a very different meaning within international relations to its traditional meaning in philosophy where it typically refers to a denial of 'objective' or 'externalist' theories. In international relations, the term refers to a theory which holds that state behaviour is, or ought to be, influenced by moral considerations.

tion given current political realities. Why do such positions merit consideration? There are several reasons. The first is theoretical. If certain highly idealistic conclusions can be shown to derive from positions to which we are now committed, this may tell us something about those commitments and how we might wish to interpret (or reinterpret) them.

Secondly, there is an important role for moral argumentation which need not, and indeed ought not, be constrained by the possibilities imposed by local political conditions. This is what I call 'aspirational moral argument'. By this I mean an argument which considers not simply what is most desirable given current constraints, but rather posits wholly alternative, and perhaps revolutionary, configurations of social, political, and legal realities. I take it that part of the task of the moral philosopher is to broaden the universe of imaginative possibility by introducing and exploring alternative visions of moral reality. The purpose of such visions is to help identify long-term moral objectives rather than immediate directives. Indeed, the most significant part of moral advancement often consists not so much in identifying right and wrong acts, or good and bad states of affairs, but in helping to realize the conditions whereby humans are enabled to behave morally and well. Nowhere is this more true than in the sphere of international relations.

The chances of realizing such moral visions can often seem impossibly remote, yet occasionally, through a confluence of intellectual, social, and political forces, remarkable things are achieved. The abolition of slavery must once have seemed a hopelessly idealistic proposition; an almost inconceivable development given prevailing political realities. Its realization in the western world has been one of the great examples of a genuine moral revolution, overturning deeply imbedded institutions and practices. While not denying that the victory against slavery reflected political, economic, and even military developments, the intellectual efforts of John Stuart Mill, Thomas Macaulay, William Wilberforce, and others in formulating the arguments and envisioning new moral possibilities cannot be ignored. The abolition of slavery is one case which should be borne in mind when philosophers make their case for 'thinking the unthinkable'.

This book has grown out of research conducted for my B.Phil. and doctorate at Oxford University. I have worked on these projects with three 'Johns' of very different philosophical convictions: John Finnis, John Lucas, and Jonathan Glover. I would like to express my appreciation and gratitude to each of them. I am particularly indebted to Jonathan Glover who has helped me greatly in crystallizing my thoughts into concrete arguments. I would like to thank Bernard Williams whose ongoing help, support, and razor-sharp criticisms have been invaluable to me. Sue Uniacke read an early version of Part I and made many valuable comments. Danesh Sarooshi and Gerry Simpson read and made comments on the chapter on international law. I have benefited deeply from innumerable conversations with my friend Pierre Van-Hoeylandt, my teacher and friend Ben Gibbs, and my father Sam Rodin. The cover design and artwork have been provided by my talented wife, Nina.

I have several institutional debts to recognize. This manuscript was completed during my tenure as Stipendiary Junior Research Fellow at Wolfson College, Oxford. I also worked on the project during a visiting fellowship at the Australian National University (ANU), funded by the New Zealand Public Advisory Committee on Disarmament and Arms Control. I would like to express my appreciation to the Committee for their support and to Wolfson and the ANU for providing convivial and stimulating working environments. I must also express my sincere appreciation to the Rhodes Trust for the scholarship which first enabled me to embark on this journey.

Finally I would like to take this opportunity to thank the American Philosophical Association for awarding this work the Frank Chapman Sharp Memorial Prize for the best unpublished essay or monograph on issues in war and peace.

D. R.
Oxford

Contents

Part II: National-Defense

Introduction

Of all the problems of moral and political philosophy there are few as difficult or as urgent as those concerning war, aggression, and violence. They are, of course, very old problems but there are two features which make them particularly challenging. The first is that they concern what we might call 'morality *in extremis*'. In war and interpersonal violence we find humans at our most fearful, most vulnerable, and also most destructive. Because of this, the issues they raise are among the most intense, difficult, disturbing, and yet characteristically human of all moral problems. Secondly, the character and nature of these problems changes with evolving historical circumstance. This fact compels us to continually re-evaluate the principles and sometimes the very concepts of our moral assessment.

At the present time the legal and moral norms of war are under extraordinary strain. The strain has come from developments in many different areas: from new weapons and strategic realities (such as the development of terrorism and guerrilla warfare); from new forms of political association (such as the European Union) and in some cases disassociation (failed states and fragmenting multinational states); and from new moral and political priorities (such as the spectacular rise in the conception of universal human rights). All of these developments raise fundamental moral and legal questions. Among them are questions about the nature of responsibility and moral agency, the status and foundation of human and community rights, and the relationship between individual and state.

This book is an attempt to explore our moral response to war and aggression through the lens of a single idea—that of self-defense. In so doing I will hope to provide a little forward illumination as to how some of these issues might productively be tackled in the twenty-first century.

I have chosen to focus on self-defense for a number of reasons. The first is a deep dissatisfaction with the way the notion of self-defense is applied in international law and international ethics. Self-defense is first and foremost a feature of personal morality and criminal codes, but it has become one of the most important elements in our thinking about the rights and wrongs of international violence. Thus self-defense is central to modern international law: it is currently the sole legal justification for the use of force by states without the authorization of the United Nations. Self-defense is also one of the lynchpins of international law's intellectual progenitor, the Just War Theory. Despite its medieval origins the Just War Theory is overwhelmingly the dominant model for the moral assessment of political violence in the western tradition. Any attempt to provide a more effective normative framework for dealing with international violence must come to terms with what works—and what does not—within this theory. It shall be my contention that a great deal in the theory and law of national self-defense does not work.

Secondly, the moral phenomenon of self-defense is highly interesting and problematic in its own right. That this is so is not immediately apparent. Self-defense is one of those deceptive conceptions that at first blush seems entirely transparent. What could be more obvious than the fact that a person who is attacked has the right to kill their attacker if this is necessary to preserve their own life? But the conception of self-defense in fact presents many difficult and perplexing problems. They are theoretical problems but they bear directly on the concrete operation of the right in criminal law. Self-defense is difficult because it stands at the centre of a tension between one of the most basic of all moral prohibitions (that against violence and the taking of human life) and an explicit and often surprising exception to that very prohibition. There are very few circumstances in which self-preferential killing is morally or legally permitted. Understanding why it is permitted in the case of self-defense is no trivial matter.

In the course of this book I will undertake two basic projects. The first is to provide a robust explanation of defensive rights in their most general form. The second is to determine whether this explanation can be used to ground a right of national self-defense. The two projects are linked by the widespread presupposition that there is a strong explanatory analogy between personal self-defense and national self-defense.

My conclusion will be that a coherent explanatory account of self-defense can be constructed around the idea of personal rights, but that the attempt to build a justification for war on the conception of self-defense faces tremendous difficulties and ultimately fails. Because self-defense is the centrepiece of the modern *jus ad bellum* (the rules specifying the conditions for a just war) this result has significant consequences for the entire enterprise of normative international relations.

The argument

The idea that there exists a right of national self-defense, correlate with the right of personal self-defense, is so old and so entrenched that these conclusions will certainly be controversial. It may help to indicate here a little of the structure and methodology of my argument. The argument has a two-part structure, the first is constructive and explanatory in mode, the second, is probing, questioning, and ultimately sceptical.

Part I concerns the search for an explanation of the right of self-defense. By explanation here, I mean an account which shows why the right of self-defense has normative force, and why it is subject to the particular limitations, restrictions, and permissions that it is. An explanation of a moral concept is thus importantly different from conceptual analysis. While analysis attempts to discern the internal structure of an idea and its proper range of reference, an explanation goes further. It helps us understand the grounding and operation of a moral concept by showing how it is related to, and draws normative support from, other relevant features of our legal, moral, and conceptual framework.

To develop such an explanation of self-defense it is necessary first to understand the broad framework ideas relevant to this part of our moral universe. These are ideas such as obligation, exculpation, responsibility, and rights. To this end more primitive normative notions such as claim, duty, liberty, justification, and excuse are identified and explored. From these basic building blocks it is possible to construct a working model of defensive rights in their most general form (of which the right of personal self-defense is but one species). The model of defensive rights is intended to be a sort of road map to the class of rights, showing what its basic elements are, and how they are related to one another. This model is used to explain some of the most important limitations which characterize the operation of defensive rights, particularly those of proportionality (the requirement that defensive measures not be out of proportion to the harm averted), necessity (the requirement that defensive measures only be taken if there is no less harmful way to avert the threatened harm), and imminence (the requirement not to engage in defensive measures unless the danger of harm is immediately present). A substantive account of the proportionality requirement is developed and defended.

All of this reveals much about the operation and content of the right of self-defense, but it does not answer the basic question: what is it about situations of self-defense that entitles the victim to act? Why is the victim permitted to kill the aggressor, but not the other way around, even though at the moment of engagement each is a threat to the life of the other? This is a difficult and complex question not least because different theoretical perspectives generate very different and often conflicting answers. Consequentialists have attempted to explain self-defense as a preference for the lesser evil. Rights theorists have sought to explain why the aggressor no longer possesses the right not to be killed, often by appealing to a theory of forfeiture. Christian thinkers have employed a doctrine of 'double effect'.[1] A number of recent theorists have appealed to notions of necessity and 'forced choice'. Each account answers to different sets of intuitions and gives very different answers to many important questions about the operation of the right. For example, is it permissible to defend oneself against non-culpable aggressors (children, the insane)? Is there a duty to retreat before killing in self-defense? What is the nature of the proportionality requirement? Is there a limit to the number of aggressors one may permissibly kill in self-defense? While each approach is in certain respects persuasive, each too has characteristic and debilitating difficulties. In my view there is currently no single account which provides a satisfactory treatment of the right of self-defense.

The last chapter of Part I is devoted to the development of a more adequate grounding for this right. The account I propose sees self-defense as arising most basically from the interaction of the rights of agents in situations of conflict. By examining basic principles and

---

[1] The double effect doctrine is prominent in Catholic moral philosophy. It is premised on the assumption that no private person may ever intentionally take human life. The right to use defensive force which results in the death of an aggressor is explained by a distinction between intended actions, and foreseeable (but unintended) side-effects. It is permissible, on this view, to defend one's life with force which one foresees will result in the death of the aggressor, provided that one does not intend the aggressor's death either as a means or as an end. I do not intend to deal directly with the double effect account of self-defense. I assume that it can sometimes be permissible to intentionally kill in defence of one's life. For good discussions of the doctrine see Anscombe, G. E. M., 'War and Murder', in Rachels, J. (ed), *Moral Problems*, New York: Harper Collins, 1979; Foot, P., 'The Problem of Abortion and the Doctrine of the Double Effect', in *Virtues and Vices*, Oxford: Basil Blackwell, 1978; Uniacke, S., *Permissible Killing, The Self-Defence Justification of Homicide*, Cambridge: Cambridge University Press, 1994, ch. 4; Glover, J., *Causing Death and Saving Lives*, New York: Penguin Books, 1977, ch. 6.

key intuitions concerning the status and operation of human rights we can gain an understanding of why, at the critical moment, the aggressor fails to possess the right to life and the defender possesses the right to kill. The explanation invokes the fault of the aggressor and innocence of the defender for the attack as well as observations about the reciprocity of moral obligation. It is an account which gives primacy to notions of respect for persons over utility, and to the notions of responsibility over diminished responsibility and excuse. The account is intended to be both explanatory and maximally (though not perfectly) consistent with our pre-theoretical intuitions.

With the explanation of defensive rights in hand we are able to examine the right of national self-defense in light of this. The idea of an explanatory analogy between persons and states is one of the oldest and most pervasive images of political philosophy and international law. Since at least the early Middle Ages there has been a persistent assumption that the right of states to engage in defensive war is intimately connected with the right of personal self-defense in such a way that personal self-defense explains or lends justificatory support to the right of national self-defense. As one modern commentator put it: 'The notions of self-defence and of just war are commonly linked: just wars are said to be defensive wars, and the justice of defensive wars is inferred from the right of personal self-defence'.[2]

I believe that the view which sees a moral connection of this kind between the right of personal self-defense and national self-defense is mistaken. I develop an argument to show that the right of national self-defense cannot be explained in terms of personal self-defense. In Part I the argument proceeds from basic moral considerations and builds towards a detailed understanding of the content and operation of the right of self-defense. In Part II the methodology is reversed—we start from a pre-existing conception of national self-defense and work backwards to determine whether it can be given an appropriate moral grounding in more basic considerations. In order that the right can be given the strongest possible hearing, it is important that we start from a characterization which is broadly based and plausible. For this reason our starting point will be the right of self-defense as it is defined in modern international law.

---

[2] Lackey, D., *The Ethics of War and Peace*, Englewood Cliffs, NJ: Prentice Hall, 1989: 18.

There are two ways in which the argument from self-defense to national-defense might be developed. The first is to attempt to understand national self-defense as a special application of the right of personal self-defense. Thus it is often said that national-defense is the 'collective form' of personal self-defense. I call such an account the 'reductive strategy'. The second is to take seriously the notion of an analogy and to provide an account of national self-defense as a state-held right analogous to the personal right of self-defense. I call this the 'analogical strategy'. Both strategies fail. The reasons for their failure are complex and take us into substantive questions of political philosophy. A large part of the reason, however, stems from what we may call 'the two levels of war'. War can at once be viewed as a relation between persons and as a relation between states or other collective entities. Every military action is ascribable to some kind of collective entity, but it is at the same time constituted by actions ascribable to particular persons. Yet both sets of entities—the collective and the individual—are conceived as moral agents, the bearers of rights and the subjects of duties. Moral assessment of acts of war requires, therefore, a dual level of analysis which confounds the simple attempt to model the rights of states on the rights of persons.

There is no analogy between personal and national self-defense, at least not one capable of providing a normative foundation for the right as it has historically been understood in international law and the Just War Theory. In Chapter 8 I develop the argument by examining the related issues of international punishment and law enforcement. I argue for three seemingly counter-intuitive conclusions. First, soldiers cannot be exempted of responsibility for their involvement in an unjust war. Secondly, independently acting states are not able to engage in wars of punishment, for punishment requires an authority to punish which is absent in the state at war. Thirdly, there is a powerful case for a minimal universal state implicit within the social contract theory of political philosophy. This argument is explored through the writings of two of the greatest social contract theorists: Hobbes and Kant.

What is required is a rethinking of some of the most basic moral and legal categories of international relations. This project will have to undertake the task of both connecting and balancing the rights of states with the rights of individual persons in alternative, finer, and more appropriate ways than at present. It is an immense and difficult task which must fully engage the resources of law, politics, political philosophy, ethics, and many other social sciences. But it is one whose prosecution could hardly be more urgent.

The status of moral claims

Before commencing with the argument, I would like to make some remarks about the nature of the claims that I shall be making in the course of this book. My goal is to criticize and clarify our ethical thinking about defensive rights and war, and to help identify the appropriate normative stance on international ethics. The end point of this enquiry is a set of claims about permissibility and impermissibility, justice, rights, and duties. What, then, is the basis for the assertion of these claims?

They are based on a process of critical reflection upon conventional moral judgements, philosophical argumentation, and criminal and international law. I take these conventional, philosophical, and legal judgements to be evidence for a system of norms that we might call our 'common morality'. The common morality is conceived as a system of shared norms which forms for us a recognizable 'moral world' which we inhabit and which guides our moral responses.

There are many problematic questions that can rightly be raised about the notion of a common morality. First, does a shared conception of morality exist? In a pluralist world, can such a notion be employed with any plausibility? Secondly, if a shared set of norms can be identified, is it coherent and internally consistent to a sufficient degree to make the kind of exploratory project that I am attempting possible? Thirdly, can the common morality be given an adequate philosophical foundation when challenged by competing meta-ethical or first-order theories such as emotivism, ethical scepticism, or Nietzschian immoralism?

These are serious and difficult questions, and though I do not intend to provide comprehensive answers to them here, I would like to say a few words to clarify the position that my argument will assume with respect to them. Taking the questions in turn, I fully acknowledge that the system of common morality appealed to in this work is historically and culturally specific. By this I mean that it comprises a system of ethical thought that has developed within what may broadly be termed 'western civilization' through, amongst other things, the great monotheistic religious traditions, the legal and jurisprudential tradition, and western philosophical reflection. It would, however, be a mistake to conclude from this, and from the existence of different and divergent moral traditions, that we are thereby committed to some form of ethical relativism. First, it is possible that a system of thought may be true, and hence non-relativistic, even though it has developed within a tradition that is historically and culturally specific. A good deal of difficult argumentative terrain must be crossed in order to arrive at the position of relativism from the brute fact of divergent belief systems. One reason for this is that there are criteria which can credibly be appealed to in making judgements between ethical systems. These criteria will include, for instance, the richness and coherence of the system of norms, the extent to which it is capable of engaging in a useful way with characteristic human problems, and the fineness and appropriateness of the distinctions it is capable of sustaining.

Moreover, though certain elements of what I will appeal to as part of the common morality (arguably even including the conception of 'rights') may be peculiar to the western tradition, there are other moral concepts and judgements which are a good deal more universal. For instance, it seems to be true that almost all cultures at all times have considered manslaughter an event of grave moral significance, such that if one is to intentionally take a human life, some very strong considerations must be provided in its justification. The more we are able to base our reasoning upon these deeper moral responses, the more universally acceptable our conclusions will be.

The second question concerns the coherence of common morality. In one sense, this is precisely the issue that the present work seeks to address. My argument will suggest that certain generally accepted judgements of common morality about the permissibility of a defensive war are, in fact, not consistent with more basic elements of our shared moral outlook, or at least that they fail to be supported by these basic elements in the way they are often thought to be. Clearly then, I do not believe that all our common moral intuitions are consistent and coherent, let alone true. Rather, what moral argument attempts to achieve is to transform our pre-reflective moral responses into a systematic whole that is, to the greatest extent possible, coherent and consistent.

As to the final question, our moral outlook does indeed require a rigorous foundation, but it will not find one here. For obvious reasons, sustained and serious reflection on the question of moral foundations is not possible in a work of this length and scope. As in other areas of intellectual endeavour, first-order enquiry cannot wait for meta-philosophical foundations.

This does not, however, mean that the question of moral foundations can be ignored, for that debate must be in the background of any first-order moral enquiry and will become important at various points in the argument. What is important at the outset is what one assumes a foundation of common morality would look like. It is tempting to think that such a defense could only be achieved by deriving its norms from, and reducing them to, one or another of the classic moral theories—consequentialism, Kantian deontology, Aristotelian virtue ethics—or some other theory. I do not, however, accept this assumption. Not only do I not attempt such a derivation, I do not give my allegiance to any of the standard theories as a working methodology.

The reason for this is that I believe that a moral exploration which has any hope of being true, will have to recognize the force of a number of different theoretical perspectives, in other words a plurality of sources of normativity. Thus, it seems to me absolutely certain that consequentialist considerations sometimes override genuine rights and duties. For instance (affirming a judgement that Kant notoriously denied), it seems to me unquestionably right to intentionally deceive a murderer who enquires where his would-be victim is hiding. On the other hand, it seems to me equally undeniable that rights and duties often stand against and override powerful consequentialist considerations. For example, it would never be right to kill an innocent man in a hospital waiting room if this were the only way to provide organs for transplant into several patients who would otherwise die. These two judgements seem to me as certain as anything can be in ethical enquiry. But to recognize this is to recognize that consequentialism and Kantian absolutism both identify powerful, overlapping, and sometimes conflicting sources of moral obligation. Any moral exploration which is alive and true to our moral experience must acknowledge the force of each, and it must do this even at the cost of admitting conflicting moral judgements and insoluble dilemmas.

To some this will appear an intolerable way of proceeding for it seems to accept a degree of inconsistency and indeterminacy at the very outset of our enquiry, whereas the most fundamental goal of philosophy is consistent and coherent explanation. However, it is difficult to see an acceptable alternative. In the absence of universally persuasive reasons for a particular moral theory, the alternative is to adhere stubbornly to a particular theory in the face of powerful conflicting intuitions. But it seems to me that such an approach can only lead to sterile and unconvincing results which fail to do justice to the richness and complexity of lived moral experience. The approach I will adopt is to explore moral conflicts and tensions, to resolve them where this is possible, and, where it is not possible, to lay bare the contours of conflict, so that we may see it clearly and better understand where its sources lie. To accept this model of ethical enquiry is to accept that there may not always be a clear and determinate answer to the question 'what ought I do?', not because the world fails to contain real and objective values or obligations, but because real values and obligations can arise from different sources and makes claims upon us in different ways.

War and consequentialism

Despite this acknowledgement, it may seem to some readers that I have given short shrift to consequentialism in the construction of my argument. If this is so, it is not because I think that consequentialism fails to identify a valid and powerful set of ethical considerations. It is rather that consequentialism is frequently a deeply disappointing guide on the basic question of the *jus ad bellum* with which we are concerned: 'when, if ever, can it be right to wage war?' The principal reason for this is that the scope of this question is simply too broad to be amenable to the kind of cost/benefit analysis that consequentialism proposes.

To see this we may take for an example the Allies' war against Nazi Germany. Many people would regard this as last century's clearest example of a justified war, yet it is by no means certain that, on purely consequentialist grounds, we should consider the war as justified. The Nazi regime was brutal and aggressive: it systematically murdered approximately 6 million innocent people, and subjected many millions more to a regime of extraordinary moral repugnance. But the war itself cost somewhere in the region of 55 million lives. In addition it made 40 million persons homeless, caused incalculable destruction to the world's cultural and material wealth, and had the after-effect of initiating the Soviet Union's brutal half-century dominion over Eastern Europe. This was an horrific price to pay for stopping Nazi Germany. It is certainly not obvious that on strict consequentialist grounds it was a price worth paying.

Of course we know that Germany would have continued and extended its policies of oppression and genocide had it not been defeated and we may speculate about the number of people who might then have lost their lives. Perhaps the costs of not fighting the war would in the end have been even higher than the costs of fighting. But the point is, 'perhaps' is the best we can say here. Even as a purely historical task, calculating the actual costs of a war has an appalling margin of error. Estimates of the number of victims of the holocaust range from 4 to 6 million, and estimates of the Soviet war casualties alone have ranged from 7 to 50 million persons.[3] As a backward-looking exercise, therefore, calculating the costs of an historical occurrence of the magnitude of the Second World War is unavoidably fraught with obscurity and unknowns. But of course the primary role of a theory of moral evaluation is not backward-looking judgement of past action, but forward-looking assessment of how one ought to act. It is on this count that consequentialism is most disappointing as a moral theory of warfare. For it is clear that almost none of the final consequences of the Second World War could have been reliably predicted in 1939 when the decision to go to war was made. The costs and the benefits of any given war, even in a metric as crude as the number of lives lost and saved, is something which is unavoidably captive to the vagaries of counterfactual history.

There are several reasons why this is the case. The first is simply that wars are hugely complex and dynamic events whose course is determined not only by large numbers of independently and antagonistically acting agents, but also by wholly unpredictable external eventualities, for example the weather. Secondly, wars have a peculiar internal dynamic of their own which often subverts the original objectives and commitments of those who initiate them. Carl Von Clausewitz described the phenomenon of escalation in war whereby each side is compelled by the other to commit ever greater resources in an attempt to grasp victory and avoid defeat.[4] For this reason

---

[3] See Hobsbawn, E., *The Age of Extremes, the Short Twentieth Century 1914–1991*, London: Michael Joseph, 1994, ch. 1; Overy R. (ed.); *The Times Atlas of the Twentieth Century*, London: Times Books, 1996: 102–3.

[4] See Clausewitz, C., *On War*, Howard, M., and Paret, P. (eds.), Princeton: Princeton University Press, 1976, bk. I, ch. 1.

assessments made at the outset of a war of its likely costs and benefits often prove to be wildly inaccurate.

Consequentialism is thus a surprisingly poor guide for assessing the morality of specific wars. As a determinant of general principles on the initiation of warfare it is even worse. It is often supposed that the rule permitting wars of national-defense is justified in an obvious way by the beneficial effects of such a rule in deterring future aggression. In fact this is often no more than a crude speculation based on vague assumptions about human behaviour. The question of what the deterrence effects of a rule permitting wars of self-defense are, and whether such effects outweigh the costs of licensing resort to armed conflict remains untested. On reflection it does not seem that there is any way, even in principle, in which the truth of such generalized principles could be reliably tested.

Consequentialism leaves us in the dark about moral questions of this level of complexity and historical scope. Moreover, there is something slightly unreal about asking questions such as whether fighting Nazi Germany had better consequences than not doing so, which suggests more than simply the impossibility of answering them. For suppose we could somehow answer the question confidently in the affirmative, would this capture what we feel to be morally most important about the Second World War? I believe that few would think so. Given this, it is natural that we look for guidance to other ways of moral thinking, and the related conceptions of rights and justice will be obvious places to begin.

At various points in the argument I invoke 'moral intuitions' in an attempt to show that consequentialism does not always provide a satisfactory explanation of important aspects of common morality. But this procedure requires justification because, for those who adhere to consequentialist theories, one of their most important features is the ability to revise and amend the intuitions of common morality in a systematic way. After all, it may be asked, what is the point of a moral theory if it leaves our ordinary intuitions and prejudices untouched? Thus a dedicated consequentialist could say that if common moral intuitions conflict with consequentialist principles, then so much the worse for moral intuitions.

This is an important response and it cannot be discounted; however, it faces the difficulty experienced acutely by John Stewart

Mill in his defense of utilitarianism.[5] If consequentialism is to be employed as a revisionary principle, then it becomes a question of vital importance what grounds we have for accepting the truth of the principle. Here we face a dilemma. If, as Mill believed, the correctly formulated consequentialist principle is normatively foundational, then it cannot be amenable to proof or justification in the ordinary sense, for the principle is itself the source of all moral derivation. But if the truth of this principle cannot be derived from more basic principles, then we seem forced back upon a reliance on intuitions: either in the sense of appealing to intuitions about the principle's independent plausibility, or appealing to the extent to which it can account for our pre-reflective intuitions. In either case it seems that our acceptance of the principle must rest on intuitions which are not different in kind from the first-order intuitions which the principle seeks to revise. What this means is that we can never make light of overriding first-order intuitions, especially if they are powerful. If an account can be found which accommodates them, this should be counted as a strong reason for its acceptance, and we should make every effort to find such an account before letting them go.

A brief word about my use of terminology before commencing. For the remainder of this text I shall reserve the term 'self-defense' for the right and act of personal self-defense. The right and act of national self-defense shall be referred to as 'national-defense'. Our general question could thus be phrased: can we understand both self-defense and national-defense as legitimate aspects of a single more general phenomenon of legitimate defensive rights? It is to this task that we now turn.

[5] Mill, J. S., *Utilitarianism*, London: Dent, 1972.

Part I
Self-Defense

1

Rights

Self-defense is referred to as a right. Why? What kind of right is it? What is its normative origin? And how is it related to other rights? In this chapter, I shall begin to answer these questions through an enquiry into the logical structure of rights. Such a project will provide a good starting point for the investigation of self-defense for two reasons. First, the notion of a 'right', of which self-defense is thought to be a species, is not immediately transparent. Secondly, from an understanding of the logical structure of rights, we can attempt to identify the structure of defensive rights in their most general form. Such an account has the potential to yield significant rewards.

Hohfeld's building blocks

A pioneer in the theory of rights is the jurist Wesley Newcomb Hohfeld.[1] Though his analysis is developed in the context of legal rights, his framework is, in many respects, relevant to moral rights and will provide a useful starting point for the moral analysis of self-defense. Hohfeld's central contribution was to show that the term 'right' is multiply ambiguous for under that heading trade a number of quite distinct yet related deontic conceptions. Hohfeld believed that these 'jural conceptions' are fundamental in the sense that they are irreducible to more primitive notions. But they could, he thought, be adequately defined through ostension and through identifying their logical relations with one another.

The most intuitive notion with which to commence is that of a duty. A duty is simply an obligation owed by some party to perform or abstain from performing a certain act. However, Hohfeld's treatment of duty differs from the way that term is sometimes used in

---

[1] W. N. Hohfeld's seminal treatise on the logic of rights is *Fundamental Legal Conceptions as Applied in Judicial Reasoning*, Cook, W. W. (ed.), New Haven: Yale University Press, 1919. I am indebted to L. W. Sumner's analysis in the following exposition (see Sumner, L. W., *The Moral Foundation of Rights*, Oxford: Oxford University Press, 1987, ch. 1).

ordinary parlance. We often talk of a duty without identifying a specific party which is its object. A Hohfeldian duty, however, is necessarily relational, in the sense that it always specifies an obligation owed by one party *to* another. It follows that for Hohfeld, a duty has three distinct elements: a subject (the party whose duty it is), a content (what it is his or her duty to do), and an object (the party to whom the duty is owed). This tripartite relationality between subject, object, and content is a feature of all Hohfeld's fundamental conceptions.

An important reason for treating the fundamental normative conceptions as relational in this way, is that it enables us to articulate very fine-grained normative positions. For example, it is only with a relational notion of duty that one can express the fact that I may have a duty to you to perform a certain action, but have no duty towards some other person for the performance of that very same action. The wider case of a universal duty or one with an unspecified object can be generated quite easily by simply iterating the relational duty over the set of all moral or legal agents. Relational normative conceptions, therefore, enable us to construct with the same conceptual tools both what the lawyers call *in personam* and *in rem* claims and obligations.[2]

We are now in a position to introduce the logical relations which may obtain between the different normative conceptions. The relations in question are *jural correlation* and *jural opposition*. Jural correlates are logical equivalents with different subjects. Jural opposites are logical contradictories with the same subject. To illustrate: the correlate of a duty is a claim. Thus, if you are indebted to me, then you have a *duty* to me to pay the specified sum of money. The correlate of this is my *claim* against you that you pay me the money. The claim and the duty are logically equivalent descriptions of the same normative relation. Each describes the relation from a different perspective—that of the subject and object of the duty respectively.

The jural opposite of a claim is a *no-claim* (simply the absence of a claim against a particular party in a particular context). The correlate of a no-claim is a *liberty*.[3] For example, if you have no claim against me that I do the dishes, then I have the liberty with

---

[2] See Waldron, J., *Theories of Rights*, Oxford: Oxford University Press, 1984: 6.

[3] Hohfeld's term here is 'privilege', but I follow standard modern legal and philosophical usage in employing the term 'liberty'.

respect to you, not to do them. My liberty consists simply in the absence of an obligation to you to act otherwise.

The relations between the first four normative conceptions can be represented in a diagram, the rows of which are correlates, and the columns and diagonals of which are opposites (see Fig. 1.1).[4]

One objection which may be raised to this logical scheme questions whether the normative relations inevitably fall into pairs of correlates and opposites. Is it the case, as Hohfeld believes, that duties and claims are 'invariable correlatives'?[5] While it is difficult to imagine a claim without a corresponding duty, there do appear to be circumstances in which there are duties with no attendant claim. For example, it may be the case that we all have a duty to give charity to the needy, but it does not seem to be the case that the needy have a right (claim) to receive it—for charity is precisely a grace.[6] How is it that charity can be a duty if it is also a grace?

The issues raised by examples such as this are not entirely straightforward, but it does seem possible to understand them in such a way that they need not be fatal to Hohfeld's system. The key is to appreciate the distinction between the recipient of the content of a duty on the one hand, and the object of a duty on the other. These two parties need not be identical. For example, if I promise you that

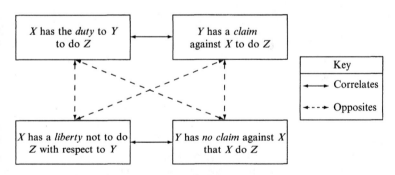

Fig. 1.1. Hohfeld's first-order jural conceptions

[4] Tables 1.1 and 1.2 are adapted from Sumner, *The Moral Foundation of Rights*, 27 and 30.

[5] *Fundamental Legal Conceptions*, 38.

[6] Think of the old joke about the merchant who fails to give his usual donation to the village pauper, explaining that business was very bad this week. 'So?', responds the beggar, 'If you had a bad week, why should I suffer!'

I will take care of your brother then my primary duty is to you, not to your brother even though he will be the recipient of the content of my duty. In this case, you have the claim against me that I give him care, but your brother has no such claim. Given this distinction, it is possible to provide an explanation of the above example. It is plausible that, in this case, the object of one's duty to give charity (and hence the holder of the claim) is not the recipient of the content of the duty, but rather some third party, which may be the community at large or even God. It is thus possible to maintain the integrity of Hohfeld's system without doing violence to our intuitions in these cases.

There is one unusual feature of Hohfeld's conception of a liberty which should be noted before proceeding. In ordinary language, to say that someone has a liberty to do something normally implies that they are free to do that thing or not, as they so choose. However, this is not an implication of Hohfeld's conception of a liberty. Since it is a bare permission to do something, a Hohfeldian liberty is compatible with (indeed it is entailed by) a duty to do that thing. Thus, one may have a Hohfeldian liberty to do a certain thing with respect to a certain party and yet have no liberty *not* to do it. This incongruity between Hohfeld's conception of a liberty and the common usage can be made good if we adopt a terminological suggestion made by Joel Feinberg. He suggests that we refer to the liberty to perform a certain action and the liberty to abstain from performing it as two 'half-liberties', and refer to their conjunction as a 'full liberty'. Thus, the normatively unencumbered choice implied by the common usage of liberty will consist in the conjunction of two logically distinct Hohfeldian (half) liberties.[7]

Claim, duty, liberty, and no-claim form the first-order deontic conceptions of Hohfeld's system. Although less important for our purposes, we should note that standing above these first-order conceptions are a set of four second-order conceptions, so-called because they concern the legal or moral ability and disability to affect changes in first-order normative relations. The second-order relations are *power* (the capacity to alter a first-order normative relation, for example, the capacity to promise is a power to impose

---

[7] Feinberg, J. *Rights, Justice, and the Bounds of Liberty,* Princeton: Princeton University Press, 1980: 157 and 237. Hart draws substantively the same distinction using the terms 'bilateral' and 'unilateral' liberty; *Essays on Bentham,* Oxford: Oxford University Press, 1982: 166–7.

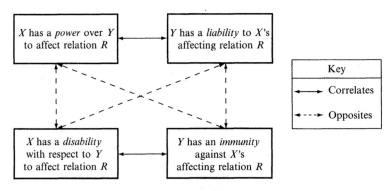

Fig. 1.2.   Hohfeld's second-order jural conceptions
Note: R refers to one of the four first-order normative relations.

a duty on oneself), *liability* (subject to having one's first-order normative relations altered by another party, for example, a criminal may be liable to be fined by a court), *disability* (lacking the power to affect or alter a certain first-order relation), and *immunity* (not being subject to having one's first-order relations altered by a particular party). Whereas the first-order relations concern the deontic modalities (required/forbidden/permissible), the second-order relations, having to do with what is within one's power, invoke the alethic modalities (necessary/impossible/possible). The second-order conceptions can also be represented in a diagram with correlates on the rows and opposites on the columns and diagonals (see Fig. 1.2).

The logical structure of rights

Now that we have the fundamental normative conceptions in hand, we can address the question: what is the relationship between these various normative conceptions and the concept of a right? Of the eight Hohfeldian relations, four in particular have an obvious application to the notion of a right. These are the relations which confer on their subject what we might call a 'normative advantage' in contrast to their correlate term, namely: claims, liberties, powers, and immunities. Whatever rights may be, it seems clear that they are a normative advantage for those who possess them. But does the concept of a right correspond to just one of these relations, or is it rather some complex combination of the four, or do rights consist of a different combination of normative relations in different circumstances?

Hohfeld himself believed that 'a right in the strictest sense' is nothing but a claim, the correlate of a duty.[8] He did, however, admit that judges and lawyers often use the term 'right' to refer to liberties, powers, and immunities, so his restrictive definition of rights as claims is probably best seen as a plea for terminological clarity rather than an attempt to provide a comprehensive analysis of the concept.

Thomas Hobbes also thought that rights, properly understood, are normatively simple, but unlike Hohfeld he argued that they were liberties rather than claims: 'RIGHT, consisteth in a liberty to do, or to forbeare; whereas LAW, determineth, and bindeth to one of them: so that Law and Right, differ as much as Obligation, and Liberty; which in one and the same matter are inconsistent'.[9]

Despite the appealing simplicity of these views, it would seem that any attempt to reduce all rights to a single normative relation will necessarily founder. This is because there are many genuine rights which undeniably consist of a complex of different normative relations. For example, any plausible conception of rights will have to treat property rights as genuine rights. Yet property rights clearly consist of a set of normative advantages including the *liberty* to dispose of one's possession as one sees fit, the *claim* against others that they not do the same, the *power* to transform ownership and restrict or permit use by third parties, and an *immunity* against others exercising such powers against the property holder. To hold a property right is to be the subject of this complex combination of normative relations.

Hobbes's position that rights are simple liberties is, moreover, vulnerable to a deeper objection. Even if we grant that the freedom to 'do or to forbear' is an important feature of many rights, an equally important feature of rights is the protection they afford against interference or maltreatment by others. If this is to be the case, rights must contain claims as well as liberties. There is, indeed, something very peculiar about the way Hobbes refers to the universal liberties possessed by agents in the state of nature as rights. For, in

---

[8] *Fundamental Legal Conceptions*, 36, 71–2.
[9] Hobbes, T., *Leviathan*, Tuck, R. (ed.), Cambridge: Cambridge University Press, 1991, ch. XIV: 91.

what meaningful way can it be said that I have a right to life if this does not include any claims against others, for instance, that they not kill or attack me?

Considerations of this kind have led some writers such as L. W. Sumner to maintain that rights are generally complex packages of Hohfeldian relations which must necessarily include some claims against others.[10] This view is motivated by the plausible assumption that to be effective, even rights principally directed towards protecting liberties require more than the deontically unconstrained choice implicit in a full liberty. They also require duties on the part of others to, *inter alia*, assist with and not to obstruct the exercise of that liberty. For example, my right to vote is, in the first instance a liberty, but it could not be an effective right if it did not contain claims against others, for example, not to obstruct my voting and against certain officials to assist me by providing voting papers.

This analysis is certainly persuasive for many moral and political rights. However, I shall argue below that it is not the case that all rights contain claims against others. For, as we shall see, there are certain simple liberties which are properly described as rights. I shall argue that the right of self-defense and defensive rights more generally are simple Hohfeldian relations which do not contain claims, and yet there are good reasons to include them in the class of genuine rights.

Having a right and being in the right

Before proceeding to this, however, there is an important qualification which must be noted concerning the Hohfeldian system considered as an analysis of moral rights. One might be tempted to adopt the Hohfeldian theory of rights as a mechanism for asserting facts about all-things-considered moral obligation. Thus, if one weighed all relevant ethical considerations in a particular circumstance and determined that X morally ought to do Y to Z, one might assume this to be logically equivalent to a statement about the rights of the persons concerned, in other words to saying that Z has a claim right against X to do Y and X has a duty to Z to do Y. Considered as an analysis of moral rights, however, such a procedure would be

---

[10] Sumner, *The Moral Foundation of Rights*, 35–53.

seriously deficient. The reason for this is that rights are not the whole of morality, and ascribing a right is importantly different to asserting an all-things-considered moral judgement.

Consider the following examples. If someone breaks in the door of your house to rescue a child from poisonous fumes, then he violates your claim-right that he not damage your property. This is the case even though it is obviously right to act as he did in the circumstances. Thus rights may be violated and a right-bearer wronged by an action which, all-things-considered, is the right thing to do. Conversely, a person may act wrongly even though he has an undeniable right to act as he does. For example a rich moneylender who needlessly causes the ruination of a poor family by refusing to extend a loan has the right to act as he does, though his action is, all-things-considered, wrong because it is heartless and uncharitable. It follows that having a right to do X and being in the right in doing X are not logical equivalents.

When we use the vocabulary of rights, we are appealing to a form of moral consideration distinct from, and potentially opposed to, other aspects of morality such as consequentialist considerations (as in the case of breaking the door to rescue the child) and virtues (as in the case of the miserly moneylender). How are we to distinguish a right from other forms of moral consideration?

Although this a complex and difficult question, there are three characteristics which can be readily identified. First, rights have a distinctive stringency, such that they generally override competing moral considerations. Secondly, they have a particular role in standing against, and placing limits upon, what may be called 'goal-based' moralities such as consequentialism. Thirdly, rights are moral considerations which have a unique relation to individual moral subjects.

Ronald Dworkin highlights two of these features in his well-known characterization of rights: 'Rights are best understood as trumps over some background justification for political decisions that states a goal for the community as a whole'.[11] The peculiar stringency of rights is powerfully illustrated by Dworkin's metaphor of a trump card. This metaphor suggests that rights are absolute ethical considerations which always override competing considerations. However, as our two examples above suggest (and Dworkin

---

[11] Dworkin, R., 'Rights as Trumps', in Waldron (ed.), *Theories of Rights*, 153.

himself acknowledges)[12], rights do not always override competing ethical considerations. Sometimes it is wrong, all things considered, to do what one has a right to do, and there may be circumstances in which it is morally right to violate a person's genuine rights. For this reason I prefer to think of rights as analogous, not to a trump card, but to a strong 'breakwater'. On the breakwater view, the function of a right is to erect a normative barrier against the infringement of individual interests and liberties. It is in the nature of this barrier to be sufficient to defeat the great majority of competing claims. However, it is always conceivable that circumstances will arise in which an individual's right is simply overwhelmed by the gravity of competing moral considerations.

The second idea implicit in Dworkin's description of rights is that they function specifically to set limits on what Dworkin has called 'goal-based' moralities. Goal-based moralities are those which are based on some interest of society taken as a whole rather than simply those of individual agents.[13] The most prominent form of goal-based morality is utilitarianism. Dworkin is right to identify this as an important feature of the morality of rights, and indeed the tension between rights and consequentialist considerations is one of the most important in moral theory. However, as the example of the miserly moneylender demonstrates, rights do not only function to place limits on goal-based moralities—they may also conflict with other aspects of morality such as the virtues.

The third way in which rights are distinguished from other aspects of morality is the special way in which they attach to particular moral subjects. As Jeremy Waldron has said: 'When a person's rights are violated, we say not only that something wrong has been done, but that the right-bearer himself has been wronged'.[14]

There is disagreement over precisely how rights relate to and protect individuals. One view, derived from Bentham and represented in the work of Joseph Raz and David Lyons, holds that a right exists where there is a determinate party who benefits, or is intended to benefit, from the existence of a normative relation. The subject of a right, on this view, is any party whose interests are intended to be served by the existence of the normative relation.[15] The rival view,

---

[12] See Dworkin, R., *Taking Rights Seriously*, Bristol: Duckworth, 1977: 90.
[13] ibid. 169–73.
[14] Waldron, *Theories of Rights*, 8.
[15] See Raz J., 'On the Nature of Rights', *Mind*, 93 (1984), 194–214.

associated with H. L. A. Hart, holds that one has a right when one has control over the normative relation in question. For example, a person who has a right against another party typically has the Hohfeldian power to insist upon or to release the other party from the obligation to perform their duty and to press for, or to forego compensation which may be due them on non-performance of the duty. On the control view, a person has a right when they possess powers of this kind over a specific normative relation. In Hart's words: 'The idea is that of one individual being given exclusive control, more or less extensive, over another person's duty so that in the area of conduct covered by that duty the individual who has the right becomes a small-scale sovereign'.[16]

Though the disagreement between these two views is far-reaching and important, both acknowledge that rights are necessarily directed towards the protection of individual subjects. This is a highly significant feature of the concept of a right and it is one which will figure significantly in the account of self-defense which I will develop in the following pages. Though my account of defensive rights is agnostic between the benefit and control theory, it seeks to build an account of defensive rights as emerging from a complex set of normative relations between two moral subjects.

Justification and excuse

Our preliminary investigation into the logical structure of rights has yielded sufficient conceptual tools to proceed with the examination of defensive rights. We must now determine whether self-defense, and defensive rights more generally, can be analysed in terms of the Hohfeldian relations.

What is self-defense? In legal terms the plea of self-defense is a defense against a charge of murder (or lesser offenses such as assault) leading, if successful, to a full acquittal. Self-defense is therefore first and foremost a form of exculpation. An exculpation is some feature or set of circumstances that serves to remove or mitigate the blame attributable to an agent for the performance of a proscribed action.

Exculpations may be of two different kinds: they may constitute an excuse for a wrongful action, or they may constitute a full

---

[16] Hart, *Essays on Bentham*, 183.

justification. Excuse and justification are quite distinct normative conceptions and each serves to make an agent *ex culpa* in different ways. The distinction between justification and excuse is medieval in origin, but for a long time the distinction appeared to have lapsed in legal theory. Interest in the legal implications of justification and excuse has revived following the publication of George Fletcher's *Rethinking Criminal Law*.[17] According to the philosopher J. L. Austin: 'In the one defence [justification] we accept responsibility but deny that it was bad: in the other [excuse], we admit that it was bad but don't accept full, or even any, responsibility'.[18] George Fletcher's legal definition asserts that claims of justification 'concede that the definition of the offence is satisfied, but challenge whether the act is wrongful', whereas claims of excuse, 'concede that the act is wrong but seek to avoid the attribution of the act to the actor'.[19]

A successful excuse leads to the withholding of punishment or blame without conferring approval. Excuses themselves may be of various different kinds each of which operates in a slightly different way. Some excuses such as physical compulsion, automatism, and mistake invoke the claim that the agent did not intend to perform the proscribed act, or did not have the intention to perform the action under the proscribed definition. Other excuses concede that the action was intentional but deny that it was voluntary. Duress, necessity, and provocation are excuses of this form. A third group of excuses involve cases in which the agent is either incapable of forming a criminal intent or lacks the capacity for full deliberation of the moral or legal issues involved; this group includes the excuses of infancy, insanity and involuntary intoxication.[20] Excuses may be of varying degrees of strength: they may partially mitigate fault for an action, or they may serve to remove it completely.

In none of these cases, however, can the notion of an excuse be analysed in terms of the Hohfeldian relations. An excuse is not a permission or liberty to perform the action in question, nor (obviously) is it a claim, power, or immunity. The reason why excuses

---

[17] Boston: Little Brown, 1978, see esp. ch. 10. For philosophical discussion of the concepts see Austin J. L., 'A Plea For Excuses', *Proceedings of the Aristotelian Society,* 57 (1956), 1–30; D'Arcy, E., *Human Acts,* Oxford: Clarendon Press, 1963: 77–85; and Uniacke, S., *Permissible Killing,* Cambridge: Cambridge University Press, 1994: 23 and 137–8.

[18] Austin, 'A Plea For Excuses', 1–30, at 2.

[19] Fletcher, *Rethinking Criminal Law,* 759.

[20] The different forms of excuse are discussed in greater detail below, at pp. 90 ff.

cannot be analysed into the Hohfeldian relations is that the latter function to provide a framework for moral evaluation—they provide a terminology for describing obligations, permissions, and requirements. But as Eric D'Arcy says, 'The effect of an *excusing* circumstance is to put the wrongful act *ex causa*, outside the court of moral verdict at all'.[21] For this reason there is little intercourse between the system of Hohfeldian relations and the idea of an excuse.

With justification, however, the situation is very different. Justification is a much stronger form of exculpation than even a fully mitigating excuse, for in contrast to excuses it concerns the rightness of the action itself. A justified action is one that would normally be wrong, but which, given the circumstances, is either fully permissible or a positive good. It is not a forgivable lapse or a regrettable action that one is none the less excused for performing; it is rather something that one is either fully entitled to do, or not prohibited from doing.

Justifying conditions may also be of different kinds and the differences between them are material to whether they may be analysed in terms of the Hohfeldian relations. Building upon the discussion in the last section, we may draw a distinction between justifications grounded in consequentialist considerations and those deriving from the rights of the persons concerned. A classic example of a consequentialist justification, is the case of the farmer who burns his neighbour's field to prevent a wild fire from engulfing a town. The neighbour has a right not to have his field destroyed, but the farmer's action is justified in the circumstances because it is overwhelmingly the lesser evil. What is distinctive about this case, however, is that the farmer does not have a simple Hohfeldian liberty to burn the field, since the neighbour's claim-right against having his property destroyed does not disappear in the face of the justification. This manifests itself in the feeling that despite the justified nature of the farmer's act, the neighbour is still owed some compensation, redress, or apology. What this implies is that justifications arising from consequentialist considerations (in particular 'lesser evil' justifications) are not reducible to a simple Hohfeldian relation.

In contrast to this, consider the case of a person whose justification for taking my car is that I have given him permission to drive it. There is no sense in which I have a residual right that my car not be taken, nor is there any implication that I should be owed redress or

---

[21] D'Arcy, *Human Acts*, 81.

apology. The justification can in fact be described entirely in Hoh-feldian terms, for it consists simply in his liberty to take my car, in the context of the background presumption of a duty to abstain from acts of that kind. More generally, justifications of this form may be defined as the liberty to perform a specified act when the act would, in normal circumstances, have been forbidden. Justifications resulting from claims of right frequently take this form.

Now is self-defense a justification or an excuse, and if it is a justification is it of the kind which may be reduced to a simple Hohfeldian liberty? We have to be careful here. Like many other actions regulated by moral and legal norms, self-defense has what we might call 'central cases' which fully or perfectly instantiate the regulated class of action, peripheral cases which share sufficient features with the central case to fall within the regulated class, and marginal or ambiguous cases which share some resemblance to the central case but about which it is an open question as to whether they properly fall within the regulated class.

I take the central case of self-defense to have the following features: (i) an aggressor makes an intentional attack on the victim's life which will succeed unless the victim uses lethal force against the aggressor; (ii) the attack is objectively unjust in the sense that the aggressor has no legitimate right to make the attack, for example, he is not a law enforcement officer acting within his duty; (iii) the aggressor is fully culpable in making the attack; (iv) the victim is wholly innocent with respect to the attack (for example, he has not provoked the aggressor in any faultworthy way). I call this the central case of self-defense because it identifies the strongest conditions for an act of homicide to be exculpated by reason of self-defense. I do not mean to suggest that these features are necessary conditions for self-defense, but they are clearly sufficient, in the sense that anyone who believes that there is a right of self-defense must certainly believe that the right is effective in these circumstances. As we proceed, we shall have to consider other peripheral and ambiguous cases but the 'central case' as here defined will remain our paradigm of justified self-defense.

If we restrict ourselves to the central case, it seems clear that self-defense is a justification not an excuse. This is clearly recognized in most legal jurisdictions.[22] In moral terms also it seems clear that

---

[22] See Simester, A., and Sullivan, G., *Criminal Law, Theory and Practice*, Oxford: Hart Publishing, 2000: 619; Williams, G., 'The Theory of Excuses', *The Criminal Law Review* (1982), 732–742, at 739.

self-defense is most appropriately classified as a justification, not an excuse. This is because self-defense in the central case is an act that falls outside the class of culpable homicide. Someone who kills in self-defense does not commit a murder for which we exempt him of liability; rather, the defensive nature of the act makes it fail to be an instance of murder at all. We do not consider self-defense to be a wrongful form of action for which the defender ought not to be held fully responsible (as we might think about someone who flies into a violent rage after being cruelly provoked). It is rather that the victim may strike back—it is right and proper for him to do so.

Moreover, when someone justifiably kills an aggressor in self-defense we say that the aggressor has been harmed but not that he has been wronged. The aggressor (or his estate) is not in a position to demand compensation or apology for the act. This strongly suggests that self-defense is a form of justification which consists in a simple Hohfeldian liberty. If this is correct then it would appear that self-defense is capable of being analysed in Hohfeldian terms. It is, in fact, a liberty to use lethal defensive force without the presence of any residual duty to refrain from so acting.

This is a significant result, but in what sense does the liberty of self-defense constitute a genuine right? After all, we are all the subject of an infinite number of liberties to perform many kinds of action, yet it would be very odd to dignify them all with the title 'right'. There are, I suggest, several reasons why the liberty of self-defense is properly viewed as a right. In part the designation marks the exceptional nature of the liberties that constitute justifications. Justifications operate in the context of a background presumption of wrongfulness; for an act to be justified it must be an act which, as we say, 'stands in need of justification'. When the justificatory features of a certain class of action are distinct, readily identifiable, and recurring, then the justification attains a special status within the moral system. Often it becomes incorporated into moral, conventional, or statutory law as an independent normative feature. When this happens justifications begin to function with the characteristics of a right.

First, like other rights, established justifications function to identify and protect a distinct class of interests and freedoms of individual persons. For example, the justification of self-defense demarcates and protects the legitimate interest a person has in their own continued survival and bodily integrity. Secondly, and related to this, justifications serve as precedents for action which people may properly rely upon in practical deliberation with respect to similar cases. Thus, if it is determined in law or morality that a particular set of circumstances justifies the use of a certain level of defensive force, then an agent can rely upon this in measuring his response in like circumstances. In this respect, justifications differ markedly from excuses which do not always function as precedents for deliberation in this way. For example, if a person studies the rulings of the courts on the excuse of necessity (sometimes called duress of circumstance) and tailors his actions to fall within these limits, then this will not guarantee an acquittal. Indeed, it may impair the chances of acquittal, for the agent's premeditated reliance on the excuse of necessity undermines his claim to have acted out of the overwhelming compulsion of the circumstances.[23] Thirdly, the liberty of self-defense tends to override or 'trump' consequentialist considerations in situations where there is a conflict between the agent's liberty to defend himself and the greater good (this point will be explored further in Chapter 3). As Dworkin has pointed out, this is a characteristic feature of a right.[24]

Self-defense, therefore, may be analysed as a right consisting in a Hohfeldian liberty. But does the right also consist in claims against others? Some authors have argued that nothing can be a right unless it imposes duties on others. As Sumner says: 'There seems little merit in the idea that a bare liberty (even a full liberty) can constitute a right since it can impose no normative constraints on others'.[25] This concern would seem to be misplaced, since, as I have suggested, there are good reasons for counting the simple liberties which function as a justification as genuine rights: They act as established exceptions to prohibitions and thereby function to protect the liberties and interests of individuals and serve as guidelines for future deliberation. None the less it is possible that the right of self-defense, properly understood, contains claims as well as liberties in its normative structure. There would seem to be two possibilities. First, the right of self-defense may contain claims against others to assist in the act

---

[23] George Fletcher provides a good discussion of this point in *Rethinking Criminal Law*, 810–11.

[24] See Dworkin, 'Rights as Trumps'. Suzanne Uniacke has suggested that another reason why the justification of self-defense is properly viewed as a right is that an aggressor who is killed in a legitimate act of self-defense is not thereby wronged and is not owed apology or compensation. See Uniacke, *Permissible Killing*, 27.

[25] Sumner, *The Moral Foundation of Rights*, 38.

of self-defense. Secondly, it may contain claims against others not to interfere. My view is that, though it can be tempting to see claims against others as part of the right of self-defense, it is more appropriate and less misleading to analyse the right of self-defense as a simple liberty without any attendant claims.

With respect to the first possibility, it may be argued that when a third party comes to the defense of a victim, their action is justified by the victim's own possession of the right of self-defense or that their right must be derived from that of the victim. On this view, the victim's right of defense is seen as complex, with the defensive duty of third parties a component of, or derivative from, the defensive right which in the first instance belongs to the victim.

But, it is not immediately apparent how the fact that the victim has a liberty to kill the aggressor could entail or justify a liberty to take the aggressor's life on the part of a third party. An entailment of this kind is certainly not a feature of liberties in general. For example, the fact that I have a liberty to draw funds from my bank account certainly does not imply that anyone else has that liberty. The derivation might be thought to turn upon the fact that, in defending a third party, one is (unlike in the bank example) assisting the victim in the exercise of his right. But this is not a necessary feature of third party defense. One may rightfully defend a third party victim even if he does not know that he is being attacked and hence is not exercising or seeking to exercise any right at all.

Moreover, there may exist a right to defend a third party even when the party defended lacks the right to defend himself altogether. Imagine a community in which the priestly class forgo the right of self-defense. Although they do not waive their right to life (it is still a crime to kill them), they do waive the right to defend themselves with violence and are subject to punishment and condemnation if they do so. There is no contradiction, however, in the supposition that lay-persons in such a society would have the right to defend a priest who was subject to an attack. In such a case the rights of the third party defender cannot derive from, or be a corollary of, the defensive rights of the victim for *ex hypothesi* he has none.

With respect to the second possibility, there is a sense in which it is true that my liberty to defend myself with lethal force is accompanied by the general claim against others that they not obstruct me in my efforts. However, this is true only in the trivial sense in which it is true of any act that I am at liberty to perform, that others have the duty not to interfere. As Hart says, there exists a general 'protective periphery of obligations' which precludes interference in the lawful activities of others.[26] It would certainly be possible to describe this protective perimeter as a logical component of each and every one of our liberties, but it would be a misleading way of proceeding. The point is that the claims of non-interference have no intrinsic connection to the right of self-defense, for they are the same set of claims which, for instance, protect my liberty to stand on my head while whistling the 'Marseillaise'.[27]

For these reasons, self-defense is best analysed as a simple liberty to commit homicide in the defence of life. This is not to say that defensive rights have no conceptual or normative relations to claims or other normative concepts. As I shall explain in the next chapter, all defensive rights are derivative and an important class of them derive from claim-rights. However, one should not confuse this assertion with the claim that they contain, as a constituent element, claims against others.

Hohfeld's scheme has provided a useful framework for analysing the right of self-defense and has enabled us to obtain a good understanding of its underlying logical structure. Self-defense is a justification, a feature which explains why a normally prohibited act is, in the circumstances, either not impermissible or is a positive good. The justification of self-defense consists in a simple Hohfeldian liberty to commit homicide (or a lesser assault). The exceptional nature of the liberty together with its recurring and readily identifiable nature enables it to function as a genuine right within legal and moral normative systems. It does this by demarcating and protecting important interests and liberties of individual persons and providing grounds for future normative deliberation.

A logical analysis of a moral concept is, however, a very different creature to a moral explanation. A proper explanation of self-defense would need to go far beyond the merely analytical approach so far

---

[26] Hart, *Essays on Bentham*, 171–3.

[27] One might object that there is a unique and graver sense in which there is a duty to abstain from interfering with another person's act of legitimate self-defense, which is distinct from the general duty not to interfere with people's legitimate exercise of their liberties. This is certainly true; however this duty derives from the fact that to actively prevent someone from acting in self-defense is generally to become an accessory to an act of culpable homicide. But of course the duty to abstain from homicide does not derive from the right of self-defense. If there is a derivation here, it rather runs in the opposite direction.

taken. It would need to answer the following questions (amongst others): why is there a liberty to kill in self-defense? In what context is the liberty operative? What is the scope of its limitations and its permissions? Normative explanation concerns not simply the structure of a moral concept but its grounding. By this I mean that it provides an account of how the concept fits with and draws normative force from other aspects of our moral universe. In Chapter 2 we will begin to put in place the basic elements of such an explanation.

2

A Model of Defensive Rights

The right to commit homicide in self-defense is not *sui generis*, a case alone unto itself. It is rather one case within a range of morally and legally justified defensive actions. It is a range which might properly include defending one's position in a queue by delivering some sharp words to an interloper, defending a valuable art work by striking a thief who is about to steal it, through to defending one's life by shooting and killing an assailant who is about to kill you. If we are able to develop a model which explains the full range of justified defensive acts in terms of an underlying moral structure, this will have great value, especially when we come to discuss the application of defensive rights to war. The requirements for such a model will be that it explains, as fully as possible, the complete class of justified defensive actions and illuminates the limitations and criteria that characterize their operation.

A three-legged stool

We have seen in the last chapter that self-defense is a specific liberty to commit homicide in the context of a background presumption against such acts. Hohfeld treats liberties as a normative relation between three elements, namely: subject (the party who possesses the liberty), content (what the subject has a liberty to do), and object (the party with respect to whom the liberty is held). In order to construct a working explanatory model of defensive rights I propose to add to this schema a further element which we may call the *end* of the right. In the following discussion the end of a defensive right will be defined as the good or value which a defensive action is intended to preserve or protect.

The moral grounding of defensive rights may be visualized as a stool with three legs. Each leg of the explanation centres on a particular normative relationship between the elements associated with the right. The first leg concerns the relationship between the agent which possesses the right and the good which the defensive

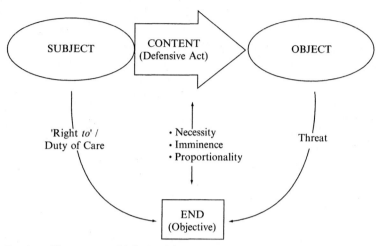

FIG. 2.1.   The structure of defensive rights

action is intended to preserve or protect; in other words between the subject and the end of the right. The second leg concerns the relationship between the good which the defensive action is intended to protect and the content of the defensive action itself; that is to say, between the end and the content of the right. The final element concerns a normative relationship between the agent which exercises the defensive right and the agent against whom it is exercised: the subject and the object of the right. When each of the appropriate justificatory elements is in place the tripod stands, and there is a legitimate right of defense. The normative structure of defensive rights may be represented diagrammatically (see Fig. 2.1).

The remainder of Part I will be devoted to exploring and explaining what these relationships amount to, and how they are capable of providing a moral explanation of defensive rights.

Defense as a derivative right

Let us begin with the relationship between the subject and end of defensive rights. Joseph Raz has distinguished between 'derivative rights' which are those that derive their normative force from some prior right or normative feature, and 'core rights' which are not so derived.[1] There seems little reason to think that defensive rights are core rights. For the content of a defensive right is the performance of an act which is frequently not an intrinsic good and which is sometimes a grave harm, such as assault or in extreme cases homicide. If they are not core rights then defensive rights must derive their normative force from some prior right or normative relation. It would seem, in fact, that all defensive rights have as part of their foundation some normative relationship between the subject and end of the defensive action. There are three different relationships which may serve as a grounding for a defensive right.

The first case is that in which the subject has a right *to* the good whose protection is the end of the defensive action. Defensive rights seem to be entailed in a very basic way by rights *to* things. Thus if I have a right to X, then it seems to follow as a simple corollary that I have the right to take measures to prevent my right to X from being violated. There are different ways in which one may have a right *to* something. Someone may have the right to an object if he owns it and therefore has property rights over it. Alternatively it may be a good to which he enjoys a liberty right or right of access, for example, the right to free speech, freedom of movement, or economic rights. Characteristically, having a right *to* something involves a combination of claims, liberties, powers, and immunities, with claims being more central to property rights and liberties more central to access rights. We say that a person has a right *to* life and this right is in some ways analogous to a property right: it has as a central element the claim against each and every other person that they not take the agent's life, or interfere with his bodily integrity.

Not all defensive rights arise, however, from property rights and rights *to* things. Consider a parent whose child is in danger from an assailant. The parent certainly has the right to defend the child, and yet there is no question of the parent having property rights over the child or of the parent's right of defense deriving from any kind of right *to* the child. Rather it would seem that the parents' right of defence arises from the duty of care that they owe towards it; the parents are obligated to protect the child and for this reason, they are at liberty to undertake the defense. Thus a second normative basis for defensive rights would seem to be an established duty of care

---

[1] 'Derived' here means 'gaining normative justification from', rather than 'logically entailed by'. Raz, J., 'On the Nature of Rights', *Mind*, 93 (1984), 194–214, at 197.

towards a certain person or object. In an analogous way, leaders are obliged and permitted to safeguard the welfare of their subordinates, museum curators to protect the artefacts entrusted to their custody, and friends to care for each other's interests. In each of these cases a right of defense may arise out of a duty of care embodied in an established moral relationship. Such relationships are a powerful source of defensive rights.

Sometimes, however, one may acquire a duty to protect or preserve a person or thing even though one has no established obligation of trust or care with regard to it. We might call these 'duties of rescue' and they arise simply from the fact that the end (being a particular good or value) is in danger, combined with the fact that one is situated so as to be able to assist. One can find oneself the subject of such duties quite unexpectedly and through no explicit action or choice of one's own, as when one discovers a drowning man or a victim of an attack. This form of duty is capable of providing a ground for defensive rights. It is from this source that the duty and right to defend the lives of third parties who are strangers arise.

In the last chapter I examined the claim that the right of third parties to defend a victim from attack is derivative of the victim's own right of self-defense and I suggested some specific objections to that view. The right to defend strangers and third parties is best seen as having its basis in an independent form of normative relationship. The right to defend one's own life derives from one's right *to* that life, whereas the right to defend a third party derives from more general considerations concerning the duty to protect the good and valuable. The term 'self-defense' is often used to cover both defense of one's own person and defense of another. This way of speaking is not normally objectionable since the two forms of defensive action share many common features. None the less it must be appreciated that there is at least one material difference between the two forms of the defensive right.

The difference concerns the question of whether defensive rights are full liberties or half-liberties.[2] It should now be readily apparent that the answer to this question will depend on their normative

[2] It will be remembered that a full liberty is complete discretion to perform or abstain from performing a given act. A half-liberty, on the other hand, is merely a Hohfeldian liberty to perform an act which is compatible with (because entailed by) a duty to perform it.

source. If a right of defense is derived from a right *to* the end of defensive action, then it will generally be a full liberty, in other words one will be free to defend the end or not as one sees fit. The reason for this is that rights *to* things are generally discretionary. As Hart has emphasized, to have a right to something normally implies the power to waive one's rights if one so wishes.[3] Thus defense of one's own life is generally thought to be discretionary rather than obligatory. What is more there may be cases in which the decision not to defend one's life would be not only permissible, but a laudable act of supererogation. Indeed Hugo Grotius held that in general: 'while it is permissible to kill him who is making ready to kill, yet the man is more worthy of praise who prefers to be killed rather than to kill'.[4] It has been an element of certain Christian teachings that we are under a duty to preserve our own life (which is why suicide is considered a sin) and that self-defense is therefore obligatory. However, the most natural way to view this position is to see the duty to protect our own lives as a duty owed to God. These cases are therefore best considered as falling under the second source of defensive rights; specific obligations deriving from explicit relationships of care, that is, the duty of care, owed to God, for the life he has entrusted to us.

Rights of defense which arise from specific or general duties of care towards the end of the defensive action, on the other hand, consist of a half-liberty combined with a duty to act in defense. The duty in question will be of varying degrees of strength depending on the circumstance. Duties deriving from explicit relationships of care such as those of a parent are generally the strongest, but even these are not absolute. For example, if a parent faced a high risk of death in an uncertain attempt to defend his child's life, then it is not clear that he would be under an obligation to act. Equally, the general duty to protect goods and values can result in extremely strong duties to act if the end in question is extremely valuable (such as human life) and the costs of action to the subject very low. However, when the risks to the subject are high, the chances of success doubtful, and the relationship between the subject and the end of the defensive action tenuous, the duty to act may become diminished until it is indistinguishable from a full liberty.

---

[3] Hart, H. L. A., *Essays on Bentham*, Oxford: Oxford University Press, 1982, 183.
[4] Grotius, H., *De Jure Belli Ac Pacis*, Kelsey, F. (trans.), New York: Classics of International Law, 1925, bk. II, ch. 1: 176.

Limits on the right: necessity, imminence, proportionality

This completes the first leg of our explanation of defensive rights. Those rights derive from rights *to*, and duties of care towards, the end of defensive action. However, to understand defensive rights is to understand that the liberties in which they consist are not absolute, but exist within determinate moral and legal bounds. The basic problematic of defensive action can be defined as the question of how far the permission to defend a particular good properly extends where the defensive measures are themselves harmful, or would otherwise be impermissible. The legal and philosophical literature on self-defense has identified three intrinsic limitations to the right. These limitations are necessity, imminence, and proportionality.[5] Each of these concepts can be explained with reference to relationships within our model of defensive rights. The limits can thus be understood as intrinsic elements of the right, grounded in its basic normative structure. This explanation will constitute the second leg of our model of defensive rights.

What do these limitations mean? Necessity in this context refers to indispensability and unavoidability rather than inevitability.[6] It expresses the requirement that one may only take a harmful measure to protect one's legitimate right if there is no less costly course of action available that would achieve the same result. Necessity thus specifies a particular relationship between the defensive act and the harm threatened against the end of the action: the defensive act is permitted only on the condition that its performance is required to prevent the achievement of the harm. For example, if one can protect oneself from harm by shooting an aggressor in the arm, then one is not permitted to shoot him through the heart, for such use of lethal force would not be necessary.

A corollary of the requirement of necessity is that there is a general duty to retreat from an aggressor, if it is possible (that is to say, readily feasible) to avoid harm in this way. It should be noted that necessity does not require that the defensive measure taken be the only possible means to avoid the violation of one's rights, but merely that there be no less harmful alternative measure that would achieve the same result. The rationale behind the limitation of necessity is

---

[5] See Fletcher, G., *A Crime of Self-Defense*, New York: The Free Press, 1988: 19 ff.

[6] Uniacke, S., *Permissible Killing*, Cambridge: Cambridge University Press, 1994: 32.

easy to discern. The liberty to perform defensive action is grounded in the fact that it is intended to protect a good or value. But general considerations of value will require us to choose the least costly course to that defense; in other words, the one which is least destructive of the good. This in turn requires us to inflict a harm only if it is necessary.

The second requirement on defensive action is that the defense may only be undertaken when the threatened act of harm is imminent. As George Fletcher puts it: 'A pre-emptive strike against a feared aggressor is illegal force used too soon; and retaliation against a successful aggressor is illegal force used too late. Legitimate self-defence must be neither too soon or too late.'[7] In legal discussions imminence is often treated as an independent requirement for self-defense; however, it would appear on reflection that imminence is conceptually derivative from necessity. The requirement not to act after harm has been successfully inflicted is a simple application of the principle of necessity (an action cannot be necessary to prevent a harm if the harm has already occurred). The requirement not to act before the infliction of harm becomes imminent, on the other hand, is simply the application of the necessity requirement subject to epistemic limitations. The point is that we cannot know with the required degree of certainty that a defensive act is necessary until the infliction of harm is imminent. If, *per impossibile*, we could know that a certain defensive act was necessary to prevent some harm long before the harm was to be inflicted, would we still have to wait until the harm became imminent before acting? It does not seem to me that we would: necessity is enough. Imminence, like the duty to retreat, is simply a component and corollary of the requirement of necessity.

If necessity and imminence require a particular relationship between the defensive act (the content of the right) and the aggressive or attacking act, proportionality requires us to balance the harmful effects of the defensive action against the good to be achieved. A classic legal formulation requires that: 'the mischief done by, or which might reasonably be anticipated from, the force used be not disproportioned to the injury or mischief which it is inflicted to prevent.'[8] Commentators sometimes explicate the idea

---

[7] Fletcher, G., *Basic Concepts of Criminal Law*, Oxford: Oxford University Press, 1998: 133.

[8] Criminal Code Bill Commission of 1879, quoted by Smith, J., *R v McKay* (1957) VR 560.

of proportionality by speaking of 'proportionate force' implying that what must be balanced in self-defense is the means of force employed. But this is misleading, for the proportionality that is required is between the harm inflicted and the good preserved, not between the type of force employed. For instance, if you are about to kill me with a knife and all I have to defend myself with is a gun or a bazooka, then my use of it is proportionate even though a bazooka is a far more forceful a weapon than a knife.

Although it may seem that the requirements of proportionality and necessity converge, they are in fact logically independent of one another. Thus, if I see from a hilltop that you are about to wrongfully read through my personal papers, and I shoot you with my high-powered rifle, this action may be necessary to protect my right to privacy, in the sense that I possess no less harmful means to prevent the violation of my right, but it would clearly be a dispro-portionate use of force. On the other hand, if I am a champion runner and can easily escape from an assailant who is trying to kill me, then shooting him would be a proportionate use of force, but it would not be necessary. Necessity, imminence, and proportionality are not sufficient conditions for an action to be justified defense, but they are necessary conditions. In both of the above examples the use of defensive force would be impermissible.

The requirements of necessity, imminence, and proportionality are the limits imposed on defensive action by justice. In practice, how-ever, it must be recognized that these restrictions operate in less than ideal circumstances for deliberation. Judgements about necessity, imminence, and proportionality must be such as to be capable of being made by frightened victims facing situations of extreme stress and danger. As Justice Oliver Wendell Holmes famously said, 'de-tached reflections cannot be demanded in the presence of an uplifted knife'.[9] The standards of necessity and proportionality must thus be interpreted with a degree of latitude and allowance for reasonable error. It is important to understand, however, that the standard of action remains an objective and not a subjective one. In other words, it is not sufficient for a victim to honestly believe that his action is necessary and proportionate; his belief must also be objectively rea-sonable. What constitutes a reasonable belief, however, must be

---

[9] Quoted in Smith, J. C., *Justification and Excuse in Criminal Law*, London: Stevens, 1989: 108.

sensitive to the strains and stresses implicit in the circumstances of a conflict situation.

The bounds of proportionality

For those accustomed to the Anglo-American legal tradition, the proportionality requirement is a deeply intuitive restriction to rights of defense. It seems obvious that certain responses to a wrongful attack are clearly impermissible because they are out of proportion to the harm which they seek to avert. However, the requirement of proportionality is more problematic than that of necessity and imminence. It requires more difficult comparative judgements about value and harm. What is more it has been a controversial requirement whose grounding is itself far from obvious.[10] Because the concept of proportionality is so important and yet so controversial in its application to self-defense, I would like to develop and defend a substantive conception of the limits of proportionate action in self-defense.

Which rights and goods would it be proportionate to defend with lethal force? Our first and clearest intuition is that it is proportionate to use lethal force in defense of life. 'Life for life' is a very clear and uncontroversial judgement[11] and it provides the basis for our understanding of proportionality. Beyond this, things become murkier. Which other rights and goods, if any, justify defense with lethal force? Plausible candidates might be defense against the loss of a limb and physical mutilation, defense against rape or sexual violation, defense of liberty, and defense of property rights.

The first claim that I shall defend is that there is a deep moral distinction between serious attacks against the person, on the one hand, and attacks against property rights, on the other, such that one may rightfully kill in the first case, but not in the second. There will, of course, be difficult borderline cases concerning what constitutes a 'serious' attack against the person, but the distinction that I have in

---

[10] Indeed certain legal jurisdictions such as those of Germany and the Soviet Union have at times not imposed a proportionality requirement at all. This seems to have stemmed from deep differences in the way they have conceived and constructed the right. See on this Fletcher, G., 'Proportionality and the Psychotic Aggressor: A Vignette in Comparative Criminal Theory', *Israel Law Review*, 8 (1973), 367–90.

[11] At least when not understood in its retributive sense.

mind would place the loss of a limb, permanently disfiguring injuries, blinding, and also rape on one side of the line, and bruises, cuts, and other readily healed injuries on the other. It should also be noted that, in my view, it is permissible to kill in defence of property upon which one's life directly depends. Thus one may, if necessary, kill a thief who is attempting to steal one's last food, or a vital piece of one's life-support machinery. These cases are merely an unusual application of the familiar right to use lethal force to defend one's life.

The principle of proportionality, as I have drawn it, will require defense in two ways: first, for its exclusion of the defense of property, and secondly, for its inclusion of non-lethal bodily harms. Let us begin with the exclusion first. The exclusion of property from rightful defence with lethal force, is a feature of English law[12] and it is enshrined in the European Convention on Human Rights.[13] It is not, however, the unanimous position of American law: in many states one is permitted to use lethal force against a burglar even if he poses no threat to life.[14]

To the extent that one finds the exclusion of property from rightful lethal defense a reasonable position, the reasoning behind this judgement might go something like this: attacks against property differ from attacks against the person because there are established and effective *post facto* means of redress in the case of property attacks which do not exist in the case of attacks against the person. Much property is insured and can be replaced in full. Thieves can be caught and prosecuted and stolen property can be recovered.

It may be objected, however, that this thought cannot identify a basic principle of justice, because the distinction is only plausible within a well-established legal order. Given the background security provided by an effective legal system, it makes sense to draw a sharp distinction between property offenses and personal attacks. However, in a state of nature there would be a greatly expanded right of defense such that it would be rightful to defend property, and perhaps any legitimate right, with lethal force.

I want to reject this claim, and maintain that the principle of proportionality that I have outlined would be valid even in the absence of an effective legal system. That this is so will be important

---

[12] See Smith, J. C., and Hogan, B., *Criminal Law*, London: Butterworths, 1992: 258: 'It can rarely, if ever be reasonable to use deadly force merely for the protection of property'.

[13] Fletcher, 'Proportionality and the Psychotic Aggressor', 367–90, at 381 n.

[14] Fletcher, G., *A Crime of Self-Defense*, New York: The Free Press, 1988: 35.

for my argument in Part II, for it is often suggested that nation states are in a state of nature with regard to one another, and it is important that we be clear about how this will affect our ideas about proportionality.

First, even in a state of nature, there is a possibility of redress and compensation for attacks on property which does not exist (or does not exist in the same way) in the case of attacks against the person. In the state of nature there is no guarantee of legal redress, but the opportunity for redress, though diminished, still exists in a way that it does not for victims of attacks against the person. For instance, a victim of theft in the state of nature might be able to re-appropriate his property, by sneaking into the thief's house late at night. The person who is maimed or disfigured by an attack, however, has no effective recourse to action of this kind. In his case, *post facto* action could only amount to retaliation and retribution, for it will not bring back lost bodily integrity. Thus, there remains a distinction based on the possibility of redress even within the state of nature, though the scope for drawing this distinction will certainly be diminished.

But it is not simply the possibility of redress that differentiates attacks against property from attacks against persons, it is also the possibility of reconstruction. A house destroyed by marauders may be rebuilt better than it was before, and a lost fortune can be reconstructed. However, after an attack which kills, mutilates, or disfigures, the original state of health or wholeness can never be reconstructed (the reconstruction of an artificial limb is not the same thing at all). What this suggests is that the harms inflicted by attacks against persons and attacks against property are not just different in magnitude; they are different in kind. It is not simply that being killed is a worse injury than being robbed of everything that one owns; it is a different kind of injury, for one inflicts damage that may be reconstructed in full, whereas for the other, this possibility does not meaningfully exist. As with the possibility of redress, the chances for effective reconstruction of property are diminished in the state of nature; however, this does not refute the claim that there exists a morally significant distinction in kind between the two harms, for that distinction is based on the possibility itself.

Now certain people will be unmoved by these considerations. After all, it might be argued, some property such as a Stradivarius violin or a Van Gogh painting cannot be replaced or reconstructed.

Yet those who feel, as I do, that there is a significant moral distinction between attacks against persons and attacks on properties will be reluctant to extend the right of lethal defense to rare paintings and musical instruments. What I think this shows is that the considerations that I have brought forward are not so much reasons for why we should value life and property in a certain way, but rather pointers to the fact that we do value them in this way. Any principle of proportionality must rest at base upon very fundamental appraisals of intrinsic value and worth. For example, we clearly judge at a basic level that the intrinsic value of a human life is of a different order from that of, say, a pair of sunglasses. It is this comparative appraisal of worth that explains why it would be disproportionate and wrong for me to shoot a pickpocket who was running off with my glasses. Such appraisals retain their force within the state of nature, for even within the state of nature a life is still a life, and sunglasses are still just glasses. It is hard to see how the appraisal could be made in any other way. Of course property is of differing value, and there is property of much greater value than sunglasses. However, I believe that at the level of appraisal I am referring to, we do attribute to life and significant bodily integrity an intrinsic value that is of a different, and higher order, than that of any and all property.

In saying this I think that we have reached a kind of ethical bedrock. That we do appraise the comparative worth of life and property in this way is, I think, something we largely discover by reflecting deeply on the case. It is difficult to know how much further beyond this argumentation can take us. For example, it has sometimes been suggested that judgements about proportionality of the kind that I am proposing may be grounded in the fact that life is a basic good whereas property is an instrumental good only. This judgement is surely correct, but what is it to make the distinction between basic and instrumental goods if not to give voice to a fundamental appraisal of value of the kind that I have been referring to? The distinction between basic and instrumental goods seems to express rather than stand as an antecedent ground for our comparative judgements of value.

I think that this represents the case that can be made for the exclusion of property from rightful defense with lethal force. Why include sub-lethal harms such as the loss of a limb or rape? Hugo Grotius suggested that one may rightly kill to prevent the loss of a limb 'especially if it be one of the principal limbs' because there is a serious risk that death will follow such injuries, for instance, from bleeding to death.[15] Although this is certainly a consideration, it does not seem to be the decisive factor, for if one has the right to defend a limb with lethal force, one surely holds the right against a malicious surgeon who would perform the amputation under meticulously hygienic conditions.

Are loss of limb and mutilation as bad as loss of life? This does not seem plausible, but we should note that proportionality does not demand equivalence between the harm avoided and the harm inflicted. It is enough that the harm be of the same order of magnitude (this is perhaps why in the legal formulation considered above, the negative phrasing is used: that the harm should 'not be disproportioned to...'). In this respect, mutilation and loss of limb share relevant features with loss of life; they are both permanent harms for which there can be no possibility of true redress, or reconstruction. This is perhaps harder to see with rape, but rape shares with the others the feature of being a severe violation of the integrity of a person. It may not leave irreparable physical harm, but there are likely to be permanent and perhaps disfiguring psychological scars, quite unlike those suffered by a victim of burglary.

What of the defense of liberty? Life and liberty are often listed together as basic human goods of central importance, and it is sometimes claimed that it is justifiable to kill in defense of liberty. These assertions derive their plausibility from the observation that liberty is a necessary condition for the shaping of any meaningful life. Liberty is both a component of, and a precondition for, many of the substantive goods that we value; in part we value life because of the liberty that it enables us to exercise. For this reason, it is conceivable that it may sometimes be proportionate to defend one's liberty with lethal force, for to deprive a person of liberty in certain contexts is to deprive them of a meaningful life.

It is extremely important, however, that we understand the limits of this claim. As Richard Norman has pointed out, there are many ways in which a person's liberty can be attacked or infringed, and the great majority of these would not make the use of lethal force proportionate. For example, if a farmer infringes your liberty by preventing you from using a public right of way, it would not be

---

[15] Grotius, *De Jure Belli Ac Pacis*, 174.

permissible to defend your liberty by shooting him dead.[16] It seems to me that it would also be disproportionate to use lethal force against someone who sought to deprive you of important political freedoms, such as the right to vote or freely express your opinions. If there is a context in which it would be proportionate to defend liberty with lethal force it would seem to be restricted to defense against enslavement, wrongful lifetime incarceration, or some similarly grave infringement of liberty. For only in such circumstances could the value of lost liberty be said to approach that of life. The difficulty of invoking a right of defense in such cases would lie with the requirement of necessity rather than proportionality, for it is often difficult to determine whether and when it is necessary to kill to escape enslavement or imprisonment. None the less the possibility that lethal force may be justified in defense against enslavement or lifetime incarceration cannot be ruled out.

I think that cases of lethal defense against significant non-lethal bodily harms and enslavement demarcate the extreme limits of what constitutes proportionate use of lethal force. I include them in the right of self-defense because of their proximity (along the axes we have discussed) to the central case. Though use of lethal force against a lethal aggressor remains the central case of self-defense, as we proceed we must bear in mind that the right also includes defence against serious non-lethal bodily attacks and enslavement in the way that I have described.

In this chapter we have explored two legs of the triad of considerations that constitute the justification of self-defense: those that revolve around the relationship between subject and the end of the right, and those that concern the relationship between the content (defensive action) and the end of the right. In doing so we have significantly illuminated the limitations and operation of the class of defensive rights. However, the most important and difficult element of the explanation remains to be put in place: that which concerns the relationship between the subject and object of a defensive right— the victim and aggressor of a conflict situation. It is this task which will form the basis for the following two chapters.

---

[16] Norman, R., *Ethics, Killing and War*, Cambridge: Cambridge University Press, 1995: 128.

3

Consequences and Forced Choice

Let us pause to take stock of what we have so far achieved. We began in Chapter 1 with some very general considerations about the nature of rights from which we were able to identify the structure of defensive rights as justifications consisting in liberties to perform acts which would otherwise be prohibited. We have begun to develop a general model of defensive rights which traces their normative grounds to rights *to* things as well as general and specific duties of care. We have introduced and explained the intrinsic limitations of necessity, imminence, and proportionality and defended a specific interpretation of them. Do we now have a satisfactory account of self-defense?

Unfortunately we do not. What we have is the beginning of an understanding of the structure and operation of the right of self-defense, of when it arises, what its intrinsic limits are, as well as its relation to other normative features. We have a partial map of the moral topology of self-defense. But an extremely important and difficult question remains unanswered.

That question concerns what happens when a defensive right rubs up against someone else's positive right. What happens if necessary and proportionate defensive action involves harming another party in such a way that the harm would in ordinary circumstances be a violation of that person's rights? What can justify a putative defender in acting in such circumstances? These questions take us beyond the explanatory power of the considerations that we have so far introduced. We have said that defensive rights arise out of rights *to* things and duties of care, but the justification provided by these relationships have definite limits. They can explain why it is the defender's business to undertake defensive measures; why he has a legitimate interest in doing so, but they don't explain what makes the aggressor, as it were, morally vulnerable to his harmful actions. Similarly the notions of necessity, imminence, and proportionality explain why the infliction of certain harms is not impermissible given a particular balancing of harms and goods. But what is missing is an explanation of why we are justified in inflicting the harm on a particular person—a person whom we can assume has interests and rights of his or her own.

The problem arises in its most dramatic form when we consider the status of the right to life of the victim and aggressor in a central case of self-defense. I have suggested that the right to defend one's own life is grounded in one's right *to* that life. Possessing the right to life, in other words, implies as a corollary the right to take measures to defend it when it is threatened. But the problem is this: as soon as a victim begins to fight back against his aggressor, he threatens the aggressor's life. If, as is commonly thought, the right to life is universal, then the aggressor must also have a right to life. But if this is the case, then it would seem to generate for the aggressor a reciprocal right to use necessary lethal force against his victim in self-defense. Yet we believe that the victim, but not the aggressor, is justified in using defensive violence.

What this problem reveals is a gap in our explanation. Part of our account of defensive rights must address the question of why the defender is justified in killing an aggressor but not vice versa. We may call this the problem of explaining the 'moral asymmetry' between defender and aggressor. It is the problem of explaining why and under what circumstances a person may become a morally appropriate object of defensive force or, in its most general form, how a person may become a morally appropriate object of violence at all. Such an explanation will constitute the third and final leg of our model of defensive rights. The first leg traced the source of defensive rights to a normative relationship between the subject and the end of the defensive action. The second concerned the limitations of proportionality and necessity which arise from the relationship between the content of the defensive action and the end of defence. If we are to find an answer to our current question then we must look to the normative relationship between the subject and the object of the defensive action. It is only here that we can hope to bridge the gap in our explanation and put the last element of our account of self-defense in place.

But the task will not be an easy one. Indeed, some authors have thought the problem of explaining the moral asymmetry between victim and aggressor in terms of rights so intractable, that it requires us to abandon the project of explaining self-defense in terms of rights altogether.[1] At this point, therefore, we must address some

---

[1] See Ryan, C., 'Self-Defense, Pacifism, and the Possibility of Killing', *Ethics*, 93 (1983), 508–24, 510; Montague P., 'Self-Defense and Choosing between Lives', *Philosophical Studies*, 40 (1981), 207–19, at 208–9.

basic questions: is self-defense best understood as arising most fundamentally from the interaction of rights? Or does it arise from some kind of consequentialist consideration? Or from some other kind of consideration entirely? In this chapter I shall consider two attempts to circumvent the difficulty by providing an answer to the asymmetry problem without substantive recourse to a conception of rights. These accounts hold the promise of providing a morally coherent explanation of self-defense without becoming embroiled in the difficulties and conundrums of a rights-based theory.

The lesser evil

Perhaps the most influential alternative to the rights-based tradition of self-defense is the view that the permissibility of killing an aggressor in self-defense can be explained as a preference for the lesser evil. Paul Robinson, a leading legal proponent of this view, begins from the general premise: 'All would agree that the criminal law seeks to prevent harmful results rather than to punish evil intent that produces no harm'.[2] He argues that the role of justification is to compensate for the limitation of laws by providing exculpating exceptions based on the public good. In his view, self-defensive homicide is analogous to a farmer justifiably burning his neighbour's field to prevent a wild fire from engulfing a town: both acts are justified as instances of rightfully choosing the lesser evil. The chief difference between the two cases, according to Robinson, is that in the case of self-defense the law has ruled in advance that the act is a lesser evil whereas the farmer must make his appeal to the lesser evil principle on a case by case basis.[3]

The lesser evil approach assimilates self-defense to a familiar and powerful form of justification; we often allow exceptions to legal or moral rules when adhering to the rule would cause more harm than good, or frustrate the intent of the rule itself. The view does not, however, accord well with the way we intuitively think of self-defense. A characteristic feature of the lesser evil justification is that frequently we feel that the party whose interests have been

[2] Robinson, P., 'A Theory of Justification: Societal Harm as a Prerequisite for Criminal Liability', *UCLA Law Review*, 23/1 (1975), 266–92, at 266.
[3] ibid. 272.

overridden is due compensation or redress. It may be right to burn a farmer's field to stop a wild fire, but still the farmer's rights have been violated (or justifiably infringed) for which he deserves some form of compensation or apology. But we do not feel this way about an aggressor who is justifiably killed in self-defense. While an aggressor is clearly harmed by the defender's acts of self-defense, we do not think of him as wronged and he (or his estate) cannot demand redress or compensation. There are important differences, therefore, between the way we conceptualize the normative consequences of self-defense and of the lesser evil justification.

A second objection is that, in the case of self-defense, the harm inflicted and the harm prevented seem to be exactly the same—that is, death. Why should it be that the death of the aggressor is a lesser evil than the death of the victim? The standard answer to this question is that the aggressor's culpability in some way devalues his or her life. The argument is that, 'as the party morally at fault for threatening the defender's interests, the aggressor is entitled to lesser consideration in the balancing process'.[4]

Now this talk of a life devalued by fault clearly sits uncomfortably with general consequentialist assumptions which are normally thought to embody the principle that 'each is to count for one and none is to count for more than one'.[5] Indeed, there are severe problems in understanding how this devaluation of the aggressor's life is supposed to work within a lesser evil account. To say that it is the aggressor's culpability that accounts for the devaluing of his life suggests that what is at issue is his moral worth. However, if this is the case, why are we not required to take the overall moral character of the aggressor and victim into account in deciding whether we may kill in self-defense? A victim who has just committed attempted murder does not forgo the right of self-defense if he is unjustly attacked, though his moral worth is presumably no greater than that of his assailant (it should be remembered that the only crime an aggressor who is killed in self-defense has committed is *attempted murder*).

Another difficulty is that, if the aggressor's life is devalued, then by how much is it devalued? Its value cannot be reduced to nothing,

---

[4] Fletcher, G., *Rethinking Criminal Law*, Boston: Little Brown, 1977: 858.
[5] See Dworkin R., 'Rights as Trumps', in Waldron, J. (ed.), *Theories of Rights*, Oxford: Oxford University Press, 1984: 154–5.

otherwise we could make no sense of the requirement to use only necessary and proportionate force in defensive actions. We evidently do think that the aggressor's death is an evil, but none the less one that we may rightfully bring about in certain circumstances. On the other hand, if the life of an aggressor is thought to retain some value, then we face a different difficulty. If a victim is attacked by more than one aggressor, there may come a point at which the combined value of the aggressors' lives outweighs that of the victim's life. And yet morality and the law allow us to kill any number of intentional aggressors in self-defense—it does not say that after a certain number (what would the number be?) we must desist from defending our life.[6]

This in turn points to an important observation about the nature of the proportionality requirement. It is apparent that the kind of balancing between the harm inflicted and good achieved demanded by the proportionality requirement is very different to that appealed to within consequentialism. A victim defending himself is not required to ensure the attainment of the greatest overall good (which might prevent him from killing a very large number of simultaneous aggressors) but he is required to ensure that the harm offered to a particular person is commensurate with the harm directly resulting from that person's actions. What this seems to imply is that the proportionality requirement is rooted in some aspect of the direct relationship between the aggressive and defending parties. In contrast to the more generalized demand of consequentialism to bring about the overall lesser evil, the proportionality requirement in self-defense imposes a set of responsibilities, restrictions, and entitlements tied to the intimate relationship between a particular victim and a particular aggressor. This is an idea to which we will return in some detail in Chapter 4.

The most telling objection to the lesser evil approach, however, is that the question of whether it is a lesser evil for the victim or the aggressor to be killed in a particular circumstance always hinges upon collateral consequences which in most cases are not relevant to whether one is morally permitted to kill the aggressor. For example, the person who attacks you may be a world-famous surgeon, or a researcher about to discover the cure for AIDS, or his death may lead

---

[6] See Wasserman D., 'Justifying Self-Defence', *Philosophy and Public Affairs*, 16 (1987) 356–78, at 359.

to violent riots, or there may be innocent people whose lives depend on his survival. Yet in neither of these circumstances would you cease to possess the liberty to kill in self-defense, even if you were fully aware of these collateral consequences. What this shows is that, far from resting on consequentialist calculations of the lesser evil, self-defense in many cases overrides or 'trumps' such considerations.

These difficulties have encouraged some authors to make a move parallel to the act/rule utilitarianism distinction. It may be that self-defense is justified, not by the fact that the death of the aggressor is a better outcome *per se* than the death of the victim, but by the fact that an overall beneficial result is achieved through endorsement of the rule allowing victims to kill aggressors. For example, Fotion and Elfstrom have argued that self-defense is permissible 'because of the anxiety and insecurity that would result if one's life could be taken at any time, for any reasons, and also because of the deterrence it provides against aggressive acts'.[7]

Such a rule-consequentialist model has certainly had great influence in Anglo-American legal thinking about justification and excuse,[8] but it too suffers from severe problems as a justification of self-defense. As several writers have noted, the justification is at once too strong and too weak.[9] It is too strong at the level of rule formation, for if it were successful, there is a significant possibility that it would justify far too much. Psychological security and deterrence might be enhanced even further by disregarding central features of the right such as the necessity and proportionality requirements, and by allowing the victim to kill an aggressor after the danger had passed, or by dispensing with the requirement to retreat if it is possible to do so safely. Yet such permissions clearly violate intuitively basic principles of the right of self-defense.

If the rule-utilitarian justification has a tendency to be too strong at the level of rule formation, it is too weak at the level of personal choice for, as Frank De Roose has pointed out, it fails to provide a moral justification for self-defensive killing in any particular instance.[10] The

---

[7] See Fotion, N., and Elfstrom, G., *Military Ethics*, Boston: Routledge Kegan Paul, 1986, quoted in De Roose, F., 'Self-Defence and National Defence', *Journal of Applied Philosophy*, 7/2 (1990), at 160.

[8] Fletcher, *Rethinking Criminal Law*, p. xix.

[9] Wasserman, 'Justifying Self-Defence', 360–1; De Roose, 'Self-Defence and National Defence', 160–1; Kadish, S. H., 'Respect for Life and Regard for Rights in the Criminal Law', *California Law Review*, 642/4 (1976), 871–901, at 883.

[10] De Roose, 'Self-Defence and National Defence', 161.

reason is that, in a particular case, the decision to kill the aggressor may not enhance the deterrence utility of the rule (perhaps no one will ever know what happened), or it may be directly inconsistent with it (killing the aggressor may incite, rather than deter, future aggression). If the only thing that justifies killing in self-defense is the usefulness of the general rule, and a particular act of killing will not support the effectiveness or usefulness of the rule, then we have no explanation for why the victim should regard himself as justified in this particular instance, given that killing is generally morally wrong.

These considerations would seem to be decisive in establishing that the 'lesser evil' approach in both its 'act' and 'rule' guises fails to yield a plausible account of our intuitive understanding of self-defense. The account makes the moral validity of self-defense depend in an inappropriate way upon contingent calculations of utility, and in so doing it fails to focus on the morally relevant features of self-defense or to capture many of our core intuitions. Self-defense, far from arising out of consequentialist considerations, in many instances seems to limit or override them. In Ronald Dworkin's terminology, it often acts as a 'trump' to consequentialist considerations, and this, as we have already seen, is a characteristic feature of moral rights.[11] This strongly suggests that an account of self-defense as rooted in a conception of rights may after all provide the best theoretical account.

Forced choice

Before reaching such a conclusion, however, we shall consider an approach to self-defense which is neither consequentialist, nor rights-based. This approach focuses on the idea of 'forced choice between lives'. It is an important account for two reasons. First, the approach has a considerable degree of plausibility as an explanation of self-defense. Secondly, understanding why the approach eventually fails provides us with important insights into the nature of self-defense and will pave the way for the final completion of our account.

Let us say that a person is in a situation of 'forced choice between lives' if and only if, through no fault of his own, he is situated so that no matter how he acts someone's life will be lost as a result of

---

[11] Dworkin, R., *Taking Rights Seriously,* Bristol: Duckworth, 1977, p. xi.

his action. Several authors have thought that this idea has central importance to the moral explanation of self-defense.[12] The reason is that the notion of a forced choice between lives seems to provide a basis for solving the problem of the moral asymmetry between aggressor and defender: the problem of how to explain why the defender is justified in killing the aggressor but not the other way around even though, at the moment of engagement, each is a threat to the life of the other. For the situation of self-defense non-controversially manifests the following asymmetry: while the defender faces a forced choice between lives, the aggressor does not, since he can withdraw at any time preventing the death of either party.

The approach based on this observation shares certain features with the consequentialist lesser evil approach. Both accounts work by phrasing the problem of self-defense, not primarily in terms of justifying a certain act (homicide), but in terms of justifying a particular distribution of harms. Whereas the lesser evil approach sees the rightfulness of distributing harm in favour of the victim as rooted in consequentialist considerations such as social utility, the forced choice approach sees it as rooted in considerations of justice.

The account I want to examine is that developed by Cheney Ryan, in a stimulating and insightful article on self-defense and pacifism.[13] Ryan introduces his argument with the following example: the occupying Nazi forces have apprehended five members of the Greek resistance and told the mayor of the local town that he must shoot one of them otherwise they will kill all five and several innocent men from the village as well. The question Ryan asks us to consider is this: if the mayor kills one of the five, is he responsible for the taking of life? According to Ryan:

While he pulled the trigger, the mayor is certainly not to blame for the fact that a resistance fighter was killed, for the Germans, not the mayor, are the ones truly responsible. (We might say: it was not his decision to *kill* that person, though it was his decision to kill *that* person.) ... The mayor was not 'justified' in his act of killing ... rather it was not *his* act of killing.[14]

[12] See Montague, P., 'Self-Defense and Choosing between Lives', *Philosophical Studies*, 40 (1981), 207–19; Wasserman, 'Justifying Self-Defense', 356–78; De Roose, 'Self-Defence and National Defence', 159–68; Richard Norman also proposes a variant of this view, see *Ethics, Killing and War*, Cambridge: Cambridge University Press, 1995: 120–32.

[13] Ryan, 'Self-Defense, Pacifism, and the Possibility of Killing', *Ethics*, 93 (1983), 508–24.

[14] ibid. 515 ff.

According to Ryan, the question of taking life in self-defense should be treated in the same way. The aggressor is responsible for the victim being in a situation where someone's life will be lost no matter what the victim does, so it is the aggressor not the victim who is ultimately responsible for the taking of life. The victim is responsible for choosing whose life will be lost, but even if he chooses incorrectly, with no justification for preferring his own life over that of the aggressor, he is not to be held responsible for homicide, for that responsibility lies elsewhere: with the aggressor.

As Ryan himself concedes, this account does not ground self-defense as a justification, but merely as an excuse. His explanation does not demonstrate that the defender is right to kill the aggressor, but only that the killing should not be counted as amongst the acts for which he is properly responsible. This is a counter-intuitive result, for, as we have seen above, self-defense is most naturally understood as a justification not as an excuse and almost all legal jurisdictions construe it in this way. But if the account is powerful in other ways, we may be willing to accept this, and modify our view of self-defense as a right constituting a full justification.

Ryan's next move is to claim that in fact there is a valid reason for the victim to prefer his own life over the aggressor's. He notes that a basic principle of the law of torts holds that 'where a loss has been incurred between two innocents, the causer pays'.[15] Applying this principle to situations of forced choice in self-defense suggests that it is rightful for the victim to sacrifice the aggressor's life rather than his own, since the aggressor, but not the victim, is the cause of the situation in which someone's life will be lost no matter what.

One perceived advantage of this account is that it only invokes the causal responsibility of the aggressor, but does not require the aggressor to be morally responsible or at fault.[16] Because of this, the account can allow defense against non-culpable aggressors (for instance, sleep-walkers or the insane) as genuine instances of self-defense.

---

[15] ibid. 516.

[16] In this respect Ryan's principle, is substantially weaker than that employed by Phillip Montague in his forced choice account of self-defense. For Montague self-defense is characterized by the presence of the following conditions: '(i) individuals $X_1, \ldots, X_n$ are situated so that harm will unavoidably befall some but not all of them; (ii) that they are so situated is the fault of some but not all members of the group; (iii) the nature of the harm is independent of the individuals who are harmed; (iv) Y, who is not necessarily included in $X_1, \ldots, X_n$ is in a position to determine who will be harmed'. Montague, 'Self-Defense and Choosing between Lives', P 215.

Some writers such as Suzanne Uniacke have thought that explaining self-defense as 'unitary right' in this way is an important theoretical requirement of any valid explanation of self-defense.[17]

The crucial question is whether Ryan's general claim about responsibility is valid: is it true that someone who kills in a situation of forced choice is not responsible for homicide? We may consider in this context Cicero's example of the two shipwrecked sailors who are both trying to hold onto a plank that will support only one.[18] Both sailors face a situation of forced choice; no matter how they respond to the situation one will die. But do we believe that because of this, if one pushes the other off the plank, or beats him to death, he would not be responsible for the taking of life—that, as Ryan says, it would not be '*his* act of killing'? It does not seem to me that we do. There are situations in which being in a situation of forced choice between lives is not a sufficient condition for being excused of homicide.

An obvious difference, however, between this case and Ryan's examples is that here the choice between lives has not been forced by any particular person—it simply resulted from an accident or caprice of nature. All of Ryan's examples, in contrast, involve cases where some other party is responsible for the existence of the forced choice (the Nazis, the aggressor). What difference should this make? Ryan's answer, and it is an appealing one, is that the person who creates a situation of forced choice in the first place is 'ultimately responsible' for the resultant loss of life.[19] The idea seems to be that if we can identify the person with ultimate responsibility for the infliction of a certain harm, then we cannot at the same time hold another person to blame for this harm. As Ryan says: 'True responsibility for the taking of life rests not with Victim, for...real blame for Aggressor's losing his life rests with Aggressor himself'.[20]

---

[17] Uniacke, S., *Permissible Killing*, Cambridge: Cambridge University Press, 1994: 8.
[18] Cicero, *De Officiis*, bk.III, sect. 23.
[19] Ryan, 'Self-Defense, Pacifism, and the Possibility of Killing', 516.
[20] ibid. It is interesting to note that this distinction between duress deriving from the threats of a responsible person and 'duress of circumstance' is explicitly rejected by the law. English criminal law recognizes no difference in the culpability of the agent responding in the two circumstances. See Smith, J. C. and Hogan, B., *Criminal Law*, London: Butterworths, 1992, 238.

The resilience of responsibility

But is this correct? Is it generally the case that if one person is 'truly', or 'ultimately' responsible for a certain action or consequence, then no other person can be responsible for that very action or consequence? It does not seem that it is. Consider a hit-man hired to kill someone. The person 'ultimately' responsible for the taking of life in this context is clearly the client who takes out the contract. To make the example precisely analogous to the forced choice situations in Ryan's examples, we can imagine that the hit will go ahead with a different killer even if the hit-man refuses the job. Therefore, in this case too, a life will be lost no matter what the hit-man chooses. Yet obviously if the hit-man does accept the job, he is fully responsible in law and in morality for the taking of life—as responsible as the person who takes out the contract. This is the case because the hit-man is an autonomous moral agent and, though he is not the ultimate initiator of the chain of events that result in death, by accepting the job he makes the act of killing his own. What this shows is that someone can bear full moral responsibility for an act of homicide, though someone else may have 'ultimate responsibility' for the fact that life is lost.

We can explore this point further by examining an actual situation of forced choice which occurred during the genocide in Rwanda in 1994. During this period, Hutu death squads would sometimes order Hutus to kill their Tutsi spouses or Tutsis to kill members of their own family. If they refused then their entire family would be slaughtered. Such was the predicament of Vénuste Hakizamungu, who was ordered to kill his older brother Théoneste. In his own words:

The interahamwe brought him back to the house. They told us that he had to be killed in order to prove that the whole family were not agents of the RPF [Rwandan Patriotic Front]. They left him in the house, knowing that he would not try to escape. He stayed there for two days. During this time, messages were coming in every hour, urging our family to kill Théoneste. The whole family was threatened with death unless we killed Théoneste... But of course none of us could bring ourselves to accept the reality of killing my brother. For four days, I struggled with the terrible thought of how the family could cope with responsibility for the death of Théoneste.[21]

---

[21] Personal interview recorded in, *Rwanda*, London: African Rights Publication, 1995: 639.

A natural response to this terrible situation is to feel that Vénuste and his family faced a genuine moral dilemma[22]—it seems that whatever he decided to do he would be guilty of an horrendous evil, for he either commits murder, or he fails to do something within his power to prevent the massacre of his family. Vénuste faced a situation of forced choice between lives analogous to that of the mayor in Ryan's example. But the critical point is, if we view his situation as a true dilemma, it must be because we think that by killing his brother it would be his act of killing—an act for which he is morally responsible. To appreciate this, consider how the full horror of the situation is not captured by the fact that he is forced to perform an awful and unpleasant act: it is that he is forced to do something evil.[23] It is revealing to observe that Vénuste himself describes the death of his brother as an event for which he and his family would have to bear 'responsibility'.

The resilience of responsibility under situations of forced choice such as these can also be grasped in a further way. Some political commentators have speculated that what motivated the death squads in Rwanda to make such demands was an attempt to implicate the Hutu population as a whole in the killings, to bind them together in a perverse brotherhood of guilt so as to create a community in which none as innocent. This pernicious political tactic is very old. It resonates with another incident of political thuggery related by Plato's Socrates in the *Apology*. During the rule of the thirty tyrants Socrates tells us that he was ordered, together with four other men, to collect Leon of Salamis for execution. Socrates refused to obey and instead went home thereby placing his own life in grave danger. Indeed he would surely have been executed had the tyrants not subsequently fallen. As Socrates astutely notes: 'This was of course only one of many instances in which they issued such instructions, their object being to implicate as many people as possible in their wickedness'.[24] If we can make sense of this idea at all (they were compelled to perform their actions and yet they were morally tainted by them)—and it seems to me to be extremely important that we can—then it must be the case that Ryan is

---

[22] See note on pp. 67–9.

[23] I mean this in the stronger sense than that implied by consequentialists when they talk of performing 'the lesser evil'.

[24] Plato, *The Apology of Socrates*, in *Plato: The Collected Dialogues*, Princeton: Princeton University Press, 1963, 32(c).

wrong, and that it is possible to be responsible, and indeed guilty, for acts of homicide undertaken under a situation of forced choice.[25]

This leads us to an important observation about the nature of moral responsibility. Ryan wants to make the point that not all acts of killing that we intentionally perform are homicides for which we are morally responsible: the state executioner killing a justly condemned person is a good example. However, the fact of being in a forced choice between lives is neither a sufficient condition for, nor does it explain, the absence of responsibility. This may be because, by electing to act, the person in a forced choice makes the act of killing his own, as in the hit-man example. It is intuitively plausible that the reason also has to do with the difference between killing and allowing to die. In situations of forced choice, someone's life will be lost no matter what the victim chooses to do, but it is not the case that irrespective of his choices the victim will kill. Without committing ourselves to the strong position that there is always a significant moral distinction between killing and letting die, we can note that this seems to make the moral difference in the cases of Vénuste and Socrates.

Thus Ryan's argument misconceives the nature of responsibility. It is interesting to compare Ryan's view with Alan Gewirth's discussion of responsibility in his article, 'Are There Any Absolute Rights?'[26] In this paper Gewirth attempts to defend an absolutist conception of rights from a proposed consequentialist counterexample. The example is one in which a man can prevent terrorists from exploding a nuclear bomb in a crowded city only by torturing to death his own mother. According to Gewirth, the right of the mother not to be tortured is absolute and is not overridden by the right to life of the people who would be saved. This follows, argues Gewirth, from the fact that the son cannot be held responsible for the deaths of the citizens if the terrorists explode the bomb. Why is this so? Gewirth explains this by appeal to what he calls 'the principle of the intervening action':

---

[25] The cases of Vénuste and Socrates are in fact more difficult than Ryan's examples for those who would resist the erosion of responsibility in situations of forced choice. For these cases not only involve a forced choice between lives, but are also examples of action under duress. It seems to me that the responsibility of the mayor for killing in Ryan's example is even clearer given his own life is never in danger.

[26] Gewirth, A., 'Are There Any Absolute Rights?', *Philosophical Quarterly*, 31 (1981), 1–16; repr. in Waldron (ed.), *Theories of Rights*.

When there is a causal connection between some person A's performing some action (or inaction) X and some other person C's incurring a certain harm Z, A's moral responsibility for Z is removed if, between X and Z, there intervenes some other action Y of some person B who knows the relevant circumstance of his action and who intends to produce Z, or produces Z through recklessness. The reason for this removal is that B's intervening action, unlike A's action (or inaction), Y is the sufficient condition of Z as it actually occurs.[27]

In other words, because the terrorists interpose their action (the detonating of the bomb) between the son's decision and the deaths of the citizens, the son's responsibility for the deaths is thereby removed.

There are, in fact, several problems with Gewirth's principle. The first is that our sympathy for the claim that there may be a permission (or duty) for the son to torture his mother does not principally derive from the thought that he would otherwise be responsible for the death of the citizens in the sense that he would somehow be violating their rights to life (as Gewirth seems to imply). It rather derives from considerations of preserving the good and from the general duty of rescue incumbent on those in a unique or privileged position to save people.[28]

The second problem is that Gewirth's principle of the intervening action is itself obviously false. This can be seen if we apply it to the case of Vénuste and the interahamwe. When Vénuste killed his brother in response to their threats, his act of killing was an intentional act which intervened between the actions of the interahamwe and the death of Théoneste; furthermore, it was a sufficient condition of the harm as it actually occurred. Under Gewirth's principle, therefore, Vénuste's action would seem to remove responsibility from the death squad for the death of Théoneste and thereby excuse them of his death. But this cannot be right. Whatever we think about Vénuste's response to his dilemma, it in no way mitigates the blameworthiness of the those members of the interahamwe for the death of his brother. In the same way, Gewirth must be committed to saying that the action of the mayor in killing one of the prisoners removes responsibility for that death from the Nazis. Both these results are obviously wrong. Moreover, the difficulty cannot be surmounted by

---

[27] Gewirth, 'Are There Any Absolute Rights?', 104.
[28] See above, p. 38.

tinkering with what it means for the intervening actor to 'intend to produce harm z'.[29]

Gewirth and Ryan thus provide us with an interesting opposition in their accounts of responsibility: Ryan believes that responsibility can be limited to ultimate causes, whereas Gewirth believes it can be limited to immediately proximate causes. But both views are mistaken, and in an important respect the error of each would seem to be the same. It is the tempting assumption that being responsible, and in particular being guilty for a wrong, is a unique attribute which can be correctly ascribed to one party only. But moral responsibility is not a unique attribute in the way that for example 'being the rightful heir to the throne' is. Rather, it is a plastic attribute operating along the twin paths of causation and intention that can extend, multiply, and infect various persons, in different ways and for differing reasons.

There is an important point here which is well worth pursuing for its implications for our account of self-defense. As we have seen, the forced choice account of self-defense seeks to avoid or diminish the victim's responsibility for the act of killing. This is made explicit in Ryan's account which denies that the victim is responsible for taking life, and hence turns self-defense from a justification into an excuse. However, the move is implicit also in other forced choice accounts such as that of Phillip Montague. In his account, the permissibility of killing in self-defense is grounded in a principle which permits a victim to 'select a distribution [of harm] which favours the innocent over those whose fault it is that there is harm to be distributed'.[30] Self-defense on this view retains the status of a justification, but if we enquire into what is actually justified, the answer is not an act of killing, but rather a certain distributional arrangement of harms, or at most the act of so distributing the harm.

---

[29] Richard Norman pursues a similar line of objection: *Ethics, Killing and War*, 96. These are not the only problems with Gewirth's argument. Even if we accept that responsibility is removed by intervening action, Gewirth's reply would not be sufficient to rescue his notion of absolute rights from this counterexample. What if the terrorists had set the bomb to explode automatically upon the son's non-compliance, so that there was no intervening action at all? Or alternatively if the son's terrible choice resulted not from the action of any persons, but from a natural occurrence? Would Gewirth suggest that the son then would be responsible for the death of the people. That would surely be absurd. As Norman points out, what we are responsible for can turn on the actions and responsibilities of others, but what I think these considerations show is that the connection is much more complicated than Gewirth's principle suggests.

[30] Montague, P., 'The Morality of Self-Defense: A Reply to Wasserman', *Philosophy and Public Affairs*, 18 (1989), 81–97, at 82.

Like Ryan's account, there is a two-stage structure to the argument. The first is to weaken the problem by distancing the victim's action from the general prohibition on killing through assimilating it to a kind of administrative decision procedure. The second is to settle this administrative question by appeal to non-controversial principles of distributional justice. This tendency is, of course, not unique to forced choice accounts of self-defense; as I have suggested it is found also in consequentialist theories of justification. It is a frequently made complaint that consequentialism treats all questions of justice and justification as administrative decision procedures. The focus of justification is the global distribution of costs and benefits and actions are relevant only as means to, and causes of, that distribution.

I would now like to bring forward some general considerations which suggest that any account premised on the erosion of the victim's responsibility in this way will fail as an explanation of self-defense, and to highlight the dangers of this tactic in moral explanation more generally. If I am right in thinking that there are strong reasons for rejecting such an eroding move as an explanation of self-defense, then this will furnish a strong case for returning to a rights-based account of self-defense.

What then is wrong with the erosion of responsibility in theorizing about self-defense? In the first place, there is a very general sense in which it is a morally desirable thing for there to be more responsibility in the world rather than less, and for this reason we should be very cautious about expanding the sphere of excuse against that of responsible action. Part of the reason for this is that the realm of responsibility coincides with that of autonomy. When people are held responsible for a particular area of action they strive to develop, and feel themselves to possess, greater control over that area and thus enlarge their sphere of autonomy. Furthermore, it is to be hoped that greater responsibility will lead to the exercise of greater moral care in these dangerous and difficult situations. In ambiguous cases, therefore, it seems to me that moral theory should work with a presumption in favour of retaining rather than eroding responsibility.

Secondly, it does not in any case seem to me that self-defense is an ambiguous case for responsibility. When I kill in self-defense, the killing is clearly something I *do*, it is my act, an act of which it is appropriate to ask of me: 'why did you do that?' This is demonstrated, I think, by the fact that we anticipate and imaginatively affirm our future responses before ever entering situations of danger where we may have to exercise self-defense. We formulate laws and even write philosophical discourses about it. It seems to me a basic fact that the act of killing in self-defense is one that we both feel ourselves to be, and truly are, responsible for. A valid moral account of self-defense must face this fact squarely.

More subtly, I believe that there is an important thought about defensive rights which can be articulated only in the context of a theory which recognizes that the victim is responsible for his defensive actions—that it is *his* act of killing. The thought is the following one: in considering the rightness of an action one must take account not only of the consequences for other persons, but also of the consequences for one's own moral self. What I mean is that, by electing to act in a certain way, one transforms oneself into the kind of person who can and will (and can will to) act in that way. Care and sensitivity to this process of moral self-transformation through action can be a source of limitation on defensive rights (and on action more generally) which goes beyond the other-regarding limitations of necessity, imminence, and proportionality. For instance, I do not think it would be legitimate to save oneself by torturing and mutilating an assailant who threatened to do these things to you, or by harming his children, or by engineering the systematic ruination of his life, even though these actions may in the context be both necessary and proportionate. The reason for these limitations seems to me to be the following: it is not possible to justify becoming the kind of person who would torture, or harm children in order to injure the parent, or systematically ruin a life. If these are genuine limitations on the justifiable extent of defensive action, and this is indeed their source, then this can only be understood within an account which recognizes, in a way that the forced choice and consequentialist accounts do not, that the victim is responsible for his defensive actions.

This idea can be approached in another way. As we have seen above, all defensive actions are directed towards the protection or preservation of some good or value. But there comes a point at which the defensive actions themselves may subvert or threaten to destroy the very good that one is trying to protect. At this point, the limit of rightful defense is reached. In the case of self-defense, the good which is protected is the continued existence of the self. But part of the reason that we value our personal self is that it embodies a certain conception of moral goods, values, and virtues which in turn we have shaped through our acts and decisions. If defensive action requires us to subvert, distort, and violate those values, then we may approach the limit of rightful self-defense. If this is correct, then it would seem that we have articulated a further limitation on the permissible scope of defensive rights, one which we can lay alongside necessity, imminence, and proportionality. But it is a limitation which we can only understand if we recognize the responsibility of the agent for his defensive act.

This consideration is particularly pertinent for those who want to extend the notion of defensive rights into the international sphere.[31] One might hold, for instance, that defensive wars are permissible because the goods embodied in our free and democratic society are worth fighting for. But, irrespective of any other doubts we may have about the right of national-defense, there is a question about what happens if defense against the aggressors necessitates a thorough-going transformation or subversion of the values of that society. If, for instance, defending the society requires mass coercion through conscription, or the systematic deception of the population, or the encouragement of hatred, intolerance, and fear, or the repeated violation of moral norms and basic human rights through the bombing of innocent civilians and torturing of enemy spies, then one may wonder what is left of the values that one was seeking to defend. This, in turn, would place limits on the rightful means of defense.

It is important to realize that this consideration is not captured by consequentialist restrictions, for it may be that the aggressor is planning to do the same or worse, nor can it be wholly subsumed within the limitations of necessity and proportionality, for the actions may satisfy both these criteria. The question is more self-directed: is it right for my society to become one that engages in such measures? Is it right for me to become the kind of person who will take such actions? Certain actions might save the self, but so transform it, as to make it a self hardly worth saving. The bleak conclusion towards which I am moving is that, just as there are genuine moral dilemmas in which no truly fault-free course of action exists,

---

[31] This is, of course, an extension with which I shall take issue below. The point is introduced here for the purpose of discussion only.

so there may sometimes be situations in which there is a duty to abstain from self-defense, a duty in other words of martyrdom.

Consequentialists might complain that this is just an example of the old obsession with moral purity in a dirty world, of lacking moral courage through an excessive preoccupation with keeping one's hands clean, or even simple squeamishness. But quite apart from the problem of why an action that consequentialists insist is rightful should be thought capable of sullying us in a moral way, I simply do not think that this is what lies behind the idea that I am trying to articulate. It is rather the darker and more paradoxical thought that, if one can defeat evil only by becoming evil, then it is impossible to defeat evil. While it is true that even this thought can be given a consequentialist interpretation, its force lies elsewhere: in the realm of responsibility.

I have given some specific objections to the initially promising account of self-defense as a forced choice. I have ended with some very general considerations, which seek to explain why, not only the forced choice, but also consequentialist accounts, remain problematic in this area. Ultimately, the realm of reduced responsibility and necessity is the wrong place to look for an explanation of self-defense. When one kills in self-defense, one is responsible for one's killing; if the act escapes condemnation, then it must be because one's killing is in the circumstances rightful. To explain this we must turn, for all their difficulty, back to rights.

NOTE

The question of how to construe moral dilemmas is extremely difficult, but from what I have said here and in the Introduction it will be apparent that I believe them to be real moral possibilities. It is instructive to reflect, in the context of this example, on how an agent may, in a practical sense, approach the issues raised by dilemmas. We may begin by observing that, if the brother, Théoneste, consents to his own death out of a desire to save his family, then Vénuste's dilemma is, if not circumvented, at least mitigated. By giving his brother permission to kill him, Vénuste's act is no longer (morally) one of murder, and on Théoneste's part, his death becomes an act of dignity rather than a means to his degradation. For Théoneste to consent in this way doesn't make things 'all right', but it does make them better, by which I mean not so much that it produces the best outcome, but that it is the best response that he could, as a human being, make to the situation. But now if this is his best response, is it also a required response in the sense that he could be faulted for not consenting? And if the answer to this question is yes, what role should this play in his brother's deliberation? Could it justify Vénuste in disregarding his failure to consent in order that he might save the family? That Théoneste has a right to life militates against such a thought. For surely if there are moral reasons directing him to sacrifice himself, then they are operative only at the internal level. He may feel compelled to do so, but we can never say to him that he is obliged to sacrifice himself and would be at fault for not doing so. None the less, the dynamic of moral reflection conspires to defeat such a quarantining of reasons. For internal reasons of this kind can be accessed in the objective sphere when we ask ourselves the question: what would we (feel ourselves compelled to) do in the circumstances? Though I am not convinced what the outcome of this thought will be, it seems to me that sensitivity to these features (internally derived obligations of sacrifice) can play a role in thinking about how to respond decently in the terrible cases where we must choose whether to murder few to save many, without tumbling headlong into an unprincipled consequentialism. In the end Théoneste, with enormous courage, did give his brother permission to kill him:

> Théoneste got up and spoke to me. 'I fear being killed by a machete; so please go ahead and kill me but use a small hoe.' He himself brought the hoe and handed it to me. I hit him on the head. I kept hitting him on the head but he would not die. It was agonising. Finally, I took the machete he dreaded in order to finish him off quickly. The interahamwe were there during the whole time, supervising what they called 'work'. When Théoneste was dead they left. The next day I buried him. (*Rwanda*, 639)

This testimony shows how morally problematic dilemmas remain even with consent of the form discussed above. What makes them genuine dilemmas is that there is no morally 'clean' way out. The testimony raises another difficult question. Though Vénuste himself describes his action as one for which he and his family must bear 'responsibility', it would seem grossly inappropriate to seek to punish him for the deed. Why? Part of the reason surely lies in the agony with which his decision was taken and the consequent suffering it brought to him. We may contrast his case with that of Dostoevsky's Raskolnikov who also suffers terribly after committing his crime, but whose suffering can only be extirpated by submitting himself to due punishment (though part of Dostoevsky's point is surely that Raskolnikov's punishment began long before he reached the prison camp). In Vénuste's case we also view his suffering as morally appropriate. Indeed it is one of the ways in which his entirely proper sense of responsibility is manifested. Yet in his case, punishment adds nothing to our sense of appropriateness and justice. What this shows, I think, is that the notion of moral responsibility cannot be restricted to the domain of punishment. Both punishment and blame are one form of external response to wrongful actions that fall within the realm of responsibility. But they are not the only possible responses; compassion and mercy also operate within this sphere. Furthermore, the notion of moral responsibility has an important internal function in regulating our response to our own action (consider the way in which the nature of Vénuste's suffering and the nature of its appropriateness differ from the way in which suffering is appropriate after a more normal family bereavement). For this reason, the fact that punishment would be inappropriate does not demonstrate that there is no room for a substantive ascription of moral responsibility.

4

Grounding Self-Defense in Rights

The most natural way to think about self-defense, for most people, is through the idea of rights. Put in its simplest terms this reflects the intuition that a man who kills in self-defense has a right to act as he does, and that moreover what underlies this is the fact that the aggressor no longer possesses the right not to be killed by him. Through his aggressive actions his right to life has been lost, negated, or somehow annulled. There is no denying that this idea captures a powerful intuition about the way the whole mechanism of defensive rights operates.

On further reflection, however, this simple conception leads to a philosophical quagmire. When applied in a principled way to particular cases it seems to generate deep contradictions and puzzles. Indeed, so difficult has it proved to provide a coherent account of self-defense through the notion of rights that, as we shall see, a number of modern theorists have decried the entire project as hopelessly ill-conceived.

None the less, a coherent rights-based explanation of self-defense can be constructed. I shall argue in this chapter that it provides the best overall approach to completing our understanding of self-defense. In demonstrating this, however, we shall need to push the account a long way from the simple thought about loss of the aggressor's rights articulated here.

Forfeiture and rights of limited scope

As suggested in the last chapter, the primary difficulty for a rights-centred account of self-defense is how to explain what I have called the 'moral asymmetry' between the defender and the aggressor. The problem can be summarized as follows: if the right of self-defense derives from the right to life, and that right is universal, why is it permissible for the defender to kill the aggressor but not the other way around, even though at the moment of engagement each is a threat to the life of the other?

In order to answer this question we shall need to explain why the aggressor loses, or fails to possess, the right to life whilst attacking his or her victim. There would seem to be two ways to do this. Either we must give a theory of forfeiture for the right to life, such that the right is seen as forfeited by engagement in aggressive attacks. Or we must give an account of the right to life as containing implicit limitations as to its scope, so that its effectiveness is contingent upon non-engagement in aggressive conduct.[1] The difficulty is that both suggestions have features which make them extremely un-attractive when used in an account of self-defense. We will need to explore these features with great care.

At the very outset it must be noted that both suggestions conflict with a widely held belief about the right to life, namely, that the right to life is 'inalienable' and possessed 'unconditionally'. If the right to life can be forfeited or is subject to limitations of scope, then this assumption cannot be correct, since the possession of the right would be conditional on non-engagement in certain kinds of conduct. This is a surprising result, but it should not be seen as a fatal objection, for many other important rights, such as the right to privacy and the right to liberty, are seen as conditional in this way. There is no reason in principle why the right to life should not be the same.[2]

There are more substantive objections to the two accounts, how-ever, which pose a greater difficulty. The first criticism could be called the circularity objection and is directed against the limited scope approach. J. J. Thomson has argued that any attempt to explain self-defense via the notion of rights of limited scope will be viciously circular.[3] There are two ways in which the idea of a limited right to

---

[1] One way to think of this approach is to see it as a denial of the distinction between justifications and prohibitions. Instead of treating the justification of self-defense as an independent normative feature, it simply treats the criteria of justification as negative elements in the prohibition against killing.

[2] An apparent alternative to talk of forfeiture and rights of limited scope is to say that the right to life, though unconditional, is prima facie only, and subject to being overridden by the victim's more stringent right. But to say this would require us to give something very much like a theory of forfeiture, for we will need to say that the stringency of the aggressor's right to life is either forfeit or contains implicit limitations. Furthermore, it just does not seem to be the case that the aggressor possesses a right to life which we legitimately override. A person whose right is justifiably overridden deserves some com-pensation, apology, or redress. But this is not how we commonly think of the aggressor in the central cases of self-defense.

[3] Thomson, J. J., 'Self-Defense and Rights', *The Lindley Lecture*, Lawrence, Kan.: Law-rence University of Kansas Publications, 1976: 7.

life could be used in an explanation of self-defense. One alternative is that the scope of the right to life is limited in moral terms. For example, it may be that the right to life consists only in the right not to be killed unjustly. On this view, the aggressor fails to possess the right to life but the defender does not, because the aggressor, but not the defender, is engaged in an unjust attack. This view, however, is viciously circular and in a rather obvious way. For what is an unjust attack? It is simply one which violates the victim's rights. But on the current view the attack only violates the victim's rights if it is unjust. Clearly neither conception gets off the ground without the other. As Thomson says, 'one does not mind all circles, but this circle is too small'.[4]

The alternative to specifying the scope of the right to life in moral terms is to specify it in factual terms. But a related problem seems to arise if this approach is taken. For the right to life would then need to contain a complicated list of factual criteria which capture all the situations in which a defender may rightly take an aggressor's life. The properly specified right to life would proceed something like this: 'persons only have the right not to be killed when not engaged in an aggressive attack, but they retain the right in cases where their victim can escape without using lethal force, and/or where their victim's use of force would be disproportionate, and/or where the threat presented is not imminent, and/or where the victim's use of force does not arise from an intention to act in self-defence and so on... (the specification would here need to be completed with a large and probably open-ended number of factual criteria)'. The problem is that in thus specifying the scope of the right to life we have simply inserted all our pre-existing intuitions about the permissible circumstances of self-defense. In doing so we sap the notion of explanatory power, for if our conception of the right to life simply reflects our prior intuitions on the permissible circumstances of self-defense, then we can hardly point to the possession or absence of the right to explain our intuitions in those cases. The rights-centred account would then become quite empty as an explanatory tool. This charge of circularity against rights-based explanations is an important objection and we shall return to it below.

The second line of criticism could be called 'the incoherence objection' and is directed against the forfeiture of rights approach.

---

[4] Thomson, J. J., 'Self-Defense and Rights', *The Lindley Lecture*, Lawrence, Kan.: Lawrence University of Kansas Publications, 1976: 7.

The objection runs as follows: if a forfeiture of the right to life on the part of the aggressor explains the defender's liberty to kill in self-defense, then many features of self-defense become extremely difficult to account for. For example, how is one to account for the requirements of proportionality, imminence, and necessity implicit in the right? If the aggressor has forfeited his right to life through his aggressive conduct, why must the victim forbear from killing him provided he can easily escape or save himself by using non-lethal force? If we want to account for these restrictions on a forfeiture approach we will need to assume that the aggressor's forfeiture of rights may depend on contingent facts about the victim. For example, we would have to say that the aggressor's right would be forfeit when he attacks a lame victim who cannot run away, but it would not be forfeit when he makes an identical attack upon a healthy victim who can easily escape. In another example introduced by J. J. Thomson, she imagines a villainous tank driver trying to run down an innocent victim. The tank driver's right to life would be regarded as forfeit, but if the tank stalls and the driver breaks his ankle jumping out to investigate the problem then his right to life would be suddenly regained despite the continued existence of his evil intent.[5] But this sounds very odd: how can the forfeiture of the aggressor's right to life be dependent upon contingent facts such as whether his ankle is broken? In order to employ the concept of forfeiture in an account of self-defense we seem compelled to divorce it from considerations of intention and fault, but in doing so it would seem that we make a nonsense of the concept.

The incoherence objection further points out that on our ordinary understanding of forfeiture, a forfeit right cannot be violated by anyone, whether they know the right to be forfeited or not. Thus if I have forfeited my right to a piece of property, then that thing cannot be stolen from me, even by someone who believes I still own it. However, an aggressor's right to life does not seem to be like that. Not just anyone may kill an aggressor while he is an unjust threat, nor may he be killed for just any reason. For example, imagine that I walk into a bar and, seeing my old enemy Bugsey, I draw my gun and shoot him. Unbeknown to me, however, Bugsey was about to murder another man with a gun concealed under the table. Had I known about Bugsey's actions and acted with the intention of foiling them,

---

[5] See ibid. 3–4.

my shooting would have constituted justified defense. Because I did not know, my action constitutes culpable homicide.[6] What this shows is that an aggressor engaged in an unjust attack can still be killed in a way that violates his rights.[7] But how can this be if engagement in such an attack forfeits one's right to life?

What I have sketched here is an attempt to construct a dilemma for the rights-based approach, by arguing that any such account will be either circular and hence vacuous, or morally incoherent. It will be circular if built around the idea of a right to life which is of limited scope, incoherent if built around the idea of forfeiture of right.

It would seem, however, that this line of argument is wide of the mark. We can begin to see why by observing that the distinction between an account constructed in terms of forfeiture and one constructed in terms of specification of the right to life is in fact a very superficial one. In the present context, these two ways of talking do not refer to any deep moral difference. Indeed, both seem to be ways of articulating the same underlying moral idea: that the right to life is subject to conditions specified in terms of facts about the mutual relationship between an aggressor and defender (or more generally between any two interacting parties). Whether we choose to describe the right to life as limited in scope or as subject to forfeiture seems, from a theoretical point of view, immaterial.[8]

Recognizing that it is this idea which lies at the heart of the rights-based account has two implications. The first is that it reminds us to focus on the normative relationship between the aggressor and defender rather than simply on the status of the aggressor's right to life. In doing so it enables us to see that one of the problems

---

[6] This principle was enshrined in the famous case of *Dadson* (1850) 4 Cox CC 358. See on this Christopher, R. L., 'Unknowing Justification and the Logical Necessity of the Dadson Principle in Self-Defence', *Oxford Journal of Legal Studies*, 15 (1995), 229–51.

[7] Another interpretation of this case would be to say that Bugsey has no right not to be killed but my murderous intent combined with my mistake of fact is sufficient only to establish attempted murder on my part. This does not seem persuasive, partly for the simple reason that my attempt is indeed a successful one. We may contrast the Bugsey example with the case of someone who shoots a person intending to murder him, but whose victim turns out to be already dead. In this case there is no murder despite the existence of murderous intent, because a corpse is just not the kind of thing that can be murdered. It would seem that if Bugsey lacks the right not to be killed, it is in a very different way to that in which a corpse lacks rights.

[8] Through the remainder of the book I shall employ the terminology of forfeiture, but I shall imply no commitment to a theory materially distinct from the limited scope approach.

with incoherence objection is that it treats the absence of the aggressor's right to life, and the victim's possession of the right to kill, in a falsely dichotomous manner. For instance, Cheney Ryan concludes on the basis of the incoherence objection that 'a forfeit on Aggressor's part is by itself insufficient to establish Victim's right to kill'.[9] In a similar vein Suzanne Uniacke argues: 'A theory which maintains that an unjust aggressor forfeits the right to life cannot ground the justification of homicide in self-defence: the fact that someone does not have a right to life does not in itself give me a positive right to inflict lethal force on him or her'.[10] But both statements reflect a confused way of proceeding. The aggressor's loss of the right to life, and the defender's possession of the right to kill are not two independent moral facts that might part company or fail to correspond in a perplexing manner. They are rather simple Hohfeldian correlates of one another; in other words, they are the same normative fact described from two different perspectives. The aggressor's right to life includes the claim against others that they not kill him. If the aggressor forfeits this right with respect to the defender then he has a no-claim against the defender that he not kill him. But this in turn is just to say that the defender has the right (liberty) to kill him. The absence of the aggressor's right to life and the defender's right to kill are thus internally connected by the logic of normative relations.[11]

The second implication stemming from this point is that we need not conceive the forfeiture of a right on the model of a universal alienation. This assumption is implicit in the incoherence objection and it is explicitly articulated by George Fletcher: 'A person who forfeits particular rights, forfeits them (1) with regard to the whole

---

[9] Ryan, C., 'Self-Defense, Pacifism, and the Possibility of Killing', *Ethics*, 93 (1983), 508–24, at 512.

[10] Uniacke, S., *Permissible Killing, The Self-Defence Justification of Homicide*, Cambridge: Cambridge University Press, 1994: 191.

[11] Suzanne Uniacke has pointed out in personal correspondence that part of her meaning in this passage is to assert that the fact that X lacks the right to life does not always by itself imply a *positive right* to kill X. For instance, a cat may not possess a right to life, but this does not necessarily imply a positive right to kill it. This is, I think, correct. As I argued in Chapter 1, the liberty to kill in self-defense is properly described as a right for a number of related reasons: it consists in a liberty to kill in the context of a background presumption against such action, it serves to demarcate and protect a legitimate interest of individual persons, and it acts as a precedent for deliberation of future action. The broader normative context is thus relevant to when a liberty constitutes a positive right. None the less self-defense fundamentally consists of a simple liberty to kill and is thus perfectly correlative with the status of the aggressor's right to life.

world, and in particular, he forfeits them (2) with regard to persons who do not know that he has forfeited them'.[12] This view, when applied to the right to life, is closely linked to the original conception of an outlaw who was literally a person whose right to life had been annulled so that they may be killed by anyone at any time and for whatever reason. This is indeed an implausible model for thinking about the rights of an aggressor in self-defense. But there is no reason to view the concept of forfeiture exclusively in these terms. Indeed, on a Hohfeldian conception of rights this is far from the most natural way to conceive of it. If we follow Hohfeld in viewing all rights as relational then it follows that forfeiture (or limitations to the scope) of a right will also be viewed in relational terms. This implies that the forfeiture of a right should be viewed as a fact about the normative relationship between two specific parties. In which case there is every reason to believe that the forfeiture of a right will turn upon facts about the status, condition, actions, and intentions of both the parties.

Once this is recognized, the incoherence objection can be quickly dispatched. For example, in the Bugsey case there is nothing incoherent or peculiar in the claim that Bugsey has forfeited his right to life to one person (who knows of his threatening status and acts in defense), but not to another (who does not). Similarly, there is nothing peculiar in the thought that the forfeiture of an aggressor's right may depend upon material facts about the defender as well as the aggressor, for instance, whether he is sufficiently fleet-footed to escape without using force. These two features of a relational conception of forfeiture—that forfeiture can be particular rather than simply universal, and that it can depend on facts about both the subject and object of a right—enable us to deal with all the supposed anomalies raised by the incoherence objection.

So far, so good. We have arrived at an understanding of how rights can be coherently employed in a normative description of self-defense. However, proceeding in this way brings the circularity objection dramatically to the fore. On the current view, the defender does not gain the right to kill because the aggressor has lost his right to life. Rather the right to kill and the absence of the aggressor's right to life are just the same moral fact described in different ways. It seems that all we have done is to drape the language of rights over the contours of self-defense without showing how the rights con-

---

[12] Fletcher, P., 'The Right to Life', *Monist*, 63 (1980), 135–55, at 143.

cerned illuminate or explain them. If our interpretation of those rights is simply chosen to fit around our pre-existing ideas of what is acceptable conduct, then the conception of rights does no work at all, and we cannot use it to explain the limits of permissible action. This would be a profoundly dissatisfying place at which to stop.

What we require at this point is some element which can give the rights-based account a deeper explanatory power. We need something to explain why, at the moment of engagement, the defender has the right to kill and the aggressor does not have the right to live. This can be achieved only by identifying some relevant feature of the relationship between the aggressor and defender. If the account is to remain committed to anchoring the permission of self-defense in a conception of rights, then the identified feature must arise directly from the rights and related normative characteristics of the parties concerned.

The role of fault

I want to begin with the suggestion that the feature which provides the required explanation for why a victim has the right to kill his aggressor is the fault of the aggressor for the aggressive attack. To be more precise, it is the combined fault of the aggressor and innocence of the victim with respect to the aggressive attack.

The idea that fault plays a material role in the explanation of self-defense is a very old one. But it is a view which has been rejected by the majority of modern lawyers and philosophers who write on self-defense.[13] None the less the idea is, I believe, substantially correct. It will require revision and qualification in ways that I shall try to bring out below, but the suggestion contains a fundamental truth and in its revised form will yield the best overall way to complete our account of self-defense.

Let me first clarify a few things about the proposal. I do not mean to imply that it is the differential in a quantitative sense between the

---

[13] See Gorr, M., 'Private Defence', *Law and Philosophy*, 9 (1990), 241–68; Kadish, S. H., 'Respect for Life and Regard for Rights in the Criminal Law', *California Law Review*, 64/4 (1976), 871–901; Levine, S, 'The Moral Permissibility of Killing a "Material Aggressor" in Self-Defence', *Philosophical Studies*, 45 (1984), 69–78; Nozick, R., *Anarchy, State, and Utopia*, Oxford: Blackwell, 1974; Ryan, C., 'Self-Defense, Pacifism, and the Possibility of Killing', *Ethics*, 93 (1983), 508–24; Thomson, 'Self-Defense and Rights'; Uniacke, *Permissible Killing*; Wasserman, D., 'Justifying Self-Defense', *Philosophy and Public Affairs*, 16 (1987), 356–78.

aggressor's guilt and victim's innocence which provides the explanation. Nor do I mean to invoke a general contrast between the overall character of the parties (as if Mother Teresa should always come out the preferred survivor in life-death struggles!). Rather, what I have in mind is the specific moral contrast between a defender and aggressor, deriving from and pertaining to the relationship of antagonism that, at that moment, binds their fates together. We might say that, at the critical moment, the aggressor's fault for the aggressive action puts him at a moral disadvantage in respect to the victim and the victim's innocence allows him to reap the advantage.

This seems an intuitively attractive idea, but is it possible to give an account of the source of this moral advantage? Cheney Ryan has spoken about what he calls the 'negative bond' which exists between an aggressor and his victim.[14] It is an apt phrase for it captures the way that the rights and obligations of persons in a situation of conflict are determined by the peculiarly intimate nature of the relationship of violence. This determination is evident in many aspects of the right of self-defense, but is most obvious in the principle of proportionality. As we have seen in preceding chapters, proportionality requires us to balance the harm inflicted on an aggressor in the course of defense with the harm prevented. But, it explicitly does not require us to balance the overall costs and benefits of the defensive act in the manner of a consequentialist calculus, for an innocent victim is apparently entitled to kill literally any number of culpable aggressors. What seems to be operating here is a principle which directly connects the rights and obligations of the two parties involved in a conflict situation. This principle is not easy to articulate but it may the one which Phillip Montague finds in Locke's *Second Treatise*: namely, that obligations should be viewed, at least in part, as reciprocal. In other words, we have the obligation to refrain from behaving in certain threatening and harmful ways to others just as long as they do the same to us or at least remain within the bounds of civility.[15] Such a principle obviously requires further explanation and analysis but it does seem to identify a consideration of some intuitive force.[16]

---

[14] Ryan, 'Self-Defense, Pacifism, and the Possibility of Killing', 508–24, at 519 ff.

[15] Montague, P., 'Self-Defense and Choosing between Lives', *Philosophical Studies*, 40 (1981), 207–19, at 215 ff.

[16] Furthermore, it in no way conflicts with the Kantian-inspired explanatory principle which I shall introduce below.

The present proposal about the role of fault provides a non-circular explanation of the moral asymmetry between the victim and aggressor. It does so in the following way: I have the right to life. Therefore, if an aggressor makes an attack upon my life, in the absence of any special justifying circumstances, he wrongs me. Because I am innocent and he is at fault for the aggression, his claim against me that I not use necessary and proportionate lethal force against him becomes forfeited (or fails to be entailed by his right to life). Therefore I have a right (liberty) to kill him. Therefore when I attack him to defend myself, I do not violate his right to life, and hence I do not wrong him. Because I do not wrong him, I do not forfeit (or fail to possess) my right to life. This account avoids the vicious circularity of the simple specification of the scope of the right to life in moral terms reviewed above. I want to suggest that this dynamic—this careful intimate moral relationship, is capable of explaining the aggressor's forfeiture of his right to life, the defender's procurement of right to kill, and the moral asymmetry between the two.

One significant advantage of this proposal is that it can account for our intuitions about culpable provocation in cases of self-defense. Consider a man who cruelly torments his long-time enemy with the intention of goading him to make an attack so that he can kill him and claim innocence by reason of self-defense. It seems clear that killing in these circumstances does not fall within the bounds of justified self-defense, and the present account can explain why. Although the provoked man is certainly not free of fault for his actions (his fault may be the same or even greater than a negligent threat to someone's life), what prevents the provocateur from claiming the right of self-defense is that he is at fault for the creation of the situation of threat to which he now responds. In less extreme cases of provocation where the attacked party is only partly responsible for the start of the fight, we will say that their ability to claim the right of self-defense is diminished to the extent of their fault. The present account provides an extremely good explanation for these features of self-defense.

Innocent threats and innocent aggressors

Now the suggestion that the culpability of the aggressor plays a material role in the explanation of self-defense is subject to an extremely powerful objection which most commentators have considered to be fatal to the account. The objection contends that it is sometimes justifiable to kill in self-defense a person who is not in any way at fault for the harm he or she offers you. The point is often illustrated by the following standard examples: imagine you are in an elevator with a mild-mannered colleague when she suddenly goes berserk and tries to stab you, having earlier drunk coffee that some villain had laced with a mind-altering psychopathological-behaviour-inducing drug. More prosaically, perhaps, your life is endangered by the movements of someone in the throes of an epileptic fit. In either case imagine that the only way that you can save your life is by using lethal force against the other person. This is the case of the 'Innocent Aggressor'.[17]

The second example is introduced by Robert Nozick: someone picks up a fat man and throws him at you down the bottom of a well. If he lands on you, he will crush you to death, though he will survive because you will cushion his fall. However, you have a ray-gun with which you can disintegrate him in mid-flight and save yourself. This is the case of the 'Innocent Threat', which Nozick characterizes as 'someone who innocently is a causal agent in a process such that he would be an aggressor had he chosen to become such an agent'.[18]

In both these cases, runs the objection, would one not be justified in using lethal force to save oneself? Moreover, would one not be justified for the same reasons as in the central case of self-defense involving a culpable aggressor? If this is so, how can the fault or moral responsibility of the aggressor play a material role in the justification of self-defense? There is a significant consensus about this result. Most modern commentators (both philosophers and lawyers) agree that one would be justified in acting against both an Innocent Aggressor and an Innocent Threat.[19] Furthermore, this

---

[17] See Fletcher, G., 'Proportionality and the Psychotic Aggressor', *Israel Law Review,* 8 (1973), 367–90, at 371.

[18] Nozick, R., *Anarchy, State, and Utopia,* Oxford: Blackwell, 1974: 34.

[19] See Thomson, 'Self-Defense', 283–311; Uniacke, *Permissible Killing;* Ryan, 'Self-Defense, Pacifism, and the Possibility of Killing', 508–24; Davis, N., 'Abortion and Self-Defense', *Philosophy and Public Affairs,* 13 (1984), 175–207; Fletcher, G., *Rethinking Criminal Law,* Boston: Little Brown, 1978, ch. 10. The consensus view is challenged by Otsuka, M. ('Killing the Innocent in Self-Defense', *Philosophy and Public Affairs,* 23, (1994), 74–94) and in some respects by Montague ('Self-Defense and Choosing between Lives', 207–19) and Norman, R. (*Ethics, Killing and War,* Cambridge: Cambridge University Press, 1995: 120–8).

view is explicitly endorsed in most legal jurisdictions[20] and was held by many of the classical authors including Grotius and Hobbes.[21]

But the consensus view is not correct: it is generally not justifiable to save oneself by killing an Innocent Aggressor or Innocent Threat, and it is certainly impermissible to kill in the circumstance of the two examples cited above. The reasons for this stem from considerations deep in the theory of rights. Understanding what these reasons are will help us to understand why it is permissible to use violence against culpable aggressors and will bring us to the most basic grounding of my theory of self-defense.

The first move that I shall make, in order to demonstrate this, is to introduce a third problem case which I shall call the case of the 'Innocent Bystander'. In this case you can save your life only by killing an innocent person who is not, him or herself, a material component of a direct threat to your life. An example would be if you could save yourself only by seizing someone from a crowd and using them as a shield against your enemy who is shooting at you (this would be a case of substituting an innocent bystander's life for your own). Another example would be shooting the wife and children of your attacker in order to distract his attention so you may escape (a case of making use of a bystander). A final example would be killing a bystander who was innocently obstructing your escape from an aggressor (a case of riding roughshod over a bystander).[22]

I take it that most would agree that it is impermissible to save oneself by killing an innocent bystander in each of these cases. Moreover, I take it that this intuition is at least as strong as our intuitions about the permissibility of acting against an Innocent Aggressor or Innocent Threat. These cases are extremely important, for they show that, *pace* Hobbes, we do not believe that 'anything goes' when it is a case of 'either him or me'. Even under the shadow of death we recognize a duty to discriminate and not to harm certain classes of person. The requirement of excluding these cases from legitimate self-defense thus marks a significant boundary for any viable account of the right.

---

[20] See Kadish, 'Respect for Life and Regard for Rights in the Criminal Law', 876 n.

[21] Grotius, H., *De Jure Belli Ac Pacis*, Kelsey, F. (trans.), New York: Classics of International Law, 1925: 172; Hobbes, T., *Leviathan*, Tuck, R. (ed.), Cambridge: Cambridge University Press, 1991, ch. 14: 69–70.

[22] This taxonomy is Thomson's: 'Self-Defence', 89 ff. The second example is derived from Nagel, T., 'War and Massacre', *Mortal Questions*, Cambridge: Cambridge University Press, 1979: 69.

Now the challenge, for those who believe that it can be permissible to kill Innocent Aggressors and Innocent Threats, but agree that it is not permissible to kill Innocent Bystanders, is to provide an account of the basis of self-defense which can differentiate these cases. What justifies harming Innocent Aggressors and Innocent Threats if it is unjustifiable to harm Innocent Bystanders?

A first attempt to answer this question might invoke the idea of causal responsibility. Innocent Threats and Innocent Aggressors are, unlike the Innocent Bystander, causally responsible for the threat facing the victim (they are sometimes referred to as 'material' threats or aggressors). The difficulty with this proposal is that the notion of 'causal responsibility' has insufficient moral substance to ground the distinction we require. What is it to be 'the cause' of a given event? Mill employed the notion of 'total cause' to refer to the sum of sufficient conditions of a given event. In this sense, the Innocent Bystander who blocks my route of escape is properly described as causally responsible for the threat to my life. He is a cause, in the sense that he is an enabling condition of the threat.

Those who want to defend a distinction between killing Innocent Bystanders and killing Innocent Threats and Innocent Aggressors will object that this is not the appropriate notion of causal responsibility. They will insist that the relevant notion is something like that of a 'direct cause'. But we may ask: why should the fact that someone is a direct cause of a threat to my life make them an appropriate object of defensive action, whereas the fact that they are an enabling condition does not? There is certainly a distinction here, but it is not at all clear that it is a morally significant distinction. In normal circumstances, being a direct cause of harm is morally significant because we take it as evidence for, and one constituent of, moral culpability. But in the present cases culpability has been ruled out *ex hypothesi*. Given this, it is difficult to see what role 'causal responsibility' could play in grounding the distinction.[23]

Appeals to causal responsibility fail to achieve the appropriate distinction between killing Innocent Threats and killing Innocent Bystanders. Further reflection reveals why this is so. There is one kind of Innocent Threat which it is uncontroversially impermissible

---

[23] For a useful discussion of issues surrounding the notion of cause see: Putnam, H., 'Why There isn't a Ready Made World', *Synthese*, 51/2 (1982), 150 ff.

to kill. These are threatening persons who are innocent because their action is justified. Examples would be the policeman using lawful force in the course of an arrest, the state executioner killing a justly condemned man, or the victim of an attack using necessary proportionate force in self-defense. With the exception of Hobbes, almost no commentator believes that it is permissible to employ force against such threats to save one's own life, even though in each case the agent has clear causal responsibility for the threat.

This draws our attention to two important points. First, the problem of killing the Innocent Threat and Innocent Aggressor in self-defense is really the problem of killing persons who are excused but not justified for their action. Secondly, appeals to a purely 'material' account of why it is permissible to kill Innocent Threats would seem doomed to failure, because any set of material conditions which these cases satisfy will also be satisfied by justified threats whom it is clearly impermissible to kill. What these two points together demonstrate is that any workable distinction must be, at core, a normative and not a factual distinction, and it must invoke some relevant differentiation between justifications and excuses.

Objective wrongdoing

The most sophisticated rights-based account of self-defense which has so far emerged is that developed (independently) by J. J. Thomson and Suzanne Uniacke. Though the two accounts are not identical, both authors squarely address the above issue. In the view of both Thomson and Uniacke, the justification for killing in self-defense is grounded most basically in the fact that the person against whom one uses lethal force 'would otherwise kill you in such a way that they would violate your right to life',[24] or in Uniacke's terms that the threat they pose to you is 'unjust'.[25] Both writers, therefore, recognize that the explanation of self-defense must invoke some normative or moral fact about the person against whom one employs defensive force. What is distinctive about their view, however, is that they give an 'objective' account of what it means to pose an unjust threat to a person's rights. In their view it is possible for a

---

[24] Thomson, 'Self-Defence', 288 and 298–303.
[25] See Uniacke, *Permissible Killing*, ch. 5.

person to violate rights without in any way being at fault. This will occur if their behaviour is excused but still objectively wrong.

The idea that an 'objectively unjust' act may justify the use of defensive force has a long history. The Just War Theory has traditionally asserted an absolute prohibition on killing 'the innocent'. But the non-innocent (those who may permissibly be killed in war) are not defined as morally non-innocent or at fault, but rather as something like 'presently harmful'.[26] The notion has received a general exposition in recent legal writing on justification and excuse stimulated by George Fletcher's seminal work, *Rethinking Criminal Law*. Fletcher has argued that because excuses exculpate the agent without rendering the behaviour rightful, they have no function in creating and negating the rights of persons in a situation of conflict: 'Whether a wrongful actor is excused does not affect the rights of other persons to resist or to assist the wrongful actor. But claims of justification do.'[27]

Fletcher intends this to be a general principle for the resolution of conflicts of rights. He illustrates it with the famous torts case of *Ploof v Putnam* in which the plaintiff sought to dock his boat in the defendant's wharf to shelter from a ferocious storm. The defendant prevented his docking and the boat was destroyed.[28] Fletcher argues that if the plaintiff's action was justified by reason of being the lesser evil, then the defendant's resistance was wrong and he is liable for the damage to the boat. On the other hand, if the plaintiff's act was merely excused because of a 'duress of circumstance' then the defendant retains the right to resist the docking and is not liable.[29] What this principle implies for self-defense is, in the words of lawyer Glanville Williams: 'one can defend oneself against, and only against, an act that is wrong, including excusably wrong'.[30]

---

[26] See Anscombe, G. E. M., 'Mr Truman's Degree', in *The Collected Philosophical Papers of G. E. M. Anscombe*, vol. iii, *Ethics, Religion and Politics*, Oxford: Basil Blackwell, 1981, n. 1; and Kenny, A., *The Logic of Deterrence*, London: Firethorn, 1985: 10. It is only through such an objective (re)definition of innocence and non-innocence that the Just War Theory is able to maintain what would otherwise appear to be an inconsistent triad of propositions: (i) soldiers on either side of a war who abide by the rules of the *jus in bello*, or war convention, are morally innocent, (ii) one is never permitted to kill the innocent, (iii) one is permitted to kill enemy soldiers in war.

[27] Fletcher, *Rethinking Criminal Law*, 760.

[28] 81 Vt 471, 71 A 188 (1908).

[29] Fletcher, *Rethinking Criminal Law*, 761.

[30] Williams, G., 'The Theory of Excuses', *The Criminal Law Review* (1982), 732–42, at 733. There is no convenient English term for the idea of an objective wrongdoing which

I want to suggest that the use to which these authors put the notion of objective wrongdoing has severe limitations. In particular, Fletcher's general claim that excuses diminish responsibility while leaving rights of defense undisturbed, cannot be sustained. Excuses do sometimes affect the right of resistance, and understanding why this is so will provide us with a deeper understanding of the nature of defensive rights themselves.

The first way to bring this out is to interrogate the claim that the actions of an excused aggressor or threat still violate rights. Both Thomson and Uniacke assert that the innocent projectile and the automaton in our two examples would, if they succeeded in killing you, violate your rights.[31]

On the surface, this does not seem a plausible claim. How could either person be said to violate your right to life when the drugged colleague is not in any way at fault, and the falling fat man does not even meet the requirements for agency—he does not *do* anything at all? The claim that innocent projectiles and automatons can violate a person's rights is not an intuitive one. None the less, Thomson has a striking argument for it. She notes that, whatever else may be true of them, the Innocent Threat and the Innocent Aggressor certainly do not have the *right* to take the victim's life: 'In Hohfeldian terms neither has . . . a privilege of killing you. For them to lack the privilege of killing you, however, is for you to have rights (Hohfeldian claims) that they do not do so, rights they infringe if they succeed in killing you.'[32] This argument is certainly tempting. If the falling fat man doesn't have the right to kill you, then he must surely violate your rights if he lands on you and thereby kills you. But on reflection we can see that the argument must contain an error. Consider this reconstruction of Thomson's argument with different premises:

1. The boulder on the hill clearly has no right to fall on you.
2. It therefore lacks the Hohfeldian privilege of falling on you.

---

includes excused action, but the German legal concept of *rechtswirdig* and the Soviet notion of *protivopravnye* both express this meaning. See on this Fletcher, 'Proportionality and the Psychotic Aggressor', 378 and 388.

[31] NB Fletcher does *not* make this claim about cases of physical compulsion such as the falling fat man. In his view (which is also mine) there is, in these cases, no act and hence wrongdoing. See Fletcher, *Rethinking Criminal Law*, 803.

[32] Thomson, 'Self-Defence', 300. In this passage Thomson is discussing Innocent Aggressors, but her comments on pp. 288 and 302 make it clear that she believes the argument can be extended to cover an Innocent Threat such as the falling fat man.

3. But, for the boulder to lack the privilege of falling on you is for you to have a claim-right against the boulder that it not fall on you.

Therefore:

4. If the boulder falls on you it violates your right that it not fall on you.

Something has gone wrong here; we have ended up with a nonsensical conclusion though the initial premise is certainly true. To understand what is wrong with the argument we must return to considerations about the basic nature of rights. Something can only violate rights if it is the subject of a duty (this is a simple consequence of the Hohfeldian logic of rights). But something can be the subject of a duty only if it has certain minimal capacities, including the capacities of acting, deliberating, choosing and intending. This is just to say that duties can only be held by moral subjects, or to put this another way, rights must be sympathetic to the limits of obligation; where the notion of obligation cannot get a footing, neither can we talk of rights or of wrongdoing.[33] The point is enough, however, to illuminate what is wrong with Thomson's argument.

The reason why the stone on the hill has no right to fall on you is that it is just not the kind of entity that could be the subject of rights and duties. From the fact that the stone fails to possess a right (liberty) to fall in this sense, it obviously cannot be inferred that it has a duty not to fall. The correct conclusion is that the stone has neither a right (liberty) to fall on you nor a duty to abstain from falling, because it is not a moral subject at all.

But precisely the same is true of the falling fat man. He is a moral subject, but *qua* falling object he is just like the stone, neither the subject of a liberty to fall on you, nor of a duty not to fall. The falling is not something he does so his falling cannot be in violation of any duties he owes you. Hence, in crushing you he violates none of your rights (though of course the person who pushed him may well do so). The case of the drugged colleague and the epileptic in the Innocent Aggressor example can be interpreted in the same way. They are not voluntary actors and since no one can be under a duty to abstain from involuntary actions, you cannot have a claim against

---

[33] Thus the old dictum *ultra posse nemo obligatur* (no one is obliged to do anything he is incapable of doing).

them that they not involuntarily kill you. Therefore it makes no sense to speak of them involuntarily violating your right to life.

What this shows is that the result of some excuses (such as physical compulsion and automatism) is to remove the harm in question altogether from the sphere of obligation and from the realm of evaluation in terms of rights and duties. This is not, of course, to say that the harm inflicted by automatons and innocent projectiles is removed from the sphere of moral evaluation. The relevant distinction is that between a moral wrong and a moral evil. When a tree is blown down in a gale and crushes a house, this is an evil in the sense that it is a bad state of affairs but it is not a wrong; it violates no one's rights. The same would seem to be true of the falling fat man and the out-of-control automaton. If, as Thomson and Uniacke believe, one is only justified in using defensive force against an unjust threat, then we are forced to conclude that it is unjustifiable to kill innocent automatons and innocent projectiles, for in neither case can it properly be said that they would otherwise violate your right to life.[34]

But not all excuses work in this way. When someone's harmful acts are excused because of mistake, infancy, or duress, it does not seem obvious that their mistaken or infantile or coerced condition removes them altogether from the realm of obligation and duty. Such agents do seem to do wrong and to violate rights through their actions, even though we do not hold them to be fully responsible for their wrongdoing. Is it permissible to kill such Innocent Threats? To answer this question, we require a more sophisticated account of what excuses are, and how they interact with the considerations that justify self-defense. We can begin this investigation, and, at the same time, finally arrive at the most basic grounds which underlie my characterization of defensive rights, by linking our enquiry with a broadly Kantian understanding of rights.

[34] Suzanne Uniacke has argued in correspondence that my treatment of these cases leaves us with an inadequate account of their nature as excuses, for we say that excused behaviour is by some standard wrong, but that the agent is not to be blamed for its performance. If what I have said is correct then the falling fat man and the automaton are subject to no duties with respect to the harm they cause and hence violate no rights. Then doesn't this turn these excuses into justifications, by implying that the agent has a liberty and hence a positive right to inflict the harm? I think that part of the answer to this objection is provided by the observation that something may require excuse because it is bad even if it is not wrong. The status of these exculpations as excuses rather than justifications also reflects the fact that they speak to questions of responsibility on the part of the agent and it reflects the fact that had the harms in question been inflicted in the course of voluntary responsible action they would certainly have constituted a violation of rights.

Moral subjects

To take the language of rights seriously, is to be committed to the idea that a person's right may be infringed or forfeited only on the basis of something that the person is or does as a moral subject. The reason for this is that the most basic function of a morality of rights is to locate certain extremely important normative considerations wholly within the sphere of the subject itself so as to make them unassailable by external contingencies such as are appealed to by consequentialism. The idea is articulated in the following way by Thomas Nagel: 'Whatever one does to another person intentionally must be aimed at him as a subject, with the intention that he receive it as a subject. It should manifest an attitude to *him* rather than just to the situation, and he should be able to recognise it and identify himself as its object.'[35]

It seems to me that this idea identifies a comprehensible and extremely important moral principle. In terms of self-defense the principle has the following consequence: if one is to be justified in inflicting harm in an act of defense, then there must be an appropriate normative connection between the wrongfulness of the threat one is seeking to avert and the person one harms; the threat must derive from him as a moral subject, not just as a physical entity. We might say that the threat we respond to must be *his* threat rather than simply a threat of the world at large which happens to manifest itself through his body.[36]

When one kills a culpable aggressor there is precisely such a connection between the existence of the wrongful threat and the person against whom one directs defensive force: the aggressor is morally responsible for the threat. It is precisely because of this connection that our violence is morally comprehensible, for it manifests an appropriate attitude to *him*, and to something he is doing. In contrast to this, the fact that a person has unwittingly become a threat to my life, as in the Innocent Aggressor and Innocent Threat

[35] Nagel, 'War and Massacre', 66.

[36] Nagel himself expresses his principle at one point by saying that when we harm a person, it must be possible to offer the justification for our action *to* the person we harm rather than simply to the world at large (Nagel, 'War and Massacre', 67–8). But a utilitarian who believed it justifiable to kill one person to save the lives of five would presumably be willing to offer this as a justification directly to the person they sought to harm and, moreover, would believe the justification to be one which their victim ought to accept. It seems to me that my formulation better articulates what is most important about the idea.

cases, is not a fact about *them* as moral subjects; it is at most a fact about their bodies understood purely as physical objects in the world.

I take the above requirement to be implicit in the very idea of a right. To say that the falling fat man has the right to life is to say that he has an interest in his living which cannot be overridden except on the basis of his own choosing, willing, or acting. He can waive his right to life, or forfeit it (for instance, by violating certain laws or obligations), but we cannot override his right simply on the basis that it would be congenial or useful or even imperative for us to do so. In Kantian terms, to do this would be to treat him as object rather than subject—to act upon him as a bare impediment, like a falling stone. The same line of reasoning serves to explain why it is impermissible to kill Innocent Bystanders. For the only reason we could have for taking their lives is that they happen to be situated in such a way that their death is necessary for our survival. But this is not a relevant fact about them as subjects and harming them on this basis could manifest no proper attitude towards them as persons.[37]

The above principle provides the best way to complete our explanation of self-defense. It provides the third leg of our normative model of self-defense. That right is grounded, not simply in the fact that the defensive action is a necessary proportionate response to an unjustified threat to life, but also in the fact that there is a sufficiently substantive normative connection between the unjustified threat and the person against whom one uses defensive force. It is this normative connection which explains the moral asymmetry between the aggressor and defender, and explains why the aggressor is morally vulnerable to the defender's use of force.

It now becomes apparent why Fletcher's general claim, that excuses do not affect the defensive rights of other persons, cannot be correct. For excuses work (in Fletcher's words) by seeking 'to avoid the attribution of the act to the actor'.[38] If excuses serve to undermine the attribution of the act to the actor and self-defense is partly grounded in precisely such an attribution, then considerations of excuse must have an effect on defensive rights.

---

[37] Or rather it would manifest towards them an attitude of *contempt*, which in this context precisely amounts to a denial of their moral personality.

[38] Fletcher, *Rethinking Criminal Law*, 759.

The variety of excuses

The question we must now address is: what constitutes a 'sufficiently substantive normative connection' between the threat posed and the object of one's defensive action? Specifically which forms of excuse render the connection too weak? This is not an easy question to answer. Excuses constitute an extremely varied and multiform collection of normative mechanisms, and a full answer would require a study of excuse more detailed than I can attempt here. What I propose to offer is an initial (and far from exhaustive) analysis which would seem to be a plausible and fruitful base for further refinement.

We may adopt a threefold classification of excuses to help delineate the relevant issues. The first category consists of excuses in which the agent lacks the intention to perform the proscribed act. The second concerns actions which are intentional but in some sense involuntary. The third consists of cases in which the agent either lacks the capacity for full and proper deliberation of the legal or ethical issues involved, or lacks the capacity to form a 'wicked intent'.

An agent may lack the intention to perform a proscribed act for the reason that he manifests no intentional attitude whatever in his bodily movements and hence strictly performs no act at all. As we have seen, this is the case with the excuses of *physical compulsion* and with some cases of *automatism*, for example, when a person lashes out in the throes of an epileptic fit. I have argued that self-defense is impermissible against such threats, because the defensive action could manifest no appropriate attitude to them as subjects.

The other form of excuse in this category concerns cases in which the agent acts intentionally, but does not intend to perform the act under the description of the crime. The relevant excuses here are *mistake* and *ignorance*. These terms cover a broad range of cases. Some mistakes are negligent, and hence do not excuse at all. It would seem that defensive force is an appropriate response to negligently mistaken aggressors, because our violence manifests an attitude towards the agent's culpable lack of care, which in turn is something for which he is responsible. At the other extreme, certain mistakes are so complete and unavoidable that they leave intact little or none of the normative connection between the harm and the agent, which I claim to be a necessary prerequisite of proper self-defense. Imagine that you are making a film in which an actor is supposed to shoot at you with a gun loaded with blanks. Unbeknown to the actor, however, someone has put real bullets in his gun.[39] It seems to me that the threat posed by the actor in such a case is morally indistinguishable from the falling fat man. He, as a subject, does not have that minimal engagement with the threat which could justify directing defensive force against him. On the other hand, many cases of mistake fall between these two extreme examples. As Austin points out, many excuses answer one charge only by admitting another, as when one says 'I was clumsy', 'confused', or 'thoughtless'.[40] The cut-off point is not easy to determine but it seems to me that one could properly respond to threats performed in these ways with defensive force.

A second class of excuse concerns actions which are fully intentional, but which are in some sense *involuntary*. The excuses here are *duress, necessity*[41] (sometimes called 'duress of circumstance'), and *provocation*.[42] These excuses all trade on an analogy with physical compulsion. They involve the claim that the agent was subject to 'internal pressure' amounting to an 'irresistible force'.[43] The definition of duress in the American Model Penal Code allows an acquittal if the defendant was coerced by threats to the point that a 'person of reasonable firmness in his situation would have been unable to resist'.[44] A leading English case on duress talks of 'the will being overborne by threats... so that the commission of the alleged offence was no longer a voluntary act of the accused'.[45]

---

[39] This is apparently how Bruce Lee's son, Brandon Lee, died during the filming of *The Crow*.

[40] See Austin, 'A Plea For Excuses', 3.

[41] 'Necessity' in the law is an ambiguous term for it can refer to either a justification or an excuse. As a justification it refers to cases in which a harmful course of action is properly chosen as the lesser evil. Aristotle's example of the ship's captain who throws his cargo overboard in a storm to save his crew falls into this category (*Nicomachean Ethics*, trans. Ross, W. D. in *The Complete Works of Aristotle*, ii, Barnes, J. (ed.), Princeton: Princeton University Press, 1984. 1110ᵃ). It is necessity as an excuse, however, that concerns us here. In this sense it refers to actions which may not be the lesser evil but which the agent was under exceptional pressure to perform. This was the issue in the celebrated case of *Regina v Dudley and Stevens* in which two shipwrecked sailors murdered and ate a cabin boy to save themselves from starvation (14 QBD 273, 1884).

[42] Provocation is probably best understood as the companion to necessity and duress, but in some circumstances it might be classed together with infancy, insanity, and intoxication as a consideration which calls into question the ability of the agent to deliberate properly about the wrongness of his actions.

[43] Fletcher, *Rethinking Criminal Law*, 821.

[44] MPC § 2.09.

[45] *Regina v Hudson* [1971] 2 All ER 244 (Crim App) 246.

Yet these analogical expositions of the excuse are all deeply problematic. For actions performed under duress, provocation, or necessity are not literally involuntary; it is not literally the case that the
agent 'has no choice'. This is underlined by the fact that English law
does not recognize duress as an excuse to murder, attempted
murder, or to some forms of treason.[46] It thus implicitly recognizes
that persons are capable of resisting grave threats, even against their
own life, no matter how difficult it may be to do so. But why, then,
do not law and morality hold fast to responsibility in these cases
rather than allowing an excuse? For it could certainly be argued that
the harder an impulse is to resist, the greater is the need for a
deterrent.

Fletcher suggests that one strand in the theory of excuses concerns
the idea of compassion: 'Excuses are motivated by compassion for
persons caught in a maelstrom of circumstance. The underlying
sentiment is that, if any one of us were forced to act at gun point or
to steal in order to survive, we would do the same.'[47] This is, I think, a
very good characterization of why we do not seek to punish those who
commit crimes under duress, necessity, or provocation. After all, who
are we to cast the first stone when the case concerns such extreme
circumstances? Yet one may recognize the force of this point and still
find in the choices and actions of such agents sufficient grounds to
employ defensive force against them. When they offer us harm, this
represents their response as moral subjects to the situation they are
facing. It is a terrible situation and we feel compassion for them, but
still they should not have chosen the response they did, and had they
been better persons they would not have done so. Our defensive force
is, therefore, an appropriate response, not just to the situation at large,
but to *them*. In my view, it is entirely permissible to defend oneself
against an aggressor who is excused by reason of necessity, duress, or
provocation.

The final category of excuse consists of *infancy, intoxication,* and
insanity. These are all cases in which the agent either lacks the
capacity for full and proper deliberation of the legal or ethical issues
involved, or lacks the capacity to form a *mens rea* or 'wicked intent'.
The excuse of infancy offers a difficult range of cases. In English law

---

[46] Smith, J. C., and Hogan, B., *Criminal Law,* London: Butterworths, 1992: 238 and
240. See also Stone, R., *Offences against the Person,* London: Cavendish, 1999: 66.
[47] Fletcher, *Rethinking Criminal Law,* 808.

a child under the age of 10 is considered to be incapable of forming a criminal intent and hence cannot be convicted of any crime.[48] Yet it seems to me that I would have the right to defend myself against a malicious 9 year old who had got hold of a gun and was shooting at me. But as one makes the child younger and less capable of moral deliberation my intuition becomes weaker. It seems to me that I would not have the right to kill an infant toddler who was about to ignorantly discharge a firearm at me in play. However, I am unable to offer a clear theory for distinguishing the exact dividing line between these cases (nor can I discover one in the literature), and perhaps the best we can do here is to employ sensitive moral intuition on a case by case basis.

Intoxication is only a defense in law if it negates *mens rea*: 'If [the defendant] had the *mens rea* for the crime charged he is guilty, even though drink impaired or negatived his ability to judge between right and wrong or to resist temptation or provocation and even though, in his drunken state, he found his impulse to act as he did irresistible'.[49] This seems correct. Drink may weaken a man's inhibitions, but the tendencies to which he then gives vent are, in some respect at least, his own. If, on the other hand, the intoxication does remove *mens rea*, then the relevant question becomes whether the intoxication was voluntary or involuntary. If one causes harm without *mens rea* after a voluntary bout of drinking, then one is at least negligently responsible for the mischief caused. But if a person becomes involuntarily intoxicated, for instance, after inhaling noxious fumes, and goes into a state of violent automatism, then the cause of the harmful behaviour would seem to be entirely external, with the subject himself contributing nothing. In such a case, it seems to me, the threat no more relates to the agent as a subject than does the threat in the case of the falling fat man, and there can be no justification for directing defensive force against him.

The most problematic excuse of all, from the point of view of self-defense, is that of insanity. The term 'insanity' covers a multitude of very distinct pathologies, and psychiatric illness may affect a person's behaviour in many different ways. It may cause the agent to suffer from insane delusions which invokes questions of mistake and ignorance. It may cause the agent to go into a state of automatism, or to experience 'irresistible impulses'. It may lead to the development

---

[48] Smith and Hogan, *Criminal Law*, 195.   [49] ibid. 225.

of a diseased moral personality, as in the case of sociopaths who are apparently unable to form normal moral judgements.[50]

Making sense of these different considerations in light of our principle that defensive force must manifest an attitude to the aggressor as a subject rather than just to the situation at large will not be easy. But a helpful distinction will be that between cases in which the cause of the mental disturbances is internal and those in which it is purely external. Suppose someone receives a blow to the head and thereafter goes into a state of violent automatism, or suffers delusions that he is being attacked and that he must defend himself with force. This case would seem analogous to the case of involuntary intoxication discussed above, in that the cause of the mental aberration is wholly external. If one accepts that defensive action must exhibit an appropriate response to something about the subject, then I cannot see anything about such a person that could justify the employment of force against him.

Yet the same may also be true of certain mental disturbances whose causes are internal, in the sense of being internal to the body of the agent. In the case of *Kemp* a man made a sudden and motiveless attack on his wife with a hammer. It appeared that his action stemmed from arteriosclerosis which had caused a congestion in his brain.[51] Under the famous McNaughton rules the cause of the mental disturbance was deemed 'internal' and therefore generated a defense of insanity rather than non-insane automatism.[52] Yet for our purposes there is an important sense in which the cause of the aberration is external, for it has its source entirely outside of the mental and psychological world of the subject. Kemp's case seems morally indistinguishable from that of automatism induced by a blow to the head, or the inhalation of fumes.[53]

---

[50] See Davison, G., and Neale, J., *Abnormal Psychology*, New York: John Wiley and Sons, 1974.

[51] *Kemp* [1957] 1 QB 399 at 406.

[52] The McNaughton rules define insanity so as to require a 'defect of reason from disease of the mind'. But this has been interpreted by the courts to include any disease of the *body* which results in a mental disturbance be it diabetes, epilepsy, or brain tumour. See Smith and Hogan, *Criminal Law*, 202 ff.

[53] There is one important way in which the cases may differ and that is that mental disturbances deriving from bodily illness may be *recurrent* rather than merely transitory. If the mental disturbances are recurrent, as in the case of epilepsy, and the agent knows he is liable to be affected by them, then he has a duty to take provisions to ensure he is not a danger to others. An agent who fails to take such provisions may be guilty of negligently causing harm.

So the distinction that we require between internal and external causes is different to that made by law in the McNaughton rules. The distinction I want to suggest is that between aberrant behaviour whose cause lies entirely outside the psychological realm of the subject, for instance, in a blow to the head or low insulin level, and disturbed behaviour which originates from, and accords with, the psychological dispositions and makeup of the subject, even if those dispositions are themselves the result of illness. It seems to me that we may not use lethal defensive force in the first kind of case, but it may sometimes be permissible to do so in the second.

I am aware that this distinction is problematic and will be controversial, but it does seem to have some force. For example, we may contrast Kemp's case with that of a sociopath, whose psychiatric illness has caused him to develop the character of a ruthless killer who formulates and carries out murderous intentions. Now perhaps Kemp also had a murderous intention at the time he attacked his wife, but I take it that for the sociopath these intentions do not simply come as a 'bolt from the blue' as they apparently did for the unfortunate Mr Kemp. They rather stem from the state of his personality and they constitute intentions he may associate with and recognize as his own. Defending oneself against a threat posed by such a person seems paradigmatic of the right of self-defense. Why? Well, his actions reflect the kind of person he is, even if he has only become this kind of person because of psychiatric illness. It does not at all seem improper to say that, in directing force towards him, one is responding to him as a subject.

Yet, one will object, how can the state and dispositions of a subject's moral personality be significant in this way, when they are themselves a product of illness? The agent did not choose mental illness and he (presumably) could not help becoming the kind of person he is.

But these considerations start us down a long road whose ending point is not easy to discern. If we are impressed by the thought that we cannot be held responsible for moral dispositions which are themselves determined, then we must face the arguments of environmental and genetic determinism and of the dependence of mental states on electrical and chemical states of the brain. There is a danger that the realm of moral personality will be wholly obliterated by the causal grasp of the world. At some point we must draw a line around the sphere of moral agency and responsibility, even if we recognize that beyond it, or below it, lies a world of determining conditions.

It will be objected, however, that my account draws that line in the wrong place, for we do not punish the criminally insane. We therefore clearly believe that there is something special about the way that their action is determined which sets it apart from the more ordinary world of responsible action. This is a difficult point to answer. In part, I think that it shows that the conditions for just punishment and for just defense are not the same (of which, more below). Moreover, we do incarcerate the criminally insane, and hence override or disregard their rights to liberty. What can justify this, if, as I have said, impinging on a person's basic rights must reflect some response to them as a subject? Perhaps we think that confining the insane is simply a case in which consequentialist considerations of protecting society from harm outweigh the rights of the innocent individual (the breakwater of the right is overwhelmed by the consequentialist flood). I think this may be partly correct. If, on the other hand, we think that the dangerously insane do not have the right not to be locked up, then we must believe that there is something about the insane as subjects which explains this loss of right. If this were correct, then I suspect that our reluctance to describe their confinement as punishment may stem from considerations of compassion which I discussed above, rather than a strict belief in the negation of responsibility. For these reasons the distinction I have drawn between disturbed behaviour whose cause lies internal to, and that which is wholly external to, the subject, though not entirely free of problems, is none the less defensible and useful.

What is evident in this discussion is that the question of whether self-defense is justifiable against an 'Innocent Threat' or 'Innocent Aggressor' is vastly more complicated than most commentators have believed. Many writers have restricted themselves to the two rather extreme examples of physical compulsion and innocent automatism and have thought that self-defense in these cases is clearly permissible. I hope to have shown that self-defense in these cases is clearly impermissible. The class of excused threats as a whole constitutes a highly complex range of cases some of which satisfy the minimal conditions for justified self-defense, and others of which do not.

One result of this discussion has been to reveal the divergence between the conditions for just self-defense and for punishment. The famous jurist Blackstone asserted the commonly perceived connection between the two ideas: 'No act may be prevented by death unless the same if committed, would also be punished by death'.[54] Indeed, it has often been supposed that an account of self-defense which employs the idea of a forfeit of right on the part of the aggressor (such as mine) must covertly assimilate self-defense to a form of punishment.[55] But what this discussion has shown is that the requirements for just punishment and the requirements for justified defense, even on a forfeit of rights account, are not identical.[56]

This is why the simple claim that the permissibility of self-defense is grounded in the culpability of the aggressor requires qualification and refinement. For if we equate 'culpable' with 'liable to be punished', then clearly one may kill certain aggressors who are not culpable. Yet self-defense is grounded in the existence of a level of normative responsibility on the part of the aggressor for the threat he poses to the defender. Where this is not present, as in the case of physical compulsion, involuntary intoxication, or unavoidable mistake, self-defense is impermissible. The level of responsibility required is delineated by a principle of respect for persons which is Kantian in spirit and which cuts through the class of excused actions. This in turn shows that, *pace* recent legal theory, questions of excuse do bear on the rights of resistance and defense.

For all I have said, however, it does seem hard justice to hold a person guilty for striking against a dangerous automaton or an unavoidably mistaken aggressor to save his life. Why should we feel this? Thomson suggests that those who agree with her that it is a requirement of self-defense that the person killed would otherwise violate your right to life (as I do) and yet disagree with her that the Innocent Aggressor and Innocent Threat would otherwise violate your right to life (as I also do in some cases) are likely to believe that you would be excused but not justified if you killed to save your life in these cases. This is a helpful suggestion, but she unfortunately does not indicate how she thinks the excuse in these cases can be accounted for. The most obvious tactic would be to invoke Hobbesian considerations about the extreme forces operating on a person face to face with the void and the enormous difficulty of abstaining from action which could save one's life. However, this cannot be, between the cases for consider this: if Hobbesian considerations

---

[54] Quoted in Fletcher, 'Proportionality and the Psychotic Aggressor', 377.
[55] See Norman, *Ethics, Killing and War*, 123.
[56] I shall return to the relationship between self-defense and punishment in Chapter 8.

show that one is excused for killing the Innocent Aggressor and Innocent Threat, then they also show that one is excused for killing a culpable aggressor. But if one's action in the central case is excused then this would seem to preclude its being justified. The relationship between justification and excuse is not one of strict logical exclusion, but there is clearly a deep tension here, for excusable acts are those for which one is not held fully responsible, whereas one talks about justification only after responsibility has been established.[57] Moreover, the notion of self-defense as a right is premised at a basic level on the assumption of responsibility and hence the possibility of abstention even in the face of death. This assumption seems to be borne out by our strong feelings that there are situations, such as those involving Innocent Bystanders, where it is impermissible to kill to save one's own life.

A better explanation of how it could be excusable to kill a dangerous automaton or mistaken aggressor is that of reasonable mistake. When faced with dangerous and threatening individuals it is reasonable to assume that the attack is malicious unless one has very good evidence to the contrary. A reasonable mistake in many of these cases will serve to make the use of lethal force excusable (though not justified). None the less, there will inevitably be cases in which the victim has unequivocal knowledge that the aggressor is innocent in one of the ways I have specified, and the conclusion we are driven to accept is that in these circumstances the victim may not kill to save himself.

All in all, the account of self-defense that we have constructed appears to be a robust one. It accounts for more of our pre-theoretical intuitions than its obvious rivals. It avoids the Scylla and Charybdis of forfeit and specification by focusing on the particular moral relationship between defender and aggressor and viewing the rights of each as interdependent. It has the advantage of being able to account for our intuitions about provocation. Most importantly, it anchors our understanding of self-defense, and in particular the moral asymmetry between aggressor and defender, in a plausible and genuinely explanatory moral principle invoking the normative contrast between the responsibility of the aggressor and the innocence of the defender.

---

[57] See Robinson, P., 'A Theory of Justification: Societal Harm as a Prerequisite for Criminal Liability', *UCLA Law Review*, 23/1 (1975), 266–92, at 275.

In this part of the book I have defended a positive account of self-defense. My strategy has been to develop a model of defensive rights in their most general form including the right to defend third parties and to defend goods of differing value. The model of defensive rights which has emerged has shown them to derive from a complex set of normative relationships between four entities: the subject (the holder of the right), the content (the defensive act), the object (the party against whom the right is held), and the end (the good or value which the defensive actions seek to protect or preserve). A right of defense exists when a subject is at liberty to defend a certain good by performing an action which would otherwise be impermissible. The moral justification for this liberty invokes the following three considerations: (i) an appropriate normative relation exists between the subject and the end of the right, consisting either of a right *to*, or a duty of care towards the good protected, (ii) the defensive act is a proportionate, necessary response to an imminent threat of harm, (iii) the object of defensive force has an appropriate degree of normative responsibility for, and the subject is innocent of, the harm threatened. We now turn to consider the right of national-defense in light of these findings.

Part II
National-Defense

5

International Law

The first part of our project is now complete. We have developed a working explanatory model of defensive rights. Our task now is to attempt to apply this model to the purported right of national-defense. Our question shall be: to what extent can national-defense be seen as a valid instance of the broader class of defensive rights which we have charted in Part I, and in particular what is its relation to the right of self-defense?[1] Before we can do this, however, we need an understanding of the content of the supposed right of national self-defense which we will hope to scrutinize. What does it encompass? How is it conceived? What is the scope of its limitations and permissions?[2]

In answering these questions, it is very important that we do not simply construct a straw-man to subsequently demolish. Any account of national self-defense, even an ultimately sceptical and destructive one such as I shall pursue, must explain why the notion has seemed so morally credible for so long and to so many people— including many great and distinguished thinkers. If we suspect a sickness in our thinking about war and peace, our procedure must be in part diagnostic as well as remedial.

The claim that there is a right of national-defense receives its principal articulation and defense in the western tradition within the Just War Theory. But the Just War Theory is, in reality, many theories. It is more accurate to talk of the 'just war tradition' rather than the 'Just War Theory', for it includes a large number of diverse yet related positions stretching from the theological writings of Augustine and Aquinas, via the legal treatises of Grotius and his contemporaries, to the modern secular account found in writers

---

[1] A quick reminder on my use of terminology: 'national-defense' is used to refer to the act or right of national self-defense by a state or nation. The term 'self-defense' is reserved for the act and right of personal self-defense.

[2] In this discussion our task is to interrogate the status and validity of a generally accepted legal and moral right: that of national-defense. Reference to 'the right of national-defense' and its correlates should not be taken to endorse the existence or validity of such a right, but merely to refer to the content of the right as most plausibly conceived by its adherents.

such as Michael Walzer. Where should one look to find a characterization of *the* right of national-defense? Since the tradition is so diverse,
I shall adopt the strategy of giving an initial characterization of the
content of the right of national-defense by examining the formulation
of the right in modern international law. This seems the most acceptable course, since international law has a certain privileged status
possessed by no philosophical treatise, in that it represents a form of
consensus amongst the world's states. Moreover, it is increasingly
international law which furnishes the context for debate amongst
policy makers on the justice of war and military action.

International law is linked to the philosophical discourse on war
in two ways. The first is through its historical source in the great
philosopher-jurists of the sixteenth, seventeenth, and eighteenth
centuries: Vitoria, Suarez, Gentili, Grotius, Pufendorf, and Vattel
who were themselves deeply influenced by the earlier philosophical
and theological writings particularly those of Aristotle, Cicero, Augustine, and Aquinas. Though it substitutes the notion *bellum legale*
(lawful war) for that of *bellum justum* (just war), international law is
recognizably a continuation of the just war tradition, providing a
treatment of the *jus ad bellum*, contiguous with earlier discussions.
The second connection is through international law's explicit
modern-day philosophical apologists, the most influential of
whom is Michael Walzer.[3] Where international law seems to err or
construe the right of national-defense in an implausible way, we may
therefore fall back on the extra-legal texts to give the right its
strongest and most reasonable hearing. This combination of international law and contemporary philosophical apology backed by a
legal, theological and philosophical tradition stretching to St Augustine and beyond, will prove a formidable adversary for our
critical project.

National-defense in international law

The current international law on the use of force by states is found in
customary law and in the various international treaties and conven-

---

[3] Walzer, M., *Just and Unjust Wars*, New York: Basic Books, 1977. Walzer describes his
theory of *jus ad bellum* as a defence of 'the legalist paradigm', which he takes to be a close
paraphrase (with certain modifications) of modern international law.

tions to which the world's states are party. Of these, by far the most important is the Charter of the United Nations, which is the founding document of the post-Second World War international legal order. The UN Charter has important antecedents in the Covenant of the League of Nations and the Kellogg–Briand Pact, but it goes further than any document before it in outlawing the recourse to violent means in international relations. Its central provision, Article 2(4) requires that: 'All members shall refrain in their international relations from the threat or use of force against the territorial integrity or political independence of any State, or in any other manner inconsistent with the purposes of the United Nations'. The Charter thus stands as a fundamental legal repudiation of Clausewitz's dictum that: 'War is the continuation of policy with the addition of other means'.[4] Military force, Article 2(4) boldly proclaims, may never be lawfully employed as an instrument of state policy. The phrase 'use of force' was preferred to 'war' so as to encompass military activities which fall short of the legal definition of war (for instance, because war was never formally declared), and also to prevent states from redefining their conflicts so as to avoid international responsibility.[5] Article 2(4) outlaws not only the use of force in international relations, but also its very threat. It is thus an extremely broad prohibition.

To this wide-ranging ban on the use of force by states, two exceptions only are recognized in the Charter. The first is that a state may use force under the auspices of the United Nations to enforce international law. This is provided for in Chapter VII of the Charter. The second is the exception of national-defense.

This right is explicitly affirmed in Article 51: 'Nothing in the present Charter shall impair the inherent right of individual or collective self-defence if an armed attack occurs against a member of the United Nations...'. The attacked state which would exercise the right of national-defense is under an obligation to immediately inform the Security Council of their actions, and the right persists only until such time as 'the Security Council has taken measures necessary to maintain international peace and security' (Art. 51).

---

[4] Clausewitz, C., *On War*, Howard, M., and Paret, P. (eds.), Princeton: Princeton University Press, 1976: 87.
[5] For example, Japan in 1931 attempted to avoid censure for its war in Manchuria by terming the conflict an 'incident'.

There has been much recent discussion about whether there may exist a third exception to the prohibition on the use of force by states, in the form of a limited right of unilateral[6] humanitarian intervention.[7] Humanitarian intervention may be defined as unauthorized military intervention in a state for the purposes of alleviating suffering or preventing the abuse of human rights.[8] There is clearly no such right in treaty law and the possibility would seem to be precluded in the strongest terms by Article 2(4) of the UN Charter. Debate hinges, however, on whether state action has now established a right in customary law, particularly in light of NATO's dramatic intervention in the Federal Republic of Yugoslavia following atrocities committed against ethnic Albanians in Kosovo in 1999. NATO states refrained from invoking a general right of humanitarian intervention, however the law in this area does seem to be in a state of flux and may well be moving towards the adoption of a more permissive approach to unilateral humanitarian intervention (with the application of strict limitations)[9]. At the time of writing, however, it is not possible to unambiguously identify a right of unilateral humanitarian intervention in international law.[10]

From this brief summary it is evident that the UN Charter institutes a legal framework which parallels the regulation of force

---

[6] i.e. not authorized by the Security Council.

[7] See Cassese, A., 'Ex iniuria ius oritur: Are we Moving towards International Legitimation of Forcible Humanitarian Countermeasures in the World Community?' *European Journal of International Law*, 10/1 (1999), 22–30; id., 'A Follow-Up: Forcible Humanitarian Countermeasures and *Opinio Necessitatis*', *European Journal of International Law*, 10/4 (1999), 791–9; Simma, B., 'NATO, the UN and the Use of Force: Legal Aspects', *European Journal of International Law*, 10/1 (1999), 1–22; Brown, B. S., 'Humanitarian Intervention at the Crossroads', *William and Mary Law Review*, 41 (2000), 1683–741; Roberts, A., 'NATO's "Humanitarian War" over Kosovo', *Survival*, 41/3 (1999), 102–23; Guicherd, C., 'International Law and the War in Kosovo', *Survival*, 41/2 (1999), 19–34.

[8] See Roberts, A., 'Intervention and Human Rights', *International Affairs*, 69/1 (1993), 429–49, at 429.

[9] Antonio Cassese has argued that any right of unilateral humanitarian intervention would be subject to cases where at least the following conditions are present: (a) a breach of human rights amounting to a serious crime against humanity is taking place; (b) the crimes are either carried out by the central government or with their connivance and support; (c) the Security Council is unable to take effective measures to resolve the situation, for example, because of a veto by one of the permanent members; (d) the action is taken by a group of states acting in concert, with at least the non-opposition of the majority of world states; (e) all peaceful measures consistent with the urgency of the situation have been attempted first; (f) use of force is strictly limited to the alleviation of the humanitarian crisis (Cassese, 'Ex iniuria ius oritur', 27).

[10] It is, of course, uncontroversial that humanitarian intervention can lawfully take place when authorized by the Security Council under Chapter VII of the UN Charter.

amongst individuals in domestic law. First, the use of force by individual states is prohibited; secondly, a central body is set up which holds a (near) monopoly on the lawful use of force; thirdly, acts of national-defense by victim states and third party allies are permitted in the event that the central body is unable to afford protection from attack in a particular case. Every act of force by states in the international arena is thus divided by the Charter into one of three legal categories: either it is an unlawful use of force, or it is lawful because performed at the request of or with the authorization of the UN, or it is a lawful response to an illegal armed attack and hence an act of legitimate national-defense.

In practice, however, the mechanism legally enacted by the United Nations Charter broke down almost immediately. A powerful central body capable of establishing a monopoly of force and effectively enforcing international law never materialized. This was largely the result of the veto enjoyed by the five permanent members of the Security Council, and the rigid bipolarity of international relations during the cold war. It is this breakdown of the UN enforcement mechanisms which explains the singular importance of the concept of national-defense to current thought on international law and international relations. National-defense is currently the sole *casus belli* explicitly recognized in law as a justification for the use of force by states without Security Council authorization. The twin conceptions of national-defense and unlawful use of force have come to dominate the debate about the justness of war in each of its legal, political, and philosophical contexts.

Part of the reason for the pre-eminence of the concept of national-defense, of course, is that it gains enormous intuitive legitimacy from the analogy with personal self-defense. This analogy has had a profound influence on just war thinking and is explicitly invoked by both international lawyers and philosophers. Hugo Grotius, one of the fathers of international law, though at times sceptical about the analogy between private and international law, draws heavily upon it in his account of national-defense. 'What has been said by us up to this point, concerning the right to defend oneself and one's possessions', he says, 'may be made applicable also to public war, if the difference in conditions be taken into account'.[11] Writing in the

---

[11] Grotius, H., *De Jure Belli Ac Pacis* [The Law of War and Peace], Kelsey, F. (trans.), New York: Classics of International Law, 1925, bk. II, ch. 1: 184.

first half of the twentieth century the international lawyer Edwin Dickinson was able to proclaim that: 'we are indebted to this analogy [between private and international law] for almost everything that is regarded as fundamental in modern international law'.[12] With the enormous development of treaty law after the Second World War that assessment is probably now somewhat exaggerated. However, the contemporary legal scholar Yoram Dinstein is still able to unequivocally assert that 'the legal notion of [international] self-defence has its roots in inter-personal relations'.[13] Michael Walzer calls the analogical argument from self-defense to national-defense the 'domestic analogy', and places it the centre of his theory of *jus ad bellum*.[14]

Indeed it would not be an exaggeration to say that the right of national-defense in international law (deeply influenced as it is by the philosophical Just War Theory) is structured so as to be isomorphic with the criminal law of self-defense. It will be helpful to explore this isomorphism in greater detail as we chart the legal content of the right. As in the case of self-defense, the right of national-defense is not defined as an independent rule, but as an exception to a prior prohibition on the use of force. The right of national-defense is thus established as a legal justification for the use of force, consisting in a Hohfeldian liberty to perform acts which would otherwise be prohibited in law. As we have already seen, this is precisely the way that the right of self-defense is structured within criminal law and inter-personal morality.

National-defense is defined as an exception to the prohibition on the use of force, but, as in the case of self-defense, it is also defined as a lawful response to the violation of this prohibition. This has two important consequences. The first is that the provisions which establish the illegality of the use of force serve also to demarcate the rights which can lawfully be defended with force. In the terminology we have developed in Part I, it specifies the permissible end of national-defense.

What then are the legitimate ends of national-defense? Article 51 states simply that the right of national-defense is effective in the face

---

[12] Dickinson, E. D., 'The Analogy between Natural Persons and International Persons in the Law of Nations', *Yale Law Journal*, 26 (1917), 564–91, at 564.

[13] Dinstein, Y., *War, Aggression and Self-Defence*, Cambridge: Grotius Publications, 1988: 166.

[14] Walzer, *Just and Unjust Wars*, 58.

of 'armed attack'. The notion of armed attack is closely linked to that of aggression which is given its general definition in the United Nation Consensus Definition of Aggression (1974) Article 1(1), in terms which recall Article 2(4) of the Charter: 'Aggression is the use of armed force by a State against the sovereignty, territorial integrity or political independence of another State, or in any other manner inconsistent with the Charter of the United Nations'.[15] Two things are made clear in this definition: first, the rights whose imminent violation justify resort to defensive force are the rights of states. Secondly, the rights in question are those which concern the state's sovereignty. While the Consensus Definition explicitly refers to sovereignty, Article 2(4) of the Charter refers only to 'territorial integrity or political independence'. As D. W. Bowett points out, however, these two rights are constitutive of state sovereignty: 'both together define the concrete existence of a state'.[16]

What is prohibited by international law and what states have the right to defend themselves against with force is, in one influential formulation: 'Dictatorial interference in the sense of action amounting to a denial of the independence of the state'.[17] Does this mean that states are permitted to defend themselves with force against actions which violate their sovereignty or independence but which do not involve a military threat or threaten territorial integrity? Some authors have thought so. Bowett has argued that states may be justified in using force against 'economic aggression' which

---

[15] It should be noted that there are some grounds in case law and state practice for a considerably more complex set of distinctions between aggression, armed attack, and illegal use of force than is suggested here. Germany's invasion of Poland was deemed in the *Nuremberg* trials to be an act of aggression. Though Iraq's invasion of Kuwait was deemed an illegal armed attack, the term 'aggression' was not applied. In the *Nicaragua Case*, Nicaragua's support of insurgents in El Salvador was found to be an illegal use of force, but not an armed attack justifying collective self-defense on the part of the United States. This makes for a complex and convoluted set of distinctions, which are far from clearly worked out in the law. The crucial point seems to be that national-defense is deemed to be justified in the face of an armed attack which violates the territorial integrity and political independence of a state. It is highly likely that all acts of aggression, as here defined, would constitute 'armed attacks' for the purposes of Article 51. In the following chapters I shall use the term aggression to refer to any actions sufficient to trigger a right of national-defense, following the non-legal and philosophical use of that term. It should be further noted that the *threat* of use of force is not grounds for national-defense, even though it is illegal under Article 2(4) of the Charter.

[16] Bowett, D. W., *Self-Defence in International Law*, Manchester: Manchester University Press, 1958, 42.

[17] H. Lauterpacht, *International Law and Human Rights*, London: Stevens, 1950: 167.

impinges on the sovereignty of the state.[18] This view, however, is difficult to substantiate in the face of Article 51's explicit reference to 'armed attack' as a condition of national-defense, and it has been rejected by the majority of commentators. A more widely accepted, though still contentious, extension of the right of national-defense is to cover the defense of nationals abroad. The classic examples of this are the Israeli raid on Entebbe Airport in 1976 carried out to rescue Israeli hijack hostages, and the American interception of an Egyptian plane carrying terrorists who had hijacked the Italian ship *Achille Lauro*. While the law does seem to endorse a limited form of the right to defend nationals abroad, it is interesting to note that the argument typically given for bringing such actions within the scope of national-defense invokes the claim that in certain circumstances an attack against a state's citizens can be tantamount to an attack on the sovereignty of the state itself.[19]

In summary, the structure of international law suggests a strong analogy between individual self-defense and national-defense: persons are constituted by their existence as organic entities and they have the claim-right against other persons not to destroy their life or interfere in their bodily integrity. States are constituted by their existence as sovereign entities and they have the claim-right against other states not to destroy their political independence or interfere in their territorial integrity. Just as individuals have the right to defend, with lethal force, their existence as organic entities, so states have the right to defend with military force their existence as sovereign entities. This is the essence of the analogical argument for national-defense.

Limits of the right

As we can see, the basic structure of national-defense in international law is closely parallel to that of self-defense in domestic law. This similarity extends also to the limitations to which the right is subject. It is universally acknowledged that the right of national-

---

[18] See Bowett, *Self-Defence in International Law*, 106.

[19] See Bowett, D. W., 'The Use of Force for the Protection of Nationals Abroad', in Cassese, A. (ed.), *The Current Legal Regulation of the Use of Force*, Dordrecht: Martinus Nijhoff, 1986, 40–1; Alexandrov, S., *Self-Defence against the Use of Force in International Law*, The Hague: Kluwer Law International, 1996: 203.

defense is bounded by the same intrinsic limitations as the right of personal self-defense, namely, those of necessity, imminence, and proportionality.[20] However, these concepts sit less easily in international law than they do in domestic law and there are significant legal problems concerning the application of each concept to the use of force between states. At this stage I shall simply note these problems and indicate the consensus position where this is possible. As we proceed I shall hope to provide some illumination as to why these problems arise in this way for international law.

The legal requirement of necessity in national-defense is delineated by the *Caroline* Doctrine of 1838 which has been called the '*locus classicus*' of the law of national-defense.[21] The *Caroline* was an American steamboat being used to smuggle arms across the Niagara river to assist rebels fighting against the British in Canada. The British army attacked the *Caroline* on American territory, set it on fire, and sent it over the Niagara Falls with the loss of several American lives. The British claimed the right of national-defense and there followed a diplomatic exchange, during which the American Secretary of State, D. Webster, articulated a test for national-defense which was to become incorporated in international law. It required a state to demonstrate: '... necessity of self-defence, instant, overwhelming, leaving no choice of means, and no moment for deliberation'.[22] This test has been frequently reaffirmed in subsequent international law.[23] The requirement of necessity is normally thought to require states to take all reasonable means to achieve a peaceful vindication of their rights through arbitration, negotiation, and non-violent sanctions.[24]

There is, however, a significant disanalogy between the application of necessity in international and domestic law. In domestic law the test of necessity is applied throughout the period of defensive action. For instance, if a victim is able to thwart an attack upon his life by knocking his aggressor unconscious, it would not be permissible to

---

[20] The requirements of necessity and proportionality were explicitly reaffirmed in the *Nicaragua* case, 1986, ICJ Reports 14, pp. 14, 94, and 103.

[21] See Bowett, *Self-Defence in International Law*, 58.

[22] Quoted in Dinstein, *War, Aggression and Self-Defence*, 227.

[23] For instance, it was invoked by the International Military Tribunal at *Nuremberg* (Dinstein, *War, Aggression and Self-Defence*, 228).

[24] See Schachter, O., 'The Right of States to Use Armed Force', *Michigan Law Review*, 82 (1984), 1635: 'Force should not be considered necessary until peaceful measures have been found wanting or when they would clearly be futile'.

proceed with the infliction of a fatal blow. In international law, however, the test of necessity is applied only to the commencement of a conflict, not throughout the war. A state fighting a legitimate defensive war is not required in law to cease hostilities when it has vindicated its rights. It may prosecute its war to final victory even after the point at which this is no longer necessary to reverse or frustrate the initial unlawful use of force which provided the justification for the war.[25]

An example of this was the Allies' campaign against Japan and Germany in the Second World War. Once the war had commenced, the Allies were legally permitted to, and did, seek the unconditional surrender of their enemies, even after they had liberated all the territories subject to the initial acts of aggression. The Allies (chastened no doubt by the legacy of the First World War) clearly feared that Germany and Japan might recommence their aggressive activities if not completely crushed. Yet it is important to realize that in the absence of a state of war, fear of potential future aggression, no matter how well founded, cannot provide legal justification for the use of force against a state. It may be thought that this departure from the analogy with domestic self-defense reveals a simple misapplication of the requirement of necessity on the part of international law. But it is also possible that it is a remnant of medieval and early modern views which connect or elide the right of self-defense with rights of punishment, reparation, and revenge.[26] The connection between self-defense and punishment, and the role of law enforcement in international relations, will be discussed in Chapter 8. At this point we need only note that the position of international law on necessity sits uncomfortably in the context of the argument about self-defense.

The requirement of imminence in national-defense is also covered by the *Caroline* Doctrine and it has similarly generated severe

---

[25] Dinstein, *War, Aggression and Self-Defence*, 233–5.

[26] The intermingling of self-defense, revenge, punishment, and deterrence is clearly evident in this passage from Francisco de Vitoria: '. . . the commonwealth cannot sufficiently guard the public good and its own stability unless it is able to avenge injuries and teach its enemies a lesson, since wrongdoers become bolder and readier to attack when they can do so without fear of punishment . . . the injured party, city or duke, may not only defend itself, but may also carry the war into its attacker's territory and teach its enemy a lesson, even killing the wrongdoers. Otherwise the injured party would have no adequate self-defence; enemies would not abstain from harming others, if their victims were content only to defend themselves', *On the Law of War*, 1.2 § 5 and § 9 in *Vitoria: Political Writings*, Pagden, A., and Lawrence, J. (eds.), Cambridge: Cambridge University Press, 1991.

difficulties of interpretation. Dispute centres on the question of whether international law allows for 'pre-emptive' or 'anticipatory' defense, in other words, military action taken against a state which has not yet commenced an aggressive attack but which seems certain to do so. Those who argue against such a right, point to the clear and deliberately restrictive wording of Article 51 which permits national-defense only on the condition that 'an armed attack occurs'. They also argue that a more liberal interpretation would have a danger-ously destabilizing effect on international peace and security, and they point to the difficulty of determining whether a state really intends to make an attack prior to its actual commencement.[27] On the other hand, those who support a right of anticipatory defense, base their argument on the claim that Article 51 does not replace the existing customary law on national-defense but merely supplements it (customary law prior to the signing of the Charter in 1945 clearly did encompass a right of anticipatory defense). They further argue that, in an age of motorized warfare, jet fighters, and intercontin-ental missiles, it would be intolerably unjust to compel a potential victim to wait till its border had been crossed and thus yield a potentially fatal advantage to its adversary.[28]

In so far as it is possible to identify a settled position in the law on this difficult question, it seems to coalesce around the distinction between *pre-emptive* and *preventive* military action.[29] Pre-emptive defense is a strike against an aggressor who has formed the intention to attack and whose attack is imminent but has not yet commenced. Preventive defense is an attack against a state which has not yet formed the intention of an aggressive attack, but which is about to achieve a decisive advantage which would seem to make a future aggressive intent likely and dangerous. State practice and the rulings of the Security Council would seem to suggest that there is a right of anticipation only in the pre-emptive but not the preventive sense. Thus the Security Council did not condemn the Israeli attack on Egypt in 1967 in circumstances in which most observers agreed that

---

[27] See Brownlie, I., *International Law and the Use of Force by States*, Clarendon, Oxford, 1963, p. 275–278; Brownlie I., 'The U.N. Charter and the Use of Force, 1945–1985', in Cassese, *The Current Legal Regulation of the Use of Force*, 499.; Dinstein, *War, Aggression and Self-Defence*, 172–6.

[28] See Bowett, *Self-Defence in International Law*, 187–93; and Walzer, *Just and Unjust Wars*, ch. 5.

[29] Ceadel, M., *Thinking about Peace and War*, Oxford: Oxford University Press, 1987: 82–3.

Egypt was poised to launch an attack on Israel, though it did condemn the Israeli air strike against an Iraqi nuclear reactor in 1981 where there did not seem to be any imminent threat of attack.[30] However, the precise dividing line between pre-emptive and preventive use of force remains a considerable source of uncertainty which is not adequately resolved in the law.

It is in respect of the requirement of proportionality, however, that international law seems least sure of foot. Proportionality was covered in the *Caroline* Doctrine: acts of national-defense may involve 'nothing unreasonable or excessive; since the act, justified by the necessity of self-defence, must be limited by that necessity, and kept clearly within it'.[31] Several authors, while noting the acknowledged centrality of proportionality to the law on national-defense, have lamented the absence of a clear legal treatment of the concept.[32] Part of the difficulty is that proportionality is a component of both the *jus in bello*, the regulations of how a war may be fought, and the *jus ad bellum*, the regulations of when a war may be fought and brought to an end. In the former context proportionality requires balancing the harm of a particular action in the course of a war against the requirements of military necessity. It prohibits military actions which are 'excessive in relation to the concrete and direct military advantage anticipated'.[33]

Our interest is in proportionality in the context of the *jus ad bellum*, and this requires a fundamentally different kind of balancing—between the harms brought about by the pursuit of a defensive war and the nature of the threat to which the war is a response. But precisely what is it that must be balanced? The International Court of Justice in the important *Nicaragua Case* has suggested that the proportionality condition requires a similarity in the 'scale and effects' of force and counter-force.[34] However, there are two

---

[30] Cassese, A., 'Return to Westphalia? Considerations on the Gradual Erosion of the Charter System', in Cassese, *The Current Legal Regulation of the Use of Force*, Martinus Nijhoff, Dordrecht, 1986, p. 515.

[31] Quoted in Dinstein, *War, Aggression and Self-Defence*, 227.

[32] Gardam, J. G., 'Proportionality and Force in International Law', *American Journal of International Law*, 87 (1993), 391–413, at 391–2; Brownlie, *International Law and the Use of Force by States*, 261 ff. See also Walzer, *Just and Unjust Wars*, pp. xv–xvii.

[33] Protocol I to the Geneva Convention of 1949, Art. 51(iii)(b), quoted in Gardam, 'Proportionality and Force in International Law', 406.

[34] *Case Concerning Military and Paramilitary Activities in and Against Nicaragua* (Merits), 1986, ICJ Reports 14, p. 103.

problems with this formulation. The first is that it seems more applicable to small-scale border skirmishes and reprisals than to warfare as such, where the scale of force is intrinsically open-ended on both sides and subject to escalation.[35] The second is that, as I have suggested in Chapter 2, such a reading misconstrues the basic nature of proportionality in defensive rights. Proportionality does not require a similarity in the *forcefulness* of the means utilized by defender and aggressor, rather it requires that the *harms inflicted* in the course of defense be commensurate with the value of the goods and rights preserved.[36]

As we have already seen, those rights which in law justify forceful defense are the state's rights to territorial integrity and political independence. The difficulty of applying the test of proportionality in the *jus ad bellum* is this: if the balance we are required to make is between the harms inflicted in the course of war (measured in terms of number of dead, destruction to property) and the protection of a state's rights of sovereignty, then it seems very difficult to know how to go about making this comparison. For, phrased in these terms, the task seems to require the comparison of incommensurables. It is little wonder that international law has found it extremely difficult to provide a clear treatment of the proportionality requirement. In practice the law has tended to simply assume that war is always a proportionate response to unlawful use of force which threatens the sovereignty of the victim state. It is an assumption we shall subject to a good deal of scrutiny in the following chapters.

The need for a normative foundation

The law of national-defense shares one final important feature with the right of personal self-defense. That is that national-defense is conceived as a 'right' in the full sense of that word. In Article 51 national-defense is referred to not only as a right but as an 'inherent

---

[35] Dinstein, *War, Aggression and Self-Defence*, 217.

[36] Roberto Ago of the International Law Commission seems to recognize this when he states: 'It would be a mistake to think that there must be proportionality between the conduct constituting the armed attack and the opposing conduct.... What matters in this respect is the result to be achieved by the 'defensive' action, and not the forms, substance, and strength of the action itself.' Quoted in Dinstein, *War, Aggression and Self-Defence*, 218.

right'. The wording in the French version of the Charter is even stronger, describing the right as 'natural'. Furthermore, this wording has been echoed numerous times in subsequent documents and treaties in international law.[37] But this raises a question of the greatest importance about how Article 51 fits into the overall legal-moral scheme of the UN Charter.

Article 1(1) specifies the fundamental purpose of the Charter: 'To maintain international peace and security, and to that end: to take effective collective measures for the prevention and removal of threats to the peace . . .'. The article identifies a powerful consequentialist consideration as a guiding principle for international law. It is one with obvious and compelling normative force. The obligation for states to abstain from the use or threat of force in Article 2(4) clearly derives directly from this objective. It is tempting to view the rule permitting national-defense in the same light, as simply deriving from the considerations in Article 1(1). Indeed, when an attempt is made to justify the right of national-defense it is often done in consequentialist terms: namely, that the right is given normative force through its role in deterring aggression and enhancing international peace and security. The argument gains credibility from recent legal developments. As Stanimar Alexandrov has shown, the legal mechanisms of national-defense have increasingly been incorporated by the Security Council into its strategy of response to international aggression.[38] A clear example of this was the Gulf War in which the Security Council's response to the Iraqi invasion of Kuwait included endorsing action by the United States and her allies under the provisions of Article 51.[39]

But to construe the normative force of national-defense as simply deriving from a consequentialist reading of the requirements of international peace and security would be a grave mistake in both moral and legal terms. There are several reasons for this. As I have suggested in the introduction, I do not believe that consequentialist considerations in either their 'act' or 'rule' guises can by themselves adequately answer the basic questions of *jus ad bellum*. Counter-factual questions such as whether peace and security would better be

---

[37] See Combacau, J., 'The Exception of Self-Defence in U.N. Practice', in Cassese, *The Current Legal Regulation of the Use of Force*, 11.; and Brownlie, *International Law and the Use of Force by States*, 254.

[38] Alexandrov, *Self-Defence against the Use of Force in International Law*, 294 ff.

[39] ibid. 263 ff.

served through a norm permitting, or one prohibiting, national-defense have no determinate answers. What is more, the attempt to invoke general assumptions about human (or state) behaviour often cuts both ways. For example, a right of national-defense may deter aggression, but it may also serve as a mask and justification for dangerous military adventurism, particularly when the right is liberally interpreted. Antonio Cassese has stressed this problem, pointing out that, throughout the post-Charter period, states have continuously attempted to utilize Article 51 to reassert some of their lost legal competence to use force by pushing the boundaries of national-defense towards the inclusion of anticipation, defense of nationals abroad, and defense against economic aggression.[40]

More important, however, is the fact that there is a basic tension between Article 51 and Article 1(1) which the consequentialist reading of Article 51 completely fails to address. Guaranteeing states' sovereignty and endorsing a right of national-defense will sometimes further the maintenance of international peace and security (by halting present and deterring future aggression), but it will sometimes have the opposite effect, acting as a destabilizing force on the international community.[41] As Hedley Bull has pointed out, in his classic study of International Relations:

International society has in fact treated the preservation of the independence of particular states as a goal that is subordinate to preservation of the society of states itself.... Thus international society has often allowed the independence of individual states to be extinguished, as in the process of partition and absorption of small powers by greater ones, in the name of principles such as 'compensation' and the 'balance of power'.... [42]

There is, in other words, a potential conflict between the defensive rights of states and the end of international peace and security. This conflict is frequently evident in the relations between great powers and smaller states. For instance, when the Soviet Union invaded Czechoslovakia in 1968 the western powers decided not to intervene to protect its sovereignty because of the calamitous results this would have had for world peace and security. Presumably the western

---

[40] Cassese, 'Return to Westphalia?'; id., *Violence and Law in the Modern Age*, Cambridge: Polity Press, 1986.

[41] See Dinstein, *War, Aggression and Self-Defence*, 196; Bowett, *Self-Defence in International Law*, 197.

[42] Bull, H., *The Anarchical Society*, New York: Columbia University Press, 1977: 19–20.

powers believed they had the right to defend Czechoslovakia even if, because of the overwhelming consequentialist considerations, they (prudently) chose not to exercise it. An appropriate way of phrasing the moral issue in this case would be to say that the rights of the Czech state were in conflict with, and had to be balanced against, the consequentialist requirements of international security. Thus there is a potential tension, between the guarantee of the sovereign rights of states, of which national-defense is a part, and the normative objective of international peace and security. It is a tension which must be accommodated in our analysis of the right.[43]

What the forgoing suggests is that national-defense is conceived, within international law and in the just war tradition, in very much the way that self-defense is conceived in domestic law and morality. It is conceived not as stemming from consequentialist considerations alone, but as a consideration of justice deriving from morally important features of statehood itself. In other words, national-defense is conceived in the full sense of the word as right—a consideration capable of asserting normative force against the consequentialist requirements such as those of peace and security, and presumably sometimes overriding them.

But this raises a difficult and important question: if not through consequentialist considerations, then how is the right of national-defense given substantive normative content? One potential answer to this question is that the right is to be viewed as implicit in the very concept of state sovereignty itself. The often quoted authority for this view is Senator Kellogg's assertion in the negotiations preceding the signing of the Kellogg–Briand Pact in 1928 that: 'That right [national-defense] is inherent in every sovereign State and is implicit in every treaty. Every nation is free at all times and regardless of treaty provisions to defend its territories from attack or invasion.'[44] Yet, as Yoram Dinstein points out, appeal to the notion of sovereignty is incapable of giving legal substance to a right of national-

---

[43] David Luban has made a consonant argument. He claims that to base one's theory of *jus ad bellum* on consequentialist considerations simply begs the question of the *jus ad bellum*: 'by giving absolute primacy to the world community's interest in peace, it does not really answer the question of when a war is or can be just; rather it simply refuses to answer it' (Luban, D., 'Just War and Human Rights', *Philosophy and Public Affairs*, 9/4 (1980), 160–81, at 165).

[44] Kellogg, 'Speech before the American Law Association on 29 April 1928', in *Documents on International Affairs 1928*, Wheeler-Bennett, J. (ed.), Oxford: Oxford University Press, 1929, 3.

defense. For the notion of state sovereignty itself 'has a variable content, which depends on the stage of development of the international legal order at any moment'. He points out that in the nineteenth and early twentieth century when states enjoyed an almost unlimited legal competence to wage war for *raison d'état*, this power was also thought to be implicit 'in the very notion of sovereignty itself'.[45]

If the notion of sovereignty is incapable of giving legal substance to the right of national-defense, it is less capable still (and for more fundamental reasons) of providing a substantive moral grounding for the right. The basic problem is that sovereignty is a factual and not a normative concept.[46] As originally developed by Jean Bodin, the doctrine of sovereignty entailed that there could be only one ultimate source of law in the land.[47] In legal terms, a state is recognized as sovereign if it is *de facto* capable of exercising sovereign power; in other words, if it is able to assert effective control within a given territory and assert political independence from dictatorial external interference.[48] But it is appropriate to ask here: why should a political entity, which as a matter of fact does enjoy these characteristics, be seen as possessing the right to them, and, moreover, the right to defend them with lethal force? It is a good question because a fundamental premise of normative political theory is that right does not (always) follow might. The concept of sovereignty is, by itself, incapable of conferring normative content on the right of national-defense because the sense of sovereignty here employed itself requires normative justification. Morally speaking, it is an empty vessel.

For these reasons, the normative aspirations of the right of national-defense in international law require a grounding in moral theory. The need for such a grounding is acute in international law because its normative aspirations are challenged in a fundamental way by the interpretation of state action offered by descriptive International Relations in its Realist form, and by Military Strategy.

---

[45] Dinstein, *War, Aggression and Self-Defence*, 170, see also Alexandrov, *Self-Defence against the Use of Force in International Law*, 10.

[46] Luban, 'Just War and Human Rights', 164.

[47] See Sabine, G. H., *A History of Political Theory*, Hinsdale, Illi.: Dryden Press, 1973: 377–9.

[48] See Brownlie, I., *Principles of Public International Law*, Oxford: Clarendon Press, 1966: 89–108.

What is distinctive about these views is that they employ the concepts of 'defense' and 'aggression' in a wholly amoral way. Realist International Relations views states as centres of power in a dynamic system, continuously asserting and defending themselves against other centres of power. For strategists, such as Clausewitz, defense is only one phase of a successful campaign, useful for its intrinsic strength and for weakening enemy forces prior to a period of attack:

> If defence is the stronger form of war, yet has a negative object, it follows that it should be used only so long as weakness compels, and be abandoned as soon as we are strong enough to pursue a positive object. When one has used defensive measures successfully, a more favourable balance of strength is usually created; thus, the natural course in war is to begin defensively and end by attacking.[49]

Because of the intrinsic interplay of defense and offense he claims that it would 'contradict the very idea of war to regard defence as its final purpose'.[50] From both of these theoretical perspectives, the attempt to draw a moral distinction between wars of aggression and wars of defense is meaningless, for both forms of military action are simply viewed as complementary components of the never-ending process of the assertion of state power.

If the concepts of defense and aggression are to serve a normative role, as they purport to do in international law and within the Just War Theory, then we must provide an account of these concepts which is not exhausted by the Realist and strategic interpretations of them. If national-defense is to be vindicated as a right, then we must find some way of understanding the defensive acts of states as more than simply that of power protecting itself; we must show how the contours of national-defense connect in appropriate ways with recognizable and substantive human goods and with other forms of justification.

It is precisely such a vindication that the analogy with personal self-defense is intended to provide. By locating the notion of national-defense within a framework of ideas generated in the context of personal defensive rights, the Just War Theorist hopes to show how a state's military action in defending its own sovereign power can be morally justified. The remainder of this book is devoted to the task of determining whether this vindication can be successfully achieved.

---

[49] Clausewitz, *On War*, 358.   [50] ibid.

We are in a good position to deliberate on this question because we now have at our disposal a detailed picture of what it is that makes defensive rights morally efficacious. In Part I, we began with basic moral considerations and worked towards a detailed conception of self-defense. Now our method will be the reverse. We start with a substantive conception of national-defense and work backwards to see if it can be linked in an appropriate way with the basic moral considerations capable of providing an appropriate grounding.

We have seen that the justification of defensive rights rests on a complex of normative relations between the different components of the right. Yet, as I shall argue in the next chapter, far from knowing whether and how these considerations can apply to war and international relations, we do not even possess a clear understanding of what the key elements of the purported right of national-defense (the subject, object, and end) *are.* If national-defense is a right, whose right is it? And if war is a normative relation, what kind of relation is it?

6

War and Defense of Persons

The two levels of war

Michael Walzer argues that war should be viewed not as a relation between individual persons, but between states: 'The war itself isn't a relation between persons, but between political entities and their human instruments'.[1] This view is shared by Ian Clark: 'The conscript in the opposing trench is at the very least relegated to the role of representative of the enemy'.[2] Thomas Nagel, on the other hand, premises his moral investigation of war on precisely the opposite assumption: 'A positive account of the matter must begin with the observation that war, conflict, and aggression are relations between persons'.[3] David Luban concurs with this judgement: 'Wars are not fought by states, but by men and women'.[4]

It seems to me that there is a profound issue here, and one which underlies a great deal of what is morally most difficult about war. For the phenomenon of war may be accessed on two distinct levels each suggesting a distinctive moral point of view: that of the rights and responsibilities of individual persons and that of the rights and responsibilities of states or other 'political entities'. War can at once be viewed as a relation between persons and as a relation between super-personal collective entities. Every military action is ascribable to some kind of collective entity, but it is at the same time constituted by actions ascribable to particular persons.

But both sets of entities—the collective and the individual—are conceived as moral agents, the bearers of rights and the subjects of duties. Which, if either, is the most basic or fundamental level for the moral analysis of war? In our moral investigation of national-defense, should we follow Walzer and Clark in giving primacy to the

---

[1] Walzer, M., *Just and Unjust Wars*, New York: Basic Books, 1977: 36.

[2] Clark, I., *Waging War: A Philosophical Introduction*, Oxford: Clarendon Press, 1990: 17.

[3] Nagel, T., 'War and Massacre', in *Mortal Questions*, Cambridge: Cambridge University Press, 1979: 64.

[4] Luban, D., 'Just War and Human Rights', *Philosophy and Public Affairs*, 94 (1980), 160–81, at 166.

moral relation between states, or follow Nagel and Luban in insisting on the primacy of the moral relations between individual persons?

These questions are of the utmost importance for us, for they suggest two possible ways forward in the project of providing a moral vindication of the right of national-defense. At the same time they indicate the great difficulties that any such account will have to overcome. The crux of the analogical argument for national-defense is succinctly summarized by Douglas Lackey: 'The notions of self-defence and of just war are commonly linked: just wars are said to be defensive wars, and the justice of defensive wars is inferred from the right of personal self-defence'.[5] But if there is an inference from self-defense to national-defense, what form does the inference take? The two levels of war suggest two broad strategies for answering this question. The first is to give primacy to war as a relation between individuals and attempt to explain national-defense reductively at the level of personal rights. Thus one might attempt to show that national-defense can be derived from, or analysed in terms of, the personal defensive rights of citizens. The second strategy is to take the notion of state rights seriously and try to give moral content to them as independent from, yet analogous to, the rights of personal self-defense. These two broad strategies will provide the basic framework for my investigation of national-defense.

In reality, however, the situation is more complicated than this simple bifurcation suggests, for both strategies can be applied independently to each of the constitutive elements of the defensive right. Thus in investigating national-defense we must address the following questions:

1. Who or what is the *subject* of the right, that is, the right's bearer? Is national-defense a right held by the state, or by individual citizens within the state? If the former is the case, then we must enquire how it is possible for a state or community to possess moral rights. We will require an account of the genesis, operation, and limitations of rights held by communities, and crucially an understanding of how they relate to the rights of individuals within the state or community.

2. Who or what is the *object* of the right, that is, the entity against which the right is held? Is the right of national-defense held

---

[5] Lackey, D., *The Ethics of War and Peace*, Englewood Cliffs, NJ: Prentice Hall, 1989: 18.

against the aggressor state, or against the individual persons engaged in the attack? As we have seen in Chapter 7, to hold a right of defense against an aggressor implies the forfeiture or limitation of some of the aggressor's rights. If national-defense is a right held against a state, what rights does the invading state forfeit? Secondly, and more problematically, how does the state's forfeiture of rights account for the loss of the right to life of individual soldiers of the invading force?

3. What is the *end* of the right, that is, the good or value which the defensive action is intended to protect and preserve? This is perhaps the most important of our three questions. For defensive rights are governed by an intrinsic limitation of proportionality, which requires us to balance the harm inflicted in the course of defense, against the good protected. Any morally justified defensive action must be grounded in a good of sufficient value to make proportionate the harm inflicted. In international law, as we have seen, the end of national-defense is defined as the protection of a state's territorial integrity and political independence. But we must seek a deeper understanding of these rights. Why are territorial integrity and political independence morally important? Is it that the continued existence of the state as a sovereign entity is itself an intrinsic good? Abba Eban has suggested that just as individuals can be killed, so states can be the victim of the crime of 'policide', meaning the destruction of a state's sovereignty through conquest.[6] Perhaps it is to forestall such a harm that defensive military force is justified. Alternatively it may be that the rights of states only have moral significance because of the role they play in securing the lives and interests of their citizens. Perhaps it is the imminent destruction of individuals threatened by an invading army which generates the right to kill in national-defense. It is important to understand that there is no necessary connection between these two suggestions, for populations can, and frequently do, survive the destruction of their state's sovereignty, and the state can survive the destruction of a large number (though clearly not all) of its citizens.

If we apply the two strategies of reduction and analogy to the three elements of defensive rights, we arrive at eight possible arrangements which could be used as a basis for understanding the right of national-defense (see Table 6.1).

---

[6] Quoted in Walzer, *Just and Unjust Wars*, 52.

TABLE 6.1. Alternative possible
structures of the right of national-
defense

1.	5.
Individual subject	State subject
Individual object	State object
Individual end	State end
2.	6.
State subject	Individual subject
State object	Individual object
Individual end	State end
3.	7.
State subject	Individual subject
Individual object	State object
Individual end	State end
4.	8.
Individual subject	State subject
State object	Individual object
Individual end	State end

These different arrangements provide us with alternative models of the normative structure of national-defense and represent different possible 'routes' to giving normative content to the right. Simply by casting one's eye over these different models, one can see their connection to familiar forms of argument and rhetoric about the justice of war. For instance, the idea that the function of the state is to protect its citizens against the violent threats of foreigners, suggests viewing national-defense in terms of models (2) or (3). On the other hand, the familiar wartime rallying cry of the need for citizens to come to the aid of their country suggests the quite different models of (6) or (7). Models (1) and (5) represent the two strategies of reduction and analogy in their purest form—(1) represents national-defense solely in terms of rights of individuals, whereas (5) represents national-defense wholly as a matter of state rights, at most modelled on or analogous to an individual right. All the other models are mixed, invoking some elements of the idea of a pure state right and some elements of personal rights. Other aspects of international relations suggest different models again. Forceful action against terrorist groups operating from a host country of which they are not themselves citizens is often justified in terms of model (8), and the protection of nationals abroad is justified in terms of model (2).

From this elementary survey we can see that there are a number of different and potentially conflicting conceptions of national-defense. But the situation is, in fact, more complicated than even this eight-fold schema suggests. I have represented the contrast between the collective and the individual levels of war as a simple dichotomy between state and individual. However, defensive rights are often ascribed to nations, communities, tribes, and other corporate entities which are not states though they may overlap or be co-extensive with them. It seems intuitively important that the account of national-defense make room for such non-state communal entities, for, during the greater part of world history, there were no states as we now understand that term. But this raises a host of further difficult questions. What is the relationship between states and communities or nations? Do states hold rights because of their connection with communities? What happens when there is divergence or antagonism between states and the national communities they claim to represent? These questions require detailed consideration and we shall return to them below. For the moment, however, I would like to put them to one side and concentrate on the contrast between the level of the individual and that of the actor principally recognized in international law—nation states.

A dispiriting level of confusion is often evident in both popular and philosophical-legal thought on the justice of war. Few authors have appreciated the distinctions between the different possible constructions of national-defense, though they manifestly differ in important ways. The failure in many discussions to specify whether national-defense is conceived as a right held by or against a state or its citizens and the precise end of the defensive right, allows a dangerous vacillation between the possible positions and the underlying logic of justification they represent. In the following discussion I shall try to disentangle and clarify some of these themes.

The question of the normative grounding of any defensive right is first and foremost a question about its end. No defensive action can be justified unless it is directed towards the protection and preservation of a good of sufficient importance to make the harmful measures undertaken proportionate. For this reason I shall begin the discussion with an analysis of the end of national-defense. I shall first consider the reductive strategy embodied in the claim that national-defense is grounded in the end of defending the lives of citizens. In the following chapter I shall consider the more complex claim that the proper end of national-defense is the defense of what we might call the 'common life' of a community.

The reductive strategy

It is often claimed that national-defense is the 'collective form' of self-defense, and the phrase surely evokes one of our dominant moral images of war. There are, I suggest, two ways in which this claim might be understood. The first, and most simple, would be to see national-defense as simply an application, *en masse*, of the familiar right of individuals to protect themselves and others from unjust lethal attack. The normative picture of defensive war that this gives us is encapsulated in model (1) above. It is this model which Walzer seems to have in mind when he writes: 'citizens defend one another.... the government is merely their instrument'.[7]

When one state forcefully violates the territorial integrity and political independence of another it is plausible to assume that the lives of individuals will be threatened. It is therefore an obvious thought that national-defense may be understood as an organized exercise of the right of self-defense by large numbers of individuals at one time. If this were correct then the term 'national-defense' would be something of a misnomer, for there would be no independent right to use lethal force in defense of the state or nation, as such, only the rights of individuals to defend their own lives, and those of others. 'National-defense' would be a kind of shorthand for a more complex way of exercising, what would remain in the final analysis, an individual right.

It is not difficult to see, however, that such an approach is incapable of providing an adequate moral justification for the right of national-defense. There are three principal reasons for this. The first is that the liberties enjoyed by soldiers of a defending state in the national-defense paradigm extend well beyond what could be justified in terms of the personal right of self-defense alone. Self-defense is the right to use necessary and proportionate lethal force against an imminent unjust threat to life. Yet soldiers fighting a defensive war are permitted to use violence against persons who pose no imminent

---

[7] Walzer, M., 'The Moral Standing of States: A Response to Four Critiques', *Philosophy and Public Affairs* (1980), 209–29, at 211.

threat to anyone. For instance, they may kill enemy soldiers who are marching, eating, sleeping, and so on, as well as uniformed support staff such as lorry drivers, cooks, and administrators. The rights of war also include the right to lay traps and mines which are clearly no part of self-defense.

The use of violence in such contexts clearly exceeds that which could be justified solely in terms of the right of individual self-defense, for this right does not include a right of pre-emptive attack; it is a right to kill to prevent the imminent violation of an innocent person's right to life. One might think of the occurrence, not un-common in war, of a defending army engaged in a confident coun-ter-offensive against an aggressor. The forces of the aggressor are broken and in disarray as they retreat and the army of the defending state pursues them, subjecting them to fire and destroying units at will as it overtakes them. If such acts of killing can in any way be understood as justified defensive acts, it is certainly not because they are acts of personal self-defense.

The second reason why the purely reductive view is inadequate is that, as we have seen, the requirement of necessity which is implicit in the right of self-defense generates a requirement for threatened persons to retreat if it is possible to avoid harm without resort to force by so doing. But if national-defense were nothing but an exercise *en masse* of self-defense, this would seem to give rise to a general requirement to appease international aggression, if it were possible to avoid bloodshed in this way. But the right of national-defense is not normally thought to entail a duty to appease aggres-sion. This strongly suggests that national-defense cannot be reduced to the defensive rights of individuals.

The third, and most decisive, reason for rejecting the reductive view is that within the Just War Theory the rights of war, including the right to kill enemy soldiers, are held equally by soldiers on both sides of a defensive war. According to the rules of *jus in bello*, the soldiers of the aggressive state have as much right to kill defending soldiers as the defending soldiers have to kill them, even though their war, taken as a whole, is illegal and unjust. The moral relationship between soldiers in battle, as envisaged by the Just War Theory, cannot be the same as that between aggressor and victim in a standard case of self-defense, for in the Just War Theory, there is no presumption of a normative asymmetry between opposing soldiers considered as individual persons. Indeed Walzer explicitly affirms the 'moral equality'[8] of soldiers, meaning both that soldiers of the aggressive state are not conceived as culpable attackers, and that the lives of the defenders receive no additional normative protection in the form of a duty to abstain from killing them.

What this shows is that the moral relationship between combatants in war must be conceived as a different and more complex one, involving the necessary mediation of personal relationships through those of the state. The purely reductive model (1) is doomed to failure. But so too are the models which construe the subject of the right in individual or personal terms—models (4), (6), and (7). This should not be surprising. The moral discourse of personal self-defense is too fine-grained to encompass the prosecution of war. Any military campaign, be it aggressive or defensive, consists of alternating periods of attack and defense. Moreover, at any particular point in a campaign, individual soldiers on both sides will be engaged in acts of defense as well as acts of attack. It is only at a much higher level of generality that a war or campaign as such can be described as defensive. Any adequate conception of national-defense, therefore, must make a necessary reference to the greater communal entity of the state.

Though a proper understanding of the right of national-defense cannot be purely reductive, it is possible that it can be construed in such a way that we continue to see the end of national-defense in personal terms even if the subject and perhaps also the object of the right must be seen as super-personal. This leads us to the second way we might understand the suggestion that national-defense is the 'collective form' of self-defense. It may be argued that the state has an obligation (and therefore a right) to defend its citizens in much the same way that a parent has the right to defend his or her child. This view was expressed, for instance, by the American Roman Catholic Bishops in their well-known Pastoral Letter of 1983 which asserted that: 'Governments threatened by armed unjust aggression must defend their people'.[9] The same idea surfaces also in Walzer: 'the government is bound to its citizens to defend them against foreigners'[10] and also in the lawyer Fernando Tesón: 'a war in response to aggression is justified as *governmental action to defend*

---

[8] Walzer, *Just and Unjust Wars*, 34.
[9] National Conference of Catholic Bishops, *The Challenge of Peace*, Washington, DC, 1983, para. 75.
[10] Walzer, 'The Moral Standing of States', 211.

the rights of its subjects, that is, the rights of individuals as victims of foreign aggression.[11] The normative conception of national-defense here invoked is that of our model (2) or model (3). Both these models view the state as the subject of the defensive right, though the lives of individual persons are viewed as the end of the right.

This view takes us some way closer to a satisfactory account of national-defense since we need no longer restrict ourselves to the unpromising task of attempting to build up a moral picture of war as a composite of individual acts of defense. However, in so far as these models assume that the right of national-defense is grounded in the end of defending the lives of individual citizens, it too must fail as an account of national-defense. I shall bring forward two arguments to show this: the first I shall call the argument from humanitarian intervention, the second I shall call the argument from bloodless invasion.

A standard definition of humanitarian intervention is: 'Military intervention in a state, without the approval of its authorities, and with the purpose of preventing widespread suffering or death among the inhabitants'.[12] Common sense tells us that humanitarian intervention is a very different creature to national-defense. They are different and indeed antagonistic because one is directed towards the maintenance of state sovereignty while the other involves an explicit permission to violate it. Yet if national-defense were a right of defense whose end is protecting the lives of individual citizens then not only would national-defense and humanitarian intervention share an underlying moral structure but the latter right could be derived from the former by this simple argument: according to the account under consideration, if the citizens of state *A* are threatened by aggressive actions of state *B*, then state *A* has the right to engage in a defensive war against *B* in order to protect its (*A*'s) citizens. Similarly any third party, state *C*, has the right to engage in war against *B* (and hence intervene in that state without the approval of its authorities) with the end of protecting the citizens of *A*. But now it would seem that humanitarian intervention is simply the application of this general principle with respect to third party intervention on the assumption that states *A* and *B* are the same state. To put the

---

[11] Tesón, F., *Humanitarian Intervention, an Inquiry into Law and Morality*, New York: Transnational Publishers Inc., 1997: 113 (emphasis in original).

[12] Roberts, A., 'Intervention and Human Rights', *International Affairs*, 69I (1993), 429–49, at 429.

point another way, if a particular military action of state *C* is justified by the fact that it defends the endangered lives of the citizens of *A*, then it should make no difference to the morality of *C*'s action whether the citizens of *A* are threatened by their own state or a third party.

But, of course, such a result flies in the face of common sense as well as the law and the moral theory of national-defense. Humanitarian intervention is no instance of the right of national-defense; it is rather a moral consideration which is in deep tension with it. When a state intervenes in another state on humanitarian grounds, one of the moral considerations weighed against this action is the defensive rights of the subject of the intervention. Thus the United Nations condemned Vietnam's 1978 invasion of Democratic Kampuchea (now Cambodia) as a breach of that state's sovereign rights, even though the intervention succeeded in bringing to a halt the murderous campaign of violence conducted by the Kampuchean state against its own people.[13] Without endorsing the UN's position, what the example clearly brings into focus is the fact that if there is a right to humanitarian intervention, then it is because the moral basis of the right of national-defense can in certain circumstances be justly overridden, not because the right of humanitarian intervention is, in some sense, an application of those moral considerations. Just as an adequate understanding of national-defense must recognize that there is a potential tension between the right of national-defense and the maintenance of international peace and security (as we saw in the last chapter), so it must recognize that there is a potential tension between national-defense and the protection of endangered citizens. It is precisely such a distinction which an account grounding national-defense in the end of protecting the lives of citizens is incapable of making.

The argument from humanitarian intervention shows that having the end of defending the lives of persons is not sufficient to bring a proportionate and necessary military action within the purview of the right of national-defense. The argument from bloodless invasion is designed to show that defending the lives of citizens is not a necessary condition for national-defense. This argument begins from the observation that the right of national-defense, as defined

---

[13] See Weisburd, A. M., *Use of Force, the Practice of States since World War II*, Pennsylvania: The Pennsylvania State University Press, 1997: 40–2.

in international law and in the just war tradition, can be effective in the face of acts of aggression which threaten the lives of no citizens of the victim state. Such a situation may arise in a number of ways. An aggressive act may violate the territorial integrity and political independence of the victim state only by annexing or intervening in a remote and uninhabited piece of territory, or by making an illegal armed incursion into a state's air space or territorial waters where no citizen is threatened. Secondly, an aggressor may invade with such an overwhelming show of force that the victim state declines to resist and the intervention is accomplished with no loss of life.

The right of national-defense is effective in international law in the face of attacks against a state's 'territorial integrity or political independence', but this condition is both logically and factually independent of the question of whether the lives of individual citizens within the state are threatened. As Montesquieu reminds us: 'The state is the association of men, not the men themselves; the citizen may perish and the man remain'.[14] If this is correct, if, in other words, there are acts of international aggression which generate a legal and moral right of national-defense and yet which threaten the lives of no citizens, then the attempt to ground national-defense in the end of defending the lives of citizens must fail.

Imminent and conditional threats

The argument from bloodless invasion and the argument from humanitarian intervention set up a powerful challenge to the attempt to ground national-defense in the defense of the lives of citizens. Together they show that having the end of protecting the lives of citizens is neither a necessary nor a sufficient condition for a military action to be a legitimate act of national-defense. However, some may feel uneasy about these results, particularly regarding the argument from bloodless invasion.

The unease may stem from a difficult question in the interpretation of defensive rights which can be put like this. Surely the crucial point, so far as defensive rights are concerned, is not whether an act of aggression violates the rights of an agent, but whether it threatens

---

[14] Baron de Montesquieu, *The Spirit of the Laws*, Nugent, T. (trans.), Berkeley: University of California Press, 1977, bk. X, ch. 3: 192.

them. The UN Charter makes it clear that action which can ground a right of national-defense must be an act of force; it must be an 'armed attack'. Therefore, even if the aggressive act does not in fact result in the death of any person, the mere fact that it is an act of force entails a readiness on the part of the aggressors to kill if, for instance, resistance is met and demands are not acquiesced to. In other words, every act of international aggression necessarily threatens the lives of citizens of the victim state, even if it does not in the end violate their rights to life. It is therefore incorrect to suggest, as the argument from bloodless invasion does, that an act of aggression justifying national-defense need not threaten the lives of persons in the defending state.

Now in one sense this observation is clearly correct. However, it must be realized that the phrases 'life threatening' and 'threat to life' are ambiguous and we need to be extremely careful about their application. In their primary sense these phrases refer to an action or event which poses an imminent danger to some person's life. Thus if X rushes at Y with a knife and tries to stab him, he is 'threatening his life'. But these terms have a secondary sense which arises in cases which I shall call 'conditional threats' to life. These cases typically involve a threat to use force if some demand is not met, for example, X tells Y that he will stab him if he doesn't hand over his wallet. In this case we also say that 'X is threatening Y's life', but the sense is very different to that of the first case, for here the harm is conditional but not imminent.

Applying this distinction, we can see that the argument from bloodless invasion invokes the first sense of 'threat' and 'threatening'; it points out that international aggression need not pose an imminent threat to any right of sufficient magnitude to make proportionate the use of defensive lethal force.[15] The counter-argument, on the other hand, points out that international aggression necessarily poses a conditional threat to such rights. The question we must now attempt to answer is this: is it justifiable to use lethal force against a threat to life (or some other central right) which is conditional but not imminent? If it is, then there is still hope for the project of

---

[15] Such rights would include rights against being killed, maimed, or enslaved. I shall call such rights 'central rights' to distinguish them from 'peripheral rights' such as property rights which are not in themselves sufficient to make defense with lethal force proportionate. See Chapter 2, Section 4, 'The bounds of proportionality'.

grounding the right of national-defense in the end of defending the lives of persons.

The question is, in fact, not an easy one to answer. It seems clear that there are cases in which it would not be justified to use lethal force in response to a conditional threat against a central right. For example, if someone approaches you in the street and threatens to take your life if you do not give him a dollar, it seems clear that you do not act rightfully if you shoot him dead. The reason would seem to be that what is demanded in this case is not of sufficient value to justify the use of lethal force—the disparity of value between a dollar and a human life is such that one ought to surrender the money rather than take the life, even though the theft is accompanied by a conditional threat to life. What this suggests is that there is no general right to use lethal force in response to a conditional threat to a central right, but rather that the right to respond is in some way proportional to the value of what is being extorted.

If we are persuaded by this line of thought, however, we will be quickly driven to the conclusion that it is never legitimate to respond to conditional threats with lethal force unless what is extorted is itself of sufficient value to justify the use of lethal force. The reason for this is that every conditional threat to life may be disaggregated into two logically distinct elements. One is the imminent attack against certain of one's peripheral rights (for example, one's property rights to the dollar). The other element is the conditional but not imminent attack against one's right to life or other central right. Consider, now, our moral position with respect to each element of the attack. To use lethal force in response to the threat to the peripheral rights may be necessary, but it would not be proportionate. To use lethal force in response to the threat to the central rights, on the other hand, would be proportionate, but it would not be necessary (you could preserve your life by surrendering the money). But legitimate acts of self-defense must be both necessary and proportionate, therefore the use of lethal force against conditional threats of this kind cannot be legitimate instances of self-defense.[16]

---

[16] Another way of putting the argument would be this: we saw in Chapter 3 that an important feature of legitimate self-defense is that the victim is in a situation of forced choice between lives. Being in a situation of forced choice is not a sufficient condition for rightfully taking life, I argued, but it does seem to be a necessary condition. The person who faces a conditional threat, however, does not face a situation of forced choice between lives, for he can avoid the death of either party by acquiescing to the aggressor's demands.

There are, however, reasons to believe that this may not be a wholly adequate analysis of the case of conditional threats. John Locke has a very different interpretation of such cases. He argues that there is a general right to use lethal force against any person who would get you in his power by the use or threat of force. It is, he says 'lawful for a man to *kill* a *Thief*, who has not in the least hurt him, nor declared any design upon his Life, any farther than by the use of Force, so as to get him in his Power'.[17] The reason is that, 'let his pretence be what it will, I have no reason to suppose that he, who would *take away my Liberty*, would nòt when he had me in his Power, take away every thing else',[18] and 'to be free from such force is the only security of my Preservation'.[19] Locke's point is that one may kill the conditional aggressor, not because of the value of what he is demanding, but because a conditional threat, by placing one under the aggressor's power, destroys the liberty that is essential for security and ultimately preservation.

Locke's argument is closely related to an argument often made in international relations about the importance of defending borders, even if a particular border be unjust, and even if a particular violation inflicts no significant harm on the victim state. Thus Walzer argues that even borders which are 'arbitrary, poorly drawn, the products of ancient wars' warrant defense because 'once the lines are crossed, safety is gone... there is no certainty this side of the border, any more than there is safety this side of the threshold, once a criminal has entered the house'.[20]

It would seem, however, that the strong conclusion that both Walzer and Locke would like to draw from these considerations (a conclusion which would establish a general right to use lethal force in response to conditional threats) is unwarranted. Locke and Walzer both assume that there is a line such that once it is crossed 'safety is gone'; in other words, that once a conditional threat has been made and acquiesced to, there can be no safeguard against further encroachment of one's rights and ultimately one's physical security. This may stem from an implausible assumption which Locke makes explicit in his argument. He says that the reason a man may kill

---

[17] Locke, J., *Two Treatises of Government*, Cambridge: Cambridge University Press, 1960, bk. II, ch. III: 279.
[18] ibid. 280.
[19] Ibid. 279, see also bk. II, ch. XVIII: 403–4.
[20] Walzer, *Just and Unjust Wars*, 57–8.

someone who would unjustly use force to get him under his power is the same reason that one may kill a wolf or lion: 'Such Men are not under the ties of Common Law and Reason, have no other Rule, but that of Force and Violence, and so may be treated as Beasts of Prey, those dangerous and noxious Creatures, that will be sure to destroy him, whenever he falls in their Power'.[21]

But this is highly suspect. A mugger who threatens one's life is not (necessarily) like a wild animal, incapable of making rational and even trustworthy assurances about his future behaviour. A conditional aggressor makes an implicit or explicit agreement with you that, if you acquiesce to his demands, he will spare your life (he may or may not also agree not to encroach further upon one's legitimate rights). There may be good reason to believe that a conditional aggressor will honour this agreement in a particular context. After all, the practice of making conditional threats would quickly break down and cease to have usefulness for assailants if they never kept their word in such situations. Similarly with border crossing, some border incursions are made with extremely specific and limited objectives in mind, and need not lead inevitably to further encroachment. A good example of this was the Soviet Union's invasion of Finland during the Second World War.[22] So the assumption made by both Locke and Walzer that conditional threats which place one under an aggressor's power necessarily threaten one's security in such a way as to justify the use of lethal defensive force is not persuasive.

These considerations are, I think, fairly conclusive in checking Locke and Walzer's strong conclusions. Nevertheless there is an important observation at work in Locke's argument, and this concerns the role played by risk. When an attacker makes a conditional threat against your life, you incur a risk; how can you be sure that the

---

[21] Locke, *Two Treatises of Government*, bk. II, ch. III: 279.

[22] In 1939 the Soviet Union became concerned about the vulnerability of St Petersburg (then Leningrad) to potential German attack through neighbouring Finland. The Russians demanded that Finland cede certain territories surrounding St Petersburg so as to push the border beyond the maximum range of heavy artillery. These demands were clearly in violation of Finland's sovereignty as a neutral state, but there does not seem to be any question as to the genuinely limited nature of the Soviet Union's intentions. The demands were made on the basis of clear and obvious security concerns. What is more, the Russians offered the Finns compensation totalling roughly twice the territory they proposed to take and even after the Soviet Union had overcome Finnish resistance in an eventual invasion, they adhered roughly to their initial territorial demands. See Hart, L., *History of the Second World War*, London: Cassell and Co., 1970: 47–52.

aggressor will not just kill you anyway, or continue to encroach upon your rights?[23] More importantly, why should you be required to assume the risk rather than proceed with lethal force? The assumption of risk is a consideration that needs to be 'factored in' to our judgements about when it is permissible to respond. If the risk of further encroachment on central rights is very high, then the case of the conditional aggressor begins to look morally indistinguishable from the central case of self-defense, and it would seem plausible that one would have an equal right to use lethal force even though what is demanded may be quite trivial. What this suggests is a right of response to conditional threats that is bounded by two factors: the value of what is extorted and the risk incurred. The greater the risk and the greater the value of what is extorted, the greater the right of response. What is clear, however, is that these comparative judgements need to be made in light of the particular circumstances of each case. *Pace* Locke and Walzer, there is no general right to employ lethal force simply on the grounds that a conditional threat to central rights has been made. This furnishes us with a more nuanced view of the right to respond to conditional threats, but it is none the less sufficient to reinforce the argument from bloodless invasion.

To summarize this argument, we have been investigating the claim that the right of national-defense is grounded in the end of defending the lives of citizens. But not all acts of international aggression justifying defensive war on the traditional understanding of national-defense violate the rights of citizens in such a way that they or a third party defender would have a right of self-defense. Not all acts of international aggression involve imminent threats to the central rights of persons. All acts of aggression do involve at least conditional threats against the lives or central rights of persons, but I have argued that there is no general right to resist conditional threats against the central rights of persons with lethal force. Whether there is a right to kill in response to conditional threats turns on the nature and value of what the aggressor demands and the level of risk assumed.

This immediately raises the question of the value of sovereignty: what exactly is the moral status of the sovereign integrity of the state and how are we to weigh its value in judgements of proportionality

---

[23] See Hobbes, T., *Leviathan*, Tuck, R. (ed.), Cambridge: Cambridge University Press, 1991, ch. 14: 66.

when an aggressor demands that we surrender it? This is a complex question which will be addressed in the following chapter. The burden of the present chapter has been twofold: first, to show that there may be a right to national-defense (as conceived by its supporters) where there is no right of personal self-defense; secondly, that the right of national-defense, if it is a genuine right, cannot be grounded in the end of defending the lives of individuals. Our conclusion must be that the reductive strategy, understood either narrowly or broadly, cannot be viable for providing a moral vindication of the right of national-defense.

War and the protection of persons

These arguments seem to be sound; nevertheless I suspect that many will find the conclusion surprising and even counter-intuitive. There is an extremely strong presumption that war is centrally concerned with defending the lives of citizens from external threat. This is a reflection of what is sometimes called the 'two dimensions' model of sovereignty, in which the state is seen as legitimated by the protection it affords its citizens both from internal anarchy and from the threat of external enemies.[24] However, laying to one side the arguments that I have brought forward in this chapter, there are several obvious features of defensive war which should cause us to treat this simple normative model with suspicion.

To begin with, there is a distinctive problem concerning escalation in war. It is a commonplace that the number of casualties sustained by an invaded nation is related to the level and nature of that state's resistance: against a determined aggressor, strong resistance will result in a greater loss of lives. But if the end of national-defense is really protecting the lives of citizens, then we are left with the paradoxical conclusion that national-defense is a form of defensive action which involves pursuing the course known in advance to result in greater loss of life amongst the very people whose lives it is one's objective to defend. That would indeed be a strange form of defense.

The problem of escalation has many facets and serves to distinguish the case of war sharply from that of personal self-defense. As

---

[24] See Brown, C., *International Relations Theory, New Normative Approaches*, New York: Harvester Wheatsheaf, 1992: 130.

Carl Von Clausewitz explains, wars have an inherent tendency to increase in ferocity as each side seeks to bring to bear a decisive exertion of violence in order to 'throw' their opponent. Though Clausewitz acknowledged that real life conflicts are often limited by contingent political and moral factors, he insists that the escalation towards extreme measures of force is a perpetual tendency in war and a theoretical reality: 'War is an act of force, and there is no logical limit to the application of that force. Each side, therefore, compels its opponent to follow suit; a reciprocal action is started which must lead in theory to extremes'.[25]

In addition to this internal momentum, wars often have a destabilizing effect on the regions in which they are fought, precipitating conflict in neighbouring states. Moreover, since victory in war goes to the strongest not to the most just adversary, wars leave legacies of resentment and instability that often sow the seed of future conflicts. Personal self-defense does not commonly lead to blood feuds, but the roots of wars are often to be found in previous conflicts, as, for example, the causes of the Second World War are bound up with the termination of the First.

In all of these ways, the violence of war is quite unlike the violence of personal self-defense. If self-defense were more like war in that it involved similar risks of escalation, it is doubtful that we would enjoy the wide-ranging permission to resort to self-defense that in fact we do. For instance, if by defending my own life from attack I risked drawing into conflict and imperilling the lives of my friends and family and also those of my aggressor, as well as making deadly confrontation more likely in the future, it is not at all clear that I would have an unequivocal right to undertake the defense.

Despite these arguments against the assimilation of the right of national-defense to the defense of persons, I should stress that it is not the case that military action can never be justified purely in terms of individual defensive rights. The actions of those who forcefully resist genocidal aggression can quite properly be understood in terms of rights of personal self-defense, even when that resistance is organized and collective in form. Thus when the Jews of the Warsaw ghetto fought against the assault of the German army, they were quite literally fighting for their lives. In such a case it

---

[25] Clausewitz, C., *On War*, Howard, M., and Paret, P. (eds.), Princeton: Princeton University Press, 1976: 77.

would indeed be possible to dispense with the vocabulary of national-defense, for it is possible to understand their actions as justified wholly within the conceptual scheme of individual rights.

But it is precisely this feature which makes resistance to genocidal aggression unique, and a poor model for understanding the right of national-defense more generally. Most wars are not genocidal in nature, therefore no satisfactory apology for a right of national-defense could tie its justification to the presence of a genocidal threat. The fact that we do employ an independent vocabulary of national-defense suggests a moral phenomenon which cannot adequately be articulated wholly in individualistic terms—one which demands an account making necessary reference to collective and super-personal entities.

A proper understanding of the right of national-defense as it emerges in the just war tradition and in international law, cannot be achieved on the assumption that the end of war is fundamentally that of defending the lives of citizens. A war of national-defense is not just a lot of people exercising the right of self-defense at the same time and in an organized fashion. Nor is it the state exercising the right of defense on behalf of its citizens. For the state can claim the right to defend itself, when none of its citizens is under imminent threat, and it can claim this right even if it thereby puts its citizens under greater threat than if no defense were mounted. The conditions justifying action in the case of national-defense are neither coextensive, nor necessarily concomitant, with those that justify action in the case of self-defense. This serves to remove from contention our models (1), (2), (3), (4), (6) and (7)—in other words, each of the normative models which interprets the end or the subject of national-defense in individual terms. We turn now to the remaining normative models of national-defense, those which posit the defense of some form of necessarily super-personal good as the end of national-defense.

7

War and the Common Life

The frontispiece to the original edition of Thomas Hobbes's *Leviathan* bears a striking illustration. The sovereign is represented as a giant human figure, towering over the landscape, whose body is itself composed of a multitude of individual persons. The implication is that the commonwealth (what today we would call the sovereign state) may usefully be regarded as an individual person writ large.[1] This is a particularly graphic example of an extremely old and pervasive idea in political thought. Michael Walzer calls this idea 'the domestic analogy' and writes about its absolute centrality to the Just War Theory.[2] The basic thesis of the domestic analogy is that the rights and duties of states can be understood on the model of the rights and duties of individual persons.

It is difficult to overstate the importance of this idea in the history of international ethics, international law, and political philosophy. The analogy has been invoked by thinkers as diverse in time and theoretical commitments as Augustine, Grotius, Hobbes, Mill, and Rawls. In Chapter 5 we were able to see how thoroughly modern international law is imbued with the analogy with private law.

In the last chapter I identified two fundamental strategies for providing an account of national-defense. The first was to attempt to explain national-defense reductively at the level of personal rights. This was the approach explored in the last chapter. The second is what we might call the 'analogical strategy'. This approach takes seriously the notion of national-defense as a right held by states and attempts to give moral content to that right as one analogous to the personal right of self-defense. It is this idea that I will examine in the current chapter. Once again I understand the challenge

---

[1] Hobbes makes this idea explicit in the introduction to that work: 'For by Art is created that great LEVIATHAN called a COMMON-WEALTH, or STATE, (in latine CIVITAS) which is but an Artificial Man; though of greater stature and strength than the Naturall, for whose protection and defence it was intended; and in which, the *Soveraignty* is an Artificiall *Soul*, as giving life and motion to the whole body...' (Hobbes, T., *Leviathan*, Tuck, R. (ed.), Cambridge: Cambridge University Press, 1991: 9).

[2] Walzer, M., *Just and Unjust Wars*, New York: Basic Books, 1977: 58–9.

principally to be one about providing an effective account of the end of the right.[3]

The way I propose to address this challenge is by exploring the purposely broad conception of what is often called the 'common life' of a community. I take the common life to consist in the set of interconnected social structures which emerge when people live together in a community. Thus understood, the common life has a character and identity over time, it grows and develops, and it is shaped, both consciously and unconsciously, by those who live within it. It is also something which may be disrupted, irreparably altered, or even destroyed. For all of these reasons the designation collective or common 'life', though metaphorical (for a society is not literally an organism), seems appropriate. The suggestion that I shall now consider is that national-defense is a right held by states and grounded principally in the end, not of defending the lives of individual citizens, but of defending the common life of the community.

How are we to understand the idea of the common life in light of the argument about national-defense? I think that it is possible to discern three viable interpretations of the common life as a potential end of national-defense. The first interpretation would be to seek an understanding of the value of the common life in an account of state legitimacy. The second would be to see the common life as the embodiment of a particular cultural and historical heritage. The third interpretation sees the common life as the arena of collective self-determination and autonomy. My intention is to investigate whether any of these conceptions is capable of identifying a value sufficient to ground the right of national-defense as a right analogous to self-defense.

Before doing this, however, I want to identify two constraints on what an acceptable account of the common life must look like. The first is an obvious one. Because our project here is apologetic in nature, the account of the common life must be such as to ground a right of national-defense substantially co-extensive with the way that right is understood in modern international law and the best interpretation of the Just War Theory. A theory which generates deeply revisionary conclusions about the right of national-defense is not the

---

[3] There are many other difficult questions raised by this approach, some of which will be treated in the next chapter.

desired outcome of our current enquiry, though it may be an interesting and legitimate undertaking in its own right.

The second constraint arises from consideration of a radical interpretation of the status of the common life which I shall reject at the outset. This interpretation attributes to the common life a moral value prior to, and independent of, the value of the individuals who compose it. We may call this the 'strong organic view' of the common life. Such a view takes the domestic analogy in its most literal form and runs it in the opposite direction to the Just War Theory. That is to say, the rights and value of individuals are seen as stemming from their relationship to, or analogy with, the community of which they are a part. It is difficult to find serious philosophical exponents of this view, but the strong organic view was a central feature of fascist thought about the state and is also suggested by certain passages in Hegel.[4] Given such a view, it is extremely simple to account for the obligation to die on behalf of, and the right to kill in defense of, the common life, for the latter is seen as an entity whose value exceeds, and is prior to, the value of any individual life.

I introduce this view for the purpose of rejecting it, and by doing so, identifying what I take to be a prerequisite of any acceptable account of the common life. The strong organic view derives what credibility it has from observations about the essential role of the community in defining and shaping the very nature of the individual. Adherents of this view are correct to point out that methodological individualism, with its picture of rational and comprehensible individuals existing prior to all society, and out of which society is fashioned, is fanciful and perhaps incoherent. People are what they are within communities, and in abstraction from them they would be unrecognizable as moral beings. As Aristotle says, 'man is a political animal', and outside community there are only beasts and gods.[5]

What cannot be accepted, however, is the claim that the common life is a source of value independent of its value for individual persons. To say this is to accept as a constraint on moral explanation what may be called the 'humanistic principle' which Joseph Raz has

---

[4] See e.g. *The Philosophy of Right*, sects. 257and 258: 155–6. Hegel claims that the state is an 'absolute unmoved end in itself', which 'has supreme right against the individual, whose supreme duty is to be a member of the state' (quoted in Brown, C., *International Relations Theory*, New York Harvester Wheatsheaf, 1992: 64.)

[5] Aristotle, *Politics*, Sinclair, J. A., (trans.), Harmondsworth: Penguin 1962: 1253ᵃ.

defined as: 'the claim that the explanation and justification of the goodness or badness of anything derives ultimately from its contribution, actual or possible, to human life and its quality'.[6] As Raz points out, such a principle does not commit us to an instrumentalist view of the state and communal goods. These goods may be intrinsically valuable in the sense that they are necessary constituents of goods that intrinsically enrich human life.[7] But the principle serves to remind us that all goods and value in human affairs derive ultimately from persons and the valuations they individually and collectively make. An adequate conception of the common life will see it as something whose value is separate from, and irreducible to, the value of the particular individuals that make it up, yet its worth must be seen as deriving from the value it has for them. The following conceptions, which I take to be plausible interpretations of the common life, all meet this requirement and it is to them that we now turn.

Political association

An obvious way to approach the problem of identifying the moral value inherent in the common life is to draw on a familiar distinction in political theory between might and authority in the analysis of the state.[8] Might is the ability to exert force, and compel obedience, within a particular geographical area. Authority, on the other hand, is might which is justified and legitimate, and thus capable of placing a normative claim of obedience upon those who are subject to it. While might is the subject of Realist analyses of politics, authority forms the subject of normative political theory. The answer to our challenge, it would seem, may be supplied through an account of state legitimacy. By explaining how the power exercised by the state is legitimated as authority, we provide an account of how the state itself is a significant centre of moral value. It would seem reasonable to expect that such a value, suitably identified and explained, may constitute an appropriate end for the right of national-defense.

---

[6] Raz, J., 'Right-Based Moralities', in Waldron, J. (ed.), *Theories of Rights*, Oxford: Oxford University Press, 1984: 183.

[7] ibid. 188 ff.

[8] See e.g. D'Entrèves, A. P., *The Notion of the State, an Introduction to Political Theory*, Oxford: Clarendon Press, 1967, ch. 1.

There are many different accounts of state legitimacy, but one particularly powerful and instructive treatment is that provided by the social contract theory of Thomas Hobbes.[9] The Hobbesian social contract is especially germane to our purposes, because it provides an extremely minimal treatment of the legitimation of the state. It therefore offers good hope of grounding national-defense as a right held universally by sovereign states, irrespective of their particular political constitution. This is a basic premise of international law and the Just War Theory.

The essence of Hobbes's argument is that the moral authority of the sovereign state derives from its ability to provide order in human affairs. We can accept the general thrust of Hobbes's account without subscribing fully to his overwhelmingly pessimistic human psychology. Thus even if we do not accept his view of the state of nature as an unqualifiedly brutal war of all against all, we can agree that without the order stemming from a political association, presided over by a sovereign power, human life would be immeasurably more degraded and miserable than it now is.

Our problem with national-defense was to find a value embodied in the state which is not simply the value of the lives of individual persons within it, and whose defense could merit the use of lethal force. The notion of a political association explicated through the idea of the Hobbesian social contract seems to provide exactly this, for the order which the political association provides is a basic human good, one without which a great majority of the goods we value would be unattainable. Can we not explain national-defense as a right to use lethal force in defense of the goods of political association?

There are two difficulties with this proposal which I would like to explore. The first is that there is a curious, almost paradoxical, incompleteness to the idea of social contract as developed by Hobbes. The basic insight of his account is that the state's sovereign power is justified because the state of nature which it replaces is so very awful; life within it is filled with danger and insecurity. The commonwealth enables the replacement of unproductive and anarchic contention, with mutuality and co-operation.

But a by-product of this escape from the state of nature between individuals is the creation of a state of nature at the level of sovereign

---

[9] Hobbes, *Leviathan*.

states, since sovereign states are, by definition, subject to no superior power capable of systematically resolving disputes between them and subjecting them to rules. By joining the political association, the individual escapes one state of nature, only to vicariously enter another, through membership of his or her state. Consequently, so long as political association remains at a state or national level, the end of the social contract remains incomplete, because individuals remain insecure, their life and projects liable to disruption at any time from the outbreak of hostilities between states.

What this suggests is that the logic of the Hobbesian social contract, rather than supporting a right of national-defense, may in fact be deeply antagonistic to it. For if we agree that the attainment of security is a basic human imperative (or 'law of nature' as Hobbes calls it), and that the establishment of a law-governed political association is the principal means to achieving this, then this reasoning suggests a prima facie case for the establishment of a universal or global political association, one which is not marred by the existence of a state of nature at any level.

But the right of national-defense stands opposed to a universal political association in a very basic way, for it enshrines the right of diverse political communities to 'political sovereignty' and hence to freedom from subjection to an external power. The right of national-defense is therefore a central moral instrument sustaining the state of nature between states. As the International Relations theorist Martin Wight observes, 'The right of individual [national-defense] is the basic principle of international anarchy'.[10] More needs to be said about the concept of a universal political association, and I shall provide a more detailed discussion of both its possibility and desirability in Chapter 8. For the moment we should simply note the existence of a prima facie universalist argument implicit in the Hobbesian account which is in deep tension with the notion of a right of national-defense for individual nation states.

The second observation I would like to make offers a more fundamental challenge to the attempt to explain the end of national-defense through an account of state legitimacy. If we accept that the political association embodied in the sovereign state is a genuine good and, moreover, a good of sufficient value to make the use of

---

[10] Wight, M., *Power Politics*, Harmondsworth: Pelican Books, 1979: 218.

lethal defensive force proportionate, there is still a difficulty in invoking this value as a ground for the right of national-defense.

The difficulty arises from the fact that the value of political association, as understood through Hobbesean social contract theory, is simply the value of order over the miseries and insecurity of the state of nature. It is, therefore, a value which accrues equally to all minimally successful political associations. While some political associations may be better at achieving civil order than others, the justification which Hobbes's social contract offers is the value of (almost) any political association over anarchy. Herein lies the problem for an account of the right of national-defense. International aggression does not typically seek to destroy political life as such, reducing the vanquished state, as it were, to a state of nature. Rather, most aggressors seek, for reasons of power or ideology, to replace the existing political order with their own. They seek, in other words, to conquer and rule.

But if national-defense were grounded in the end of protecting the good of order embodied in the political association, it is difficult to see how there could be a right to defend against aggressors who seek to conquer and rule. For their threat is not to political association as such, but to the particular form of a given political association, and we as yet have no account of why one form of stable political life should be preferred over any other. Indeed, according to Hobbes, no harm befalls a vanquished population who are made the subject of a new sovereign.[11]

Certainly the period of conquest is likely to be disorderly and dangerous, but if anything this would seem to generate a duty to capitulate swiftly, so as to usher in the new order quickly and painlessly. These considerations are particularly pertinent to any community facing invasion by an aggressor organizationally superior to itself, as, for instance, would have been the case with many of the tribes inhabiting territories absorbed into the Roman Empire. It is difficult to see how such a community could justify a right of defense against invasion in light of an account of national-defense based on the Hobbesian theory of state legitimacy.

---

[11] See Airakson, T., 'The Whiteness of the Whale: Thomas Hobbes and a Paradox of War and Fear', in Bertman, M. A. (ed.), *Hobbes: War among Nations*, Aldershot: Avebury Press, 1989: 63.

One response to this argument would be to claim that the Hobbesian account of state legitimacy is simply too minimal and therefore too permissive. Not every sovereign power capable of providing a basic level of order and stability should be seen as an equal centre of value. It may be, for instance, that state legitimacy requires the achievement of a more substantive set of political goods, and on these grounds we may find that only a subset of the world's states (perhaps, for example, the liberal democratic states) will qualify as legitimate. On this interpretation only states which are legitimate in this stronger sense would have full defensive rights and the rightfulness of their defense would be grounded in the superiority of their form of political association.[12] But there are two problems with this suggestion. The first is that we shall still require an account of why legitimate states should be viewed as having defensive rights against other equally legitimate states, for example, why would it be wrong for one liberal democratic state to conquer and rule another? It would certainly be possible to claim that states which engage in international aggression are *ipso facto* illegitimate. However, not only does this seem intolerably ad hoc, but it fails to explain how even consistently aggressive states may have defensive rights if they are the victim of unjustified aggression.

The second problem is that such an account would not meet our first precondition for an interpretation of the common life: that it support an understanding of national-defense which maps closely to the consensus view on the laws of war. Far from constituting a defense of the traditional paradigm of national-defense as it is enshrined in international law, such a view would be a very radical departure from it. In international law states have rights against aggression *qua* sovereign states, not because they embody a particular form of political order. The law is neutral between different forms of political constitution. Indeed, I have focused on the Hobbesian contract theory precisely because its minimal account of state legitimacy held the possibility of accounting for the legitimacy, and thereby defensive rights, of all sovereign states. But for the reasons given it would appear that a minimal account of legitimacy which

---

[12] An argument along these lines is made by David Luban and Fernando Tesón. See Luban, D., 'Just War and Human Rights', *Philosophy and Public Affairs*, 9/4 (1980), 160–81; Tesón, F., 'The Kantian Theory of International Law', *Columbia Law Review*, 92 (1996), 53–102.

meets this requirement is not capable of grounding a right to defend a particular political association.

If we are to understand the right of national-defense as it has traditionally been conceived, then the right cannot simply be grounded in an account of state legitimacy and the value of political association. To justify national-defense we require a moral reason not simply to defend order, but to defend a particular form of order; to defend *our* order. This will require us to look in a different direction for our account of the end of national-defense.

The character of common lives

What the forgoing argument (that the value of political association *per se* provides no reason for defending a particular common life) masks, of course, is the special relationship that each person has to the common life of his or her own community. What people value in their common life is not just that it is an essential precondition for stable and tolerable life but the fact that it is a community with a distinctive character. For those who participate in a common life, the shared values and laws, language and literature, history and traditions, as well as the less tangible expectations and understandings which together constitute the cultural identity of the group come to be special and cherished possessions. In short, people attach value to the particular character of the common life to which they belong.

Why do we value the particular character of our common life? Any answer to this question must make reference to two quite general features of social experience. The first is that many of the goods which give meaning to our lives are dependent on our participation in a community. Even such seemingly personal activities as forming judgements of value, the creation of and reflection upon works of art, and characteristic forms of human relationship such as love and friendship are only made possible by a shared linguistic and conceptual framework embodied in a community or common life.

The point is not simply that such goods necessitate participation in some form of common life, for this would invite a response in the spirit of my last argument, namely, that any common life could in principle fulfil this function. Why should we feel justified in defending a distinctive form of common life when humans are evidently capable of locating their lives within new and different cultural communities, as immigrants often do? But the point cuts deeper than this. By providing a cultural and linguistic background to our personal lives, the common life becomes part of who we are. We are committed to the particular form of the common life we participate in, because its character has become interwoven with our own. We are who we are partly because our shared community is the way it is. This is why we have a commitment, not simply to the existence of a system of shared values and practices, but to the particular form of shared practices within which our life is conducted and has been shaped.

The second reason why we are committed to the particular character of our common life stems from our need as humans for an ongoing history or 'story' within which we can locate our lives and from which they can draw meaning. The common life is able to fill this need because it is an ongoing historical entity which has integrity over time, which existed before we were born, and will continue after we die.[13]

These two functions of the common life—that of providing a shared repository of language, values, and practice which enable and inform many of the substantive goods which compose an individual's life, and the provision of an ongoing historical narrative within which we are able to locate our lives and give them meaning—are both things which we are committed to regarding as goods of the first order. Moreover, these goods connect with the integrity of the state in two important ways. The first is that the state purports to protect and foster the unique character of the common life which exists within its borders. The second is that the state purports to instantiate the shared values and commitments of the community, by embedding them within its political forms and legal structures. In this way it is possible to build up an account of how the particular character of the common life can properly function as the end of the right of national-defense.

There is clearly an intuitive appeal to such an account of national-defense, but we must be wary of its dangers, the chief of which is that it brings us perilously close to a relativism of value. To see this we must distinguish between subjective and objective values. A subjective value I take to be one capable of being recognized only within a

---

[13] Stanley Hauerwas emphasizes this point in his stimulating essay *Should War be Eliminated?* Milwaukee: Marquette University Press, 1984.

particular community or common life. An objective value is one capable of being recognized as such by all persons universally, irrespective of community membership. The idea that there can be objective values has become very unfashionable recently, but there is good reason to believe that trans-culturally valid values can indeed exist. The Hobbesian values of societal order and political association which we have considered in the previous section seem to be values of precisely this kind—they speak to universal human needs and seem capable of being recognized as goods by persons across cultural boundaries.

Why is the idea of an objective value important to the concept of national-defense? It is important for two reasons. The first is that the proportionality requirement inherent in defensive rights is itself an objective requirement. It is not sufficient for a defender to believe that a particular good is sufficiently valuable to justify a certain measure of defensive force: it must really be so. This entails, as a minimum, that the good is such that its value could be recognized by a neutral independent observer and also the aggressor himself provided he viewed the situation fairly and objectively. Secondly, national-defense is a right which is, by its very nature, asserted across national boundaries by one state against another. Therefore, in light of the objective nature of the proportionality requirement, the basis for the right's assertion must be a value capable of being recognized across communal boundaries.

The problem is that the value attached to the particular character of a common life is principally a subjective, not an objective, value in the sense outlined above. It is a judgement accessible primarily from the internal perspective of those within the common life in question, rather than one capable of being recognized universally. We are all committed to the value of the common life in which we participate because, as I have said, it is our own. But it is not apparent why someone who is not a participant in that particular common life should recognize its distinctive form as a good and a value.[14]

The difficulty can be seen most clearly when we consider common lives or political communities which, from an objective view, are immoral, oppressive, or unjust. I am not here referring to communities whose conduct is so horrendous as to make them potential

---

[14] Other than the broadly based and somewhat vague objective value that we place upon a world with cultural diversity.

candidates for humanitarian intervention. It is possible to argue that a limited doctrine of humanitarian intervention has developed, or is in the process of developing, which would permit intervention in states that engage in widespread violations of human rights against their own citizens.[15] However, the conditions for the exercise of such a putative right have been strictly limited to abuses of human rights which are so severe that they 'shock the conscience of mankind',[16] typically involving genocide, mass expulsion, or starvation. In contrast to such cases there exist numerous states which fall below the threshold for potential humanitarian intervention yet which display a systematic and pervasive level of corruption, brutality, and disregard for human rights. States such as Nigeria, Burma, North Korea, China, and many others routinely torture, intimidate, wrongfully kill, imprison, invade privacy, and discriminate on ethnic, sexual, and political grounds.[17] Under current international law and most interpretations of the Just War Theory such states, as sovereign entities, undeniably possess the right of national-defense.

But these cases raise a difficult question for the doctrine of national-defense. If such states are held to possess a right of national-defense, then we must explain in what this right is grounded. As I have argued, we must identify an objective value adhering to these states which can serve as an appropriate end of their defensive action. The crucial point is that if there is such an objective value underlying the right of national-defense in these cases, then it cannot be the value of the particular character of the communities in question, for those political communities are *ex hypothesi* corrupt, brutal, and immoral. If they do possess defensive rights, it cannot be because we believe that there is some distinctive form of political culture or common life which is an objective value and which deserves defense and preservation.

It is of course possible (and even natural) that members of oppressive communities attribute value to their community and its particular character. As Marx has shown through his theory of

---

[15] See Cassese, A., '*Ex iniuria ius oritur*: Are we Moving Towards International Legitimation of Forcible Humanitarian Countermeasures in the World Community?' *European Journal of International Law*, 10/1 (1999), 22–30; Brown, B. S., 'Humanitarian Intervention at the Crossroads', *William and Mary Law Review*, 41 (2000), 1683–741.

[16] This classic formulation is Oppenheim's: *International Law*, vol. i, Lauterpacht, H. (ed.), 8th edn., London: Longmans, Green and co., 1955: 312.

[17] For an excellent but disturbing summary of just how widespread such abuses are see Human Rights Watch, *Human Rights Watch World Report*, New York, 2001.

false-consciousness, even the victims of oppression themselves may sometimes falsely value the social structures which serve to oppress them. But clearly this is a subjective or internal value judgement as I have defined it above. It is one conditioned by, and only plausible within, the community in question. Seeking to ground an objective right to defense (one purporting to have normative force across cultural boundaries) upon such a subjective value judgement (one which is valid only within a particular culture or common life) is a relativist and illegitimate form of argument. Appeal to the particular character of the common life cannot provide the required grounding for national-defense because it does not provide a sufficiently objective account of the value underlying defensive action.

There is, however, a response to what I have said which treats the idea of a relativism of value, not as an obstacle to the understanding of the norm of national-defense, but as one of the fundamental grounds of that norm. This view challenges the contention that we are able to make any objective value judgements at all about the justice and value of different forms of common life. All value judgements are held to be radically conditioned by the cultural and linguistic context in which they are made. It is therefore deemed illegitimate to utilize the values embodied in one form of common life (respect for human rights, participatory political institutions, and the like) as a basis for criticizing, or intervening in, other forms of common life. On this view, it is precisely our inability to make objective value judgements which grounds the obligation not to interfere in the activities of other communities or common lives. The right of national-defense is viewed as a corollary of this fundamental norm of non-intervention, itself derived from the premises of a relativism of value.

There are, however, well-known and decisive objections to an account of national-defense built on such a view. As I have already pointed out, the norm of national-defense requires the possibility of objective value judgements in a very basic way. To say that a state has the right to engage in acts of national-defense is not to say that the state's action is, or ought to be, exempt from the moral assessment of outsiders. It is rather to make precisely such an objective moral assessment by affirming that the state's acts of resistance are right and just, and have a claim to be recognized as such both by the international community and the aggressor itself.

It is only on the basis of an objective claim such as this that a norm of non-intervention or a right of national-defense could form the basis of international law or any regulatory system of international norms, for any relativist account of international ethics faces the problem of how to deal with communities which are themselves unashamedly aggressive and interventionist. If the relativist thesis is correct, then it must be illegitimate to judge or seek to restrain such communities on the basis of norms external to that culture. Thus the norm of non-intervention is interpreted in a way that renders it inherently inoperable and un-enforceable. To avoid this conclusion, the position must be amended to hold that there exists no objective moral judgements except for the single moral judgement which underlies the norm of non-intervention. While not strictly incoherent, such a position is ad hoc to the point of absurdity. In general, all attempts to derive an objective obligation of non-intervention from a position of meta-ethical relativism would seem to be guilty of objectifying the respect for difference into an overriding value and covertly asserting this as a universal norm, while at the same time denying the possibility of any such judgements.

An account of national-defense grounded in the end of defending the particular character of the common life could only succeed by illegitimately conflating objective and subjective judgements of value. It must assume that the internal and subjective value which each community places on the character of its own common life, is at the same time capable of grounding an objective norm legitimizing the use of defensive force. This it manifestly cannot do.

Communal integrity and self-determination

The last two sections set up what I take to be the basic problematic of explaining how the common life can function as an appropriate end of national-defense. The value which grounds national-defense must be particular in the sense that it provides a reason for defending one form of common life against another, but its value cannot be so particular as to be simply subjective. Our first interpretation of the value of the common life sought an explanation in terms of state legitimacy, but the value of political association understood through the Hobbesian social contract or similarly minimal theory of legitimation could provide no reason to defend a particular order against others. Our second attempt focused on the particular character of communities, but this provided us with a reason for defending a particular common life only at the cost of relativizing those reasons themselves. What we require is a value that is both objective and particular—it must be objective and recognizable as valid across cultures, yet still provide a reason for defending a particular state or community.

Freedom, autonomy, and self-determination are objective trans-cultural goods in this way. I do not mean by this that persons in all societies could agree on some substantive political conception of freedom or self-determination. Rather I mean that in so far as each person pursues projects which they are committed to regarding as good, they are also committed to regarding the freedom necessary to the attainment of those projects as a good. Humans cannot flourish or obtain full well-being, without the ability to shape their own lives in accordance with their own conception of the good.

Michael Walzer, drawing heavily on an essay by John Stuart Mill, has fashioned from this observation a vigorous defense of the moral importance of state sovereignty.[18] Both authors begin from the premise that in addition to the familiar individual or personal form of autonomy, there is an important realm of self-determination which is necessarily collective. When a community shapes its common life and political institutions, it exercises a valuable form of autonomy which cannot be realized outside the communal sphere. As Walzer says: 'In the individual case we mark out a certain area for individual choice; in the communal case we fix a certain area for political choice. Unless these areas are clearly marked out and protected, both sorts of choices are likely to become problematic.'[19] It is the process of collective self-determination which foreign intervention disturbs and disrupts. Intervention is always wrong, even if it is directed towards assisting or liberating citizens of an oppressive state, because it violates the rights of peoples to determine collectively the form and nature of their own common life. This collective self-determination is, according to Walzer, a value sufficient to make proportionate the use of lethal force in defense.

This idea would seem to overcome the dilemma generated in the last two sections. Unlike the value of order embodied in the

---

[18] See Mill, J. S., 'A Few Words on Non-Intervention', in *Dissertations and Discussions Vol. III*, London: Longman Green Reader and Dyer, 1875. Walzer spells out his views in Walzer, *Just and Unjust Wars*, ch. 6. and especially in id., 'The Moral Standing of States: A Response to Four Critiques', *Philosophy and Public Affairs* (1980), 209–29.

[19] ibid. 224.

Hobbesian political association, collective self-determination can provide us with a reason to defend a particular form of common life. Unlike the purported value of the character of particular common lives, it does not lead us to a form of relativism, for we can recognize the objective value of a community's right to choose, even if this requires us to accept that the agents in question will sometimes choose badly. Thus it could be argued that even a common life whose form we find strange or morally distasteful has an integrity which can be viewed as a value. For what deserves respect and protection is not its form or character as such, but the process of collective choosing which lies behind it. Moreover, the idea has affinities with an attractive account of the value of human life. Richard Norman has argued that what informs the moral presumption against killing people is not simply the fact that they are alive, but that they *have* a life. By this he means that humans have a capacity to shape a meaningful life as a distinctive ongoing project.[20] What Walzer and Mill both assume is that communities are similarly capable of shaping themselves as ongoing meaningful projects, and that it is the value represented by this process that underlies the rightfulness of their engaging in acts of national-defense.

In order to assess this view, the notion of communal self-determination must be probed further. One objection to this line of argument is to claim that although collective self-determination is indeed an important good, it is something that is only realized with the establishment of democratic rights. Only in a democratic society can persons in a community be said to freely shape their common life and enjoy the good of collective self-determination. If this were the case then we would find ourselves in the embarrassing situation of excluding non-democratic regimes (a substantial proportion of the world's states) from enjoyment of the right of national-defense. Clearly such a view could not form the basis of an apology for the right of national-defense as it is currently conceived in the Just War Theory and enshrined in international law.

This objection, however, misses the substance of Walzer's thesis. The kind of collective self-determination that he has in mind is not wholly captured by the exercise of democratic rights; 'self-determination and political freedom are not equivalent terms'

---

[20] See Norman, R., *Ethics, Killing and War*, Cambridge: Cambridge University Press, 1995, ch. 2.

says Walzer.[21] As he sees it, an important part of collective self-determination is the capacity to choose a political system commensurate with one's national culture, even if this results in an illiberal and authoritarian regime. Collective self-determination is the right of people 'to express their inherited culture through political forms worked out amongst themselves'.[22]

But here the account becomes strained: what exactly does this process of 'working out' consist of, if not the exercise of democratic processes? Walzer's response is that it is an eminently political process. It involves the manoeuvring of interest groups, the mobilizing of social and economic forces, and, in its most extreme form, civil war. A crucial aspect of the kind of self-determination Walzer has in mind is the right of citizens to rebel against their government if the state is not representing and defending their common life—if there is no 'fit' between the common life and the state.[23] Walzer says that civil war is a clear example of the phenomenon he has in mind when he talks of collective self-determination. This is why he insists that it is always illegitimate for foreign powers to intervene in favour of one faction in a civil war.[24]

There are, however, deep problems here, for Walzer seems to be reducing collective self-determination ultimately to coercion and the balance of force.[25] Walzer seeks to avoid this result by making the assumption, that, in a civil war, the faction with greatest normative legitimacy (i.e. greatest 'fit' with the intrinsic common life of the population) will in general be victorious. The reason for this, he says, is that victory in civil war reflects the support of the majority of the people: 'Armies and police forces are social institutions; soldiers and policemen come from families, villages, neighbourhoods, classes. They will not fight cohesively, with discipline, or at length unless the regime for which they are fighting has some degree of social support.'[26]

But this position is clearly unacceptable. The outcome of a civil war reflects far more than the support of a majority of the population. It

---

[21] Walzer, *Just and Unjust Wars*, 87.

[22] Walzer, 'The Moral Standing of States', 211.

[23] ibid. 214.

[24] The sole exception being an intervention which balances, but does no more than balance, the prior intervention of another foreign power.

[25] Gerald Doppelt makes this point: 'Walzer's Theory of Morality in International Relations', *Philosophy and Public Affairs*, 8 (1978), 3–26, at 13.

[26] Walzer, 'The Moral Standing of States', 221.

reflects, among much else, access to armaments and military training at the commencement of the conflict and the preparedness to use brutality and terror, all too often against members of the civilian population. It seems facile to suppose that a military outcome can serve as an accurate proxy for a normative process such as self-determination and normative judgements such as legitimacy. Walzer's account remains deeply problematic to the extent that it depends on such implausible assumptions.

The myth of discrete communities

These difficulties arise for Walzer because he has retreated from a straightforwardly political conception of collective self-determination as consisting in the exercise of democratic rights, and replaced it with a looser account in which collective self-determination arises out of the undisturbed operation of organic social processes of contention and dispute. But the approach has two problems. The immediate problem is that it is highly doubtful whether such processes can be viewed as embodying a form of autonomous decision-making, when they so often involve or depend upon patterns of political, social, and military coercion. The more fundamental difficulty is that the position depends upon highly dubious assumptions about the organic unity of national communities and the nature of their relationship to states.

As we have already seen, the right of national-defense as it is defined in international law is a right possessed by states. Yet it will be noted that in the last two sections the ground of the right of national-defense has been sought, not in an account of the value of the state as such, but in the value of the communities or nations associated with states. In Walzer's view, for example, the state's right of national-defense derives from the rights of communities to integrity and autonomy. In the preceding section the value of the particular character of a community was held to underlie the right of national-defense. Now both approaches are vulnerable to a number of serious objections, the most fundamental of which is that human communities do not coincide with the boundaries of states. No community is ever fully integrated within a particular state and no territory ever nurtures but a single community. This is an obvious point, but it is one with significant consequences. The discontinuity between communities and states substantially undermines the attempt to ground the right of national-defense on an account of the rights of communities.

The discontinuity between communities or nations on the one hand and states on the other takes different forms and can be approached in different ways. On the political level, the mismatch between states and nations is evident in the existence of multinational states such as the United Kingdom and in nations which exist across the boundaries of several states, for example the Kurds. On the sociological level, the problem stems from the fact that communal life is far richer and more varied than the simple division into sovereign states would suggest. Social life is not broken into discrete units which might potentially coincide with the boundaries of states. Rather, it consists of an intersecting network of communal affiliations, each of which defines a form of common life and contributes to individual identity. Communities are nested within others—the so-called 'Russian doll effect'. I am a member of the community defined by my family, my neighbourhood, my city, my national region, my country, my international region, and perhaps also the global community of mankind. In different contexts any one of these communal associations may be most important to me and each plays a significant role in defining my identity. The situation is yet more complicated still, for cutting across these vertically nested communities are numerous horizontally ordered communities and affiliations: social classes, ethnic and racial groups, churches, clubs, professional associations, trade unions, colleges, and so on. Our lives are embedded within an indefinite number of common lives, many of which criss-cross national boundaries, each of which possesses an ongoing character, and each of which constitutes a value for those who participate in it.

The problem for an account of national-defense is clear. If it is the value of communities (or the realm of collective autonomy that they make possible) which serves as the end of national-defense, then it is unclear why those rights should be attributed to states, whose relationship to these communities is often one of ambivalence and sometimes one of antagonism. The problem has two aspects. The first is that there are circumstances in which the end of protecting a community can directly conflict with a state's right to national-defense. This situation will arise most clearly in cases of humanitarian intervention in which an international agent violates the sovereignty of a state for the declared purpose of protecting the rights of a specific minority or community. Humanitarian intervention of this kind provides a clear example in which the rights of communities to autonomy and integrity do not underlie and support the defensive rights of states but rather stand in direct conflict with them.

The second aspect of the problem is that an explanation is needed of why the right to use collective violence should be limited to states and not attributed also to communities which are not sovereign states. The right to defend communal integrity with lethal force has been asserted not only by proto-states such as national liberation movements, but also by more marginal communities such as extremist religious sects, cults, and anti-government militias. Marxists, employing the notion of class war, view social class, not sovereign states, as the primary focus for the application of justified collective force. Such claims are not recognized by current international law and the dominant interpretation of the Just War Theory. But because the present account locates the grounding of the right of national-defense in the existence of a genuine community capable of exercising a form of collective autonomy, it is difficult to see why such groups should be denied an analogous right to defend their integrity with force.

The Just War Theorist may respond that the state is justified in defending itself whereas other communal entities are not, because historically it has been the state which has been able to command military allegiance. But this argument puts the cart before the horse. People are evidently increasingly prepared to die and kill for non-state community affiliations. What is more, the historic importance of national identity in our social consciousness stems, to a large extent, from the nation state's conventional ability to command legitimate military defense. Once this presumption in favour of legitimate military defense is established, the state is able to bring into play a series of powerful coercive and propaganda devices to bolster the importance of national identity in the eyes of its citizens.

A further problem with grounding the right of national-defense in the rights of communities is that it implausibly assumes that communities are discrete entities with clear criteria of identity and individuation. But, unlike states whose existence can be defined in reasonably clear legal terms, no plausible and determinate criteria exist for the identity and individuation of communities. This issue is of great importance for Walzer and Mill because their theory requires that we be able to determine with the highest degree of certainty whether a given conflict is occurring between different communities or within a single community. It is on this basis that they seek to determine when it is legitimate for an external power to intervene in the conflict. Military intervention is legitimate if the conflict is one between different communities, but it is illegitimate if the conflict is one within a single community, because in that case the war is to be regarded as a form of communal self-determination which must be protected from outside interference.[27]

The view, therefore, requires identity and individuation criteria of the strongest kind, for we must suppose that even when a community is so factionalized that it has divided into warring parties, it is still possible to identify a single continuing common-life whose rights of collective self-determination must be respected. But it is difficult to see what grounds we could ever have for making such a judgement. Notoriously, the concepts typically employed in this context, for example, the concept of a 'nationhood', have proved stubbornly resistant to analysis. As one observer says: 'Historically speaking, most nations have always been culturally and ethnically diverse, problematic, protean and artificial constructs that take shape very quickly and come apart just as fast'.[28]

Two conditions would have to be fulfilled if an account of the value of communities were to provide an effective underpinning for the right of national-defense as that right is defined in international law and in the Just War Theory. First, we would need clear criteria for settling the identity and individuation of communities. Secondly, the communities thus identified would have to be substantially co-extensive with the states. Neither condition is satisfied in the real world and it is difficult to imagine how they ever could be, given the realities of human communal life. It would seem, therefore, that

---

[27] See Walzer, *Just and Unjust Wars*, ch. 6; id., 'The Moral Standing of States', 209–29. Interestingly, the Ancient Greeks had something of a composite conception of the conflicts that occurred between Greek city states. While those wars were clearly seen as inter-communal, they were also, in so far as they consisted in hostilities between Greeks, viewed as intra-communal. Thus different and stricter regulations pertained to conflicts between Greeks than to wars against non-Greek 'barbarians'. See Draper, G. I. A. D., 'Grotius' Place in the Development of Legal Ideas about War', in Bull, H., Kingsbury, B., and Roberts A. (eds.), *Hugo Grotius and International Relations*, Oxford: Clarendon Press, 1992: 177.

[28] Linda Colley quoted in Franck, T., 'Clan and Superclan: Loyalty, Identity and Community in Law and Practice', *American Journal of International Law*, 90 (1996), 359–83, at 365.

the task of grounding national-defense in an account of the value of the common life is as problematic as the attempt to ground it in the end of protecting individual persons was seen to be in the previous chapter. The analogical strategy has proved as problematic and unpersuasive as the reductive strategy.

The argument which draws a connection between personal self-defense and national-defense is at once beguilingly simple and intuitively appealing. It has informed moral and philosophical thinking on warfare since at least the time of the Christian Fathers and has had a powerful influence on the development of modern international law. But I have argued that the analogy cannot be philosophically sustained. National-defense cannot be reduced to a collective application of personal rights of self-defense, and it cannot be explained as a state-held right analogous to personal self-defense. Because the right of national-defense has always been the central 'just cause' for war within the Just War Theory, and because the analogy with self-defense has always been its central justification, this result must be seen as a serious challenge to the traditional Just War doctrine of international morality.

I take this to be a surprising and disconcerting result, one which challenges us to revisit some of the basic normative conceptions of international relations. If the defensive rights of states cannot be simply modelled on the rights of persons, then we must work to develop new or amended conceptions for dealing with the problems of war, conflict, and aggression. The remaining two chapters explore some of the consequences of this result for our thinking about the ethics of war and peace.

8

War, Responsibility, and Law Enforcement

Our results so far have been largely negative—that the argument from self-defense to national-defense, in both its analogical and reductive forms, fails. It might be supposed that the only conclusion we can draw from this result will be a form of pacifism. In this chapter, however, I shall develop an argument for the positive conclusion that military action against an aggressive state could potentially be justified, not in terms of self-defense, but as a form of law enforcement. I shall argue, however, that such a justification is unlikely to prove effective without the establishment of something like a minimal universal state, and I shall attempt to show that there is a plausible contractarian argument for the justice of such a state. But before I can argue for this conclusion there is an important obstacle that must be navigated. If any form of military action (be it a defensive war, or a legitimate act of law enforcement) is to be justified, then we must provide a moral explanation of why the soldiers against whom one fights are appropriate objects of violence.

A paradox in the Just War Theory

Nowhere does the phenomenon of the two levels of war generate greater difficulties and paradoxes for the Just War Theory than in the task of explaining how it can be permissible, in a defensive war, to kill the soldiers of an aggressive state. In other words, how does the Just War Theorist get from a right of national-defense held against a state to a right to kill held against a particular person? From our investigation of defensive rights in Part I, we have learned that if one is to be justified in harming a person in defense, then it must be the case that the object of the defensive force has forfeited or fails to possess a right against being harmed. I argued that an aggressor can only forfeit or fail to possess rights against being harmed if there is an appropriate normative connection between him as a subject and the threat posed—the object of defensive force must bear some level of normative (as opposed to merely causal) responsibility for the threat posed.[1]

Yet the moral and legal discourse of national-defense typically proceeds almost exclusively at the level of state agents, for example, aggression is defined in international law as a crime committed by states against other states.[2] The Just War Theory maintains that by culpably attacking the territorial integrity and political independence of another state, the aggressor state forfeits certain of its own rights to territorial integrity and political independence. But the question is this: how can a forfeiture of sovereign rights on the part of a state explain the forfeiture on the part of its soldiers of their right to life? There is a gap in the moral explanation between a right to act against an aggressive state, and the right to act against the persons who are its soldiery—a conceptual lacuna between the two levels of war.

It is not at all apparent how this gap can be bridged. Having a right against an organization does not in general entail having a right against the members or agents of that organization. Thus if Company X owes me 5 dollars, it doesn't follow that Joe, being an employee of Company X, owes me 5 dollars (or anything else for that matter). How, then, can it follow from the fact that I have a liberty to infringe against the sovereign rights of State Y, that I have a liberty to take the life of Jim, being a soldier of Y?

It is of course true that if Joe is an officer of Company X and it falls within his official function (for example, because Joe is treasurer), then it is Joe's obligation to render to me that money. The point is, however, that the 5 dollars Joe is under a duty to render to me aren't his 5 dollars, they are the company's. It would be improper (to say the least) for me to try and redeem my debt against the company by gaining access to Joe's personal finances. The problem with killing soldier Jim on the basis of a right held against his state is that the life we thereby take belongs to Jim, not to State Y. The question therefore remains; if an aggressive state has forfeited certain

---

[1] Just War Theorists have sometimes advanced the position that one may permissibly kill those who are 'non-innocent', where this is understood not to mean 'morally at fault', but rather 'currently offering harm'. I argued in Chapter 4 that this position is not tenable; an 'objective' account of wrongdoing can provide no justification for the application of defensive force. See above, at pp. 83 ff.

[2] See the United Nation Consensus Definition of Aggression (1974) Article 1(1).

rights, how can this explain that its soldiers forfeit rights in such a way that it is permissible to kill them?

Perhaps the answer is that the soldier's life should in some sense be regarded as the property of the state. Perhaps the soldier implicitly conveys his right to life over to the state when he joins the army. His life becomes an asset of the state to be disposed of as it will, and like any asset, the soldier's life may be forfeited by improper conduct on the part of the state.

There is clearly something very unsettling about this idea. For a start, we may have severe reservations about whether persons are normatively empowered to conveyance away their right to life in this way. In our society one is not empowered to sell oneself into slavery, and presumably the considerations which weigh against this would count also against alienating one's right to life in this way. Furthermore, those who enter the army through conscription clearly consent to no such alienation of their rights, yet the rights of war presumably extend to the killing of conscripts. If the state claims to own the lives of conscripts this can only be because it has, as it were, 'nationalized' them. But if the right to life rules out anything at all, then it stands against such a possibility. No agent, not even the state, may appropriate the life of another person for its own interests (nor even for the collective interest). Indeed this would seem to explain what is so very pernicious about conscription, for the state thereby treats its citizens as if they were a simple resource capable of being nationalized, and this is a clear violation of the rights and dignity of the person.

The responsibility of soldiers

Now the above analogy concerning a company and its debt is of course only plausible if we imagine a certain moral distance between the agent and his organization. If we instead imagine a debt incurred because of a collapsed business for which Joe held particular responsibility, or that, instead of a large firm, Company X was a small co-operative venture or partnership, then it may indeed be appropriate to seek redress from Joe personally. To acknowledge this is to raise the question of personal responsibility for collective projects.

Indeed, such an idea would seem the most promising way of explaining why soldiers of an aggressive state are appropriate objects of violence. Surely if it is justifiable to inflict harm against the soldiers of an aggressive state, this is because they share responsibility for the wrongfulness of the aggressive war. What is curious is that the Just War Theory precludes appeal to such considerations since it denies that ordinary soldiers are personally responsible for fighting in an unjust war. Walzer, in a representative statement, claims that there exists a 'moral equality' between soldiers, entailing for both sides an equal set of military permissions and restrictions. 'The enemy soldier', says Walzer, 'though his war may well be criminal, is nevertheless as blameless as oneself', at least so long as he has adhered to the rules of *jus in bello*.[3] So the Just War Theory will not permit reference to the personal responsibility of soldiers for an aggressive war in an explanation of why they may permissibly be killed in national-defense.

But why should soldiers escape responsibility for the unjust wars in which they fight? It is, on the surface, a less than intuitive claim. Here are men killing each other on the field of battle. If there is such a thing as a just war, then it is perhaps possible to understand how a subset of these men are behaving rightly. But how can soldiers whose very war is unjust be engaged in an activity for which they are free of fault?

There is a fascinating intellectual history behind these questions, and confronting them will enable us to apprehend a tension which goes to the very heart of the Just War Theory. It is a tension implicit in the distinction between *jus in bello* and *jus ad bellum*. These two sets of rules, the former specifying what one may rightly do in war, the latter when one may rightly go to war, are presented by lawyers and Just War Theorists as two components of a unified moral and legal framework of war. But in reality they are two very different ways of thinking about the justice of war, each making very different assumptions. Put simply, *jus ad bellum* begins from the assumption that war is an illegal activity whose legitimate use is limited to, at most, one side of a given dispute. *Jus in bello*, on the other hand, assumes that war is a law-governed and hence implicitly lawful activity with entitlements and restrictions that accrue equally to both sides.

There are strong historical reasons for the antagonism between these two ways of thinking about war, and strong pragmatic reasons

---

[3] Walzer, M., *Just and Unjust Wars*, New York: Basic Books, 1977: 34–41.

for their intermingling. Historically, the two sets of rules derive from different sources.[4] *Jus in bello* is the product of the medieval chivalric code, the self-regulation of the warrior classes. *Jus ad bellum*, on the other hand, is the invention of churchmen and lawyers and represents a fundamental challenge to the assumptions built into chivalry; the assumption that military life and warfare are an acceptable and potentially noble form of activity. The old medieval pun equating *militia* with *malitia* is the central attitude of *jus ad bellum*. Pragmatically, however, combining the two ideas enables lawyers and humanitarians to regulate and mitigate the evils of war twice over; once through restrictions on the recourse to war, and again (with the knowledge that the first set of restrictions will often be ineffective) through restrictions on the conduct of war.

The pragmatic aim is laudable, but the conjunction leads to philosophical contradiction as soon as we consider the issue of personal responsibility. If, as *jus in bello* suggests, there is a 'moral equality' between soldiers, implying that the armed forces of each side are entitled to commit acts of war against the other, how exactly can it be that one side is fighting illegally and their war a crime? If an aggressive war is fought within the bounds of *jus in bello*, then the Just War Theory is committed to the seemingly paradoxical position that the war taken as a whole is a crime, yet that each of the individual acts which together constitute the aggressive war are entirely lawful. Such a war, the Just War Theory seems to be saying, is both just and unjust at the same time. The solution to this conundrum proposed by the theory is a kind of moral division of labour—monarchs and those who command the sovereign power of the state are assigned exclusive responsibility for recourse to aggressive war, that is, for matters of *jus ad bellum*, whereas the responsibility of soldiers is limited to the use of proper methods of fighting and other issues of *jus in bello*.

So the curious position that soldiers are not personally responsible for participating in an unjust war is necessitated by the historical

---

[4] For good discussions of the historical development of the Just War Theory see: Clark, I., *Waging War: A Philosophical Introduction*, Oxford: Clarendon Press, 1990: 37–48; Barnes, J., 'The Just War', in Kenny, A., Kretzmann, N., and Pinborg, J. (eds.), *Cambridge History of Later Medieval Philosophy*, Cambridge: Cambridge University Press, 1988; Draper, G. I. A. D., 'Grotius' Place in the Development of Legal Ideas about War', in Bull, H., Kingsbury, B., and Roberts, A. (eds.), *Hugo Grotius and International Relations*, Oxford: Clarendon Press, 1992.

intermingling of two quite different conceptions of the justice of war. But can this position be philosophically sustained? Many Just War Theorists have thought so and the claim has received vigorous defense throughout the theory's history. It is worth taking the time to examine these arguments.

Augustine argued that it is just for a soldier to fight only where his fighting is authorized, 'in obedience to God or some proper authority'.[5] A corollary of this, for Augustine, is that so long as a soldier's acts of war are properly authorized he is not to be blamed for them: 'He to whom authority is delegated, and who is but the sword in the hand of him who uses it, is not himself responsible for the death he deals'.[6] It is part of the order of nature that monarchs have the authority to make war and 'the servant's duty is to obey'.[7]

This duty of obedience is allowed to become overriding for Augustine; in particular it is allowed to override the duty to refrain from participating in a potentially unjust war, because the relationship between servant and master is itself underwritten by the moral authority of God. Monarchs rule by divine authority, and even if the ruler in question is an 'ungodly king', 'the iniquity of giving the orders will make the king guilty while the rank of a servant in the civil order will show the soldier to be innocent'.[8] Moreover, Augustine believed that the actions of the wicked are turned by God so as to accord with his 'secret penal arrangement and unfathomable judgements':[9] 'God is not the author but he is the controller of sin; so that sinful actions, which are sinful because they are against nature, are judged and controlled and assigned their proper place and condition'.[10]

In Augustine's framework, therefore, there exists a kind of moral safety net for the soldier or servant, which guarantees that he will not act wrongly so long as he obeys on matters for which his master has competence. In this way Augustine is able to provide a coherent

---

[5] St Augustine of Hippo, *Contra Faustus Manichaeum*, in Schaff, P. (ed.), *Nicene and Post-Nicene Fathers*, 1st series, vol. iv, Grand Rapids, Mich.: Eerdmans, 1974, bk. 22.74.

[6] St Augustine of Hippo, *De Civitate Dei*, in Schaff, P. (ed.), *Nicene and Post-Nicene Fathers*, 1st series, vol. ii, Grand Rapids, Mich.: Eerdmans, 1974: 1.21 (p. 15). Curiously the scriptural text that Augustine refers to here is the story of Abraham and Isaac. However, as Aquinas points out, this interpretation of the scripture would seem to justify violating the prohibition on killing the innocent. See *Summa Theologica*, part II. ii. 64.

[7] Augustine, *Contra Faustus Manichaeum*, in *Nicene and Post-Nicene Fathers*, 22.71.

[8] ibid. 22.75.

[9] ibid. 22.78.

[10] ibid. 22.78.

account of what I have called the moral division of labour in war. But the argument is premised on existence of God, and it is clear that his position has little to recommend it once it is removed from its theistic context. If, as we now believe, rulers and political institutions gain authority not from divine right, but from morally legitimating features of their rule, then the presumption in favour of obedience will only be as strong as the moral credentials of their rule. In which case, a duty to disobey a king issuing 'unrighteous commands'[11] on the prosecution of an unjust war would seem to remain a permanent moral possibility.

The position which Augustine formulated in theistic form became embedded in a Just War Theory which was increasingly secular in its context and application. The great transformation of the law of war from theological code to secular international law was achieved during the sixteenth, seventeenth, and eighteenth centuries by scholars, many of whom struggled to make sense of the moral division of labour. Francisco de Vitoria, famous for his defense of the rights of American Indians, stood at the very beginning of this process, and his arguments on the issue are worth examining. Vitoria says that a soldier may not fight in a war if he believes it to be 'patently unjust'.[12] But, he says, common soldiers are not required to examine the justice of the wars in which they fight and if they are in doubt they must fight. In this sense Vitoria says a soldier is in an analogous position to an officer of the law who 'must carry out the sentence of a judge even if he doubts its justice'.[13]

This is an interesting analogy. We may indeed excuse an executioner who kills a wrongly condemned man if the judicial system within which he works is generally fair and the case is genuinely a difficult one. It might then be right for him to suspend his personal reservations for the greater utility of the functioning of the system as a whole. But suppose an executioner worked within a system which is radically flawed: he knows that at least half of the men he is asked to kill are innocent because the judges are incompetent and the system corrupt. A man who continued to kill in these circumstances would be something like a murderer. But this is precisely the calculus

---

[11] ibid. 22.75.
[12] Vitoria, F., *De Indis Relectio Posterior, Sive de Jure Belle* [On the Law of War], in *Vitoria: Political Writings*, Pagden, A., and Lawrence, J. (eds.), Cambridge: Cambridge University Press, 1991: 2.2 § 22 and § 25.
[13] ibid. 2.3 § 31. See also Walzer, *Just and Unjust Wars*, 39.

with which we are presented in the case of war. As Hugo Grotius rightly points out: 'a war cannot be just on both sides... the reason is that by the very nature of the case a moral quality cannot be given to opposites as to doing and restraining'.[14] Therefore, even if a soldier is in doubt about the justice of a particular war, or does not consider himself competent to judge the issues involved, he can know with certainty that there is at least a 50 per cent chance that he is fighting on the unjust side.[15] In such circumstances it would seem to be an act of the most extreme moral recklessness to adopt Vitoria's policy of 'in case of doubt, fight'.

Vitoria argues that ordinary soldiers are not required to examine the justice of the wars in which they fight because unlike 'senators, magnates... and those called to attend royal council', they can do nothing to prevent the war even if they conclude it to be unjust.[16] But this is an old chestnut. They may not be able to prevent the unjust war, but what they are able to prevent is their participation in the proscribed activity. If a man is charged with accessory to murder, it is no defense to demonstrate that the crime would have proceeded without his help and that he could not have prevented the crime had he tried. What he is responsible for is his participation.

The Just War Theory achieves a wholly secular treatment in the arguments of Michael Walzer, and he too seeks to defend the moral division of labour. Augustine's account had emphasized the notion of authority to wage war, which he took to stem ultimately from God. A soldier acts rightly, argues Augustine, if he is a 'sword in the hand' of proper authority. In Walzer's writing the instrumentalist imagery remains, but it has been transformed in accordance with modern liberal principles into an argument about consent. He argues that if a soldier is really an 'instrument' in the hands of the state, then he does not act in the full sense at all, and therefore cannot be held responsible for his killing.[17] This condition of re-

---

[14] Grotius, H., *De Jure Belli Ac Pacis*, New York: Classics of International Law, 1964, bk. ii: 565; see also Vitoria, *De Indis Relectio Posterior, Sive de Jure Belle*, 2.4 (p. 313). This is also the position of modern international law: 'Under no circumstances can the actual use of force by both parties to a conflict be lawful simultaneously.' (Dinstein, Y., *War, Aggression and Self-Defence*, Cambridge: Grotius Publications, 1988: 168.)

[15] In reality the likelihood that his war will be unjust is far higher because, while a war cannot be just on both sides in the Just War Theory, it can (and frequently is) unjust on both sides.

[16] Vitoria, *De Indis Relectio Posterior, Sive de Jure Belle*, 2.2 § 24 and § 25.

[17] Walzer, *Just and Unjust Wars*, 36.

duced responsibility obtains, argues Walzer, because soldiers on both sides fight without consent, either because they are coerced by conscription, or because they are constrained to fight by their own conscience and loyalty. 'When [soldiers] fight without freedom', he argues, 'their war is not their crime'.[18]

The difficulty with this argument, however, is that it is simply too weak. The essence of the position is that soldiers can properly enter a plea of duress against the charge that they have wrongfully killed the innocent, that is, committed murder. Yet duress is not generally thought to provide a legal or moral excuse for wrongful killing. In English law, duress is never a defense against a charge of murder or attempted murder. When threatened with death, the law holds that a man ought rather to die himself, than escape by performing a wrongful act of killing.[19] This principle seems intuitively correct, and serves to refute Walzer's diminished responsibility argument.[20]

But even if one thinks that threat of death can furnish an excuse for unlawful killing, this is in any case not the situation faced by most soldiers. Soldiers characteristically fight for a complex set of reasons including duty, peer pressure, and fear of shame, social stigma or punishment. Though these factors clearly bring great pressure to bear on an agent, they are neither singly nor conjointly sufficient to override the duty not to participate in wrongful killing. Consider a Mafia killer. He may be non-consenting in the terms which Walzer uses to describe the predicament of most soldiers; he may dislike his job, may want to be elsewhere at the time, may only be doing it for reasons of fear or honour. But, clearly, these

---

[18] ibid. 37.

[19] See Smith, J. C., and Hogan, B., *Criminal Law*, London: Butterworths, 1992: 238 and 242.

[20] The position does, however, raise difficult questions about the status of duress as an excuse. If, as is normally supposed, extreme threats generate an excuse because they so overpower an agent's will that his actions are no longer deemed to be under his control, then it makes no sense to distinguish between murder and less serious crimes such as theft or assault in this regard. If the agent's act is really involuntary in the one case, then it must be involuntary in all cases. The result of this is that the preservation of one's own life becomes an excuse for any necessary actions, including the killing of officers taking one to lawful execution and (presumably) the killing of innocent bystanders. In my view, the theory of duress needs to be amended along the following lines: where the harm one inflicts under duress is less than the harm with which one is threatened, then this may generate a justification on the grounds of being the lesser evil. In cases in which the harm inflicted is greater than or equal to the harm threatened, there may still be room for a limited form of excuse. In this case the excuse will be based on considerations of compassion rather than involuntariness (see above, p. 92).

considerations are not sufficient to deflect our judgement that he is a murderer.

Perhaps out of recognition of these weaknesses, Walzer extends his argument in a radically different direction. As we have noted, he holds that soldiers on both sides of a war have a 'moral equality' which entails first and foremost an equal entitlement to kill the enemy.[21] This position, however, is a significant departure from the argument we have just considered; it shifts from claiming that soldiers are excused for killing because their lack of consent means they are not responsible, to the claim that their killing is justified because they possess an entitlement to kill. Indeed, it is difficult to see how the two claims could both be true of the same action, for excusable acts are those for which one is not fully responsible, whereas one talks about justification only after responsibility has been established.

The relationship between these two arguments is even more paradoxical because, when we ask where the mutual entitlement to kill could derive from, it looks very much as if it could only arise out of the kind of mutual consent to combat which Walzer has already denied in respect of soldiers. For instance, boxers have a mutual entitlement to hurt each other, but this derives from their free agreement to fight, and mutual acceptance of risk. Do soldiers in a war similarly consent to their enemy's attempts to kill and harm them? They may accept it as an inevitable part of the endeavour in which they are engaged, but they surely do not consent to it. Soldiers fight knowing they may be killed, but they do not thereby permit their enemies to kill them; they do not say to their enemies 'you may kill me if you can'. In this sense Walzer is right; soldiers do not consent to their wars in the way that boxers consent to a bout.

But, if not through consent, then how could combatants come to possess a mutual entitlement to kill? It is a difficult question because most entitlements to harm derive from some kind of normative inequality between agents and are therefore held exclusively by one party against another. Self-defense is a prime example of this. It derives, as we have seen, from a normative asymmetry between aggressor and defender. It is true that there may be deviant cases of self-defense in which two parties are each justified (or perhaps excused) in defending themselves against the other. Gladiator slaves forced to fight each other may well be in such a situation. Perhaps this is how Walzer

---

[21] *Just and Unjust Wars*, 34.

pictures soldiers at war: compelled to fight and yet possessing a mutual entitlement to kill in self-defense. But I have already argued that the right of personal self-defense cannot justify the full range of wartime activities undertaken by soldiers. What is more, the right (if it is a right) of gladiator slaves to kill their opponents persists only to the extent that they are under the control of and in fear of their masters. Presumably this implies that their primary moral duty is to try to confound their masters by escaping or rebelling if they are able. This model, therefore, hardly provides a useful paradigm for war.

Walzer's argument is thus pulling in two different and incompatible directions—one built on the presupposition that soldiers do not consent to their warring, the other on the presupposition that they do. Neither argument is sufficient in its own terms. Soldiers do not consent to fight in a way that could ground a mutual entitlement to kill. But neither is their will constrained sufficiently to generate an excuse of duress. Our brief historical survey of the Just War Theory helps to explain why Walzer's argument experiences these tensions. The requirement that soldiers not be held responsible for the justice of the wars in which they fight derives from an historical combination of two radically different conceptions of justice in war. The position thus foisted upon the Just War Theory could be sustained within the theistic framework of Augustine and Aquinas. But the position has been inherited by modern secular Just War Theory and international law which no longer have the resources to maintain it.

It seems plausible to conclude that soldiers, and not just sovereigns, are responsible for the aggressive wars in which they engage. This is true in the sense that anyone who participates in, and contributes towards, a larger communal project is responsible for the legality or morality of that project: they are responsible for their contribution. This is a common-sense position and, as we have seen, it is the arguments to the contrary that strain plausibility. Given this, it would seem that a long-standing tenet of Just War Theory must be abandoned—soldiers fighting an unjust war have no permission to kill, and there is no 'moral equality' between soldiers.

War and law enforcement

If the argument of the preceding section is correct, it would seem to suggest a different possibility for conceptualizing the moral status of killing in a defensive war. If soldiers may be held personally account-able for the aggressive wars in which they fight and, moreover, neither self-defense nor national-defense can serve as an appropriate justification for harming them, then there may be a different way of justifying the violence of war. For in fighting an aggressive war soldiers are doing something wrong and it may, therefore, be pos-sible to justify the violence inflicted on them in the course of defensive wars as law enforcement or punishment. It is this idea I would now like to examine.[22]

The idea that defensive wars may be a form of law enforcement has a long and distinguished history. Both Augustine and Aqui-nas argued that war may have a legitimate punitive function. Grotius argued that the world's states constitute a society, in which members are collectively responsible for the enforcement of the law.[23] The Grotian conception of an 'international society' of states has had a profound influence on modern international law, international rela-tions theory, and Just War Theory. It is evident in Walzer's argument that a war of self-defense is also a form of law enforcement since, as he says, in the absence of a global sovereign power 'police powers are distributed among all the members'[24] of the international com-munity.

Moreover, the idea that states may have the right to punish one another through war receives substantial support from the political theory of John Locke and his contemporary followers such as Robert Nozick.[25] Locke argues that in the state of nature each person has the private right to punish breaches of the natural law. This 'natural executive right' is only lost when persons transfer their personal right to punish to the sovereign through the social contract. Indeed, for Locke, it is the 'inconveniences... which necessarily follow from every man's being judge in his own case' which provide the principal

---

[22] Law enforcement is of a course a broader category than punishment, for it includes actions taken to prevent the commission of unlawful acts and intervention to stop crimes that are already in progress. Though much of the philosophical discussion centres on the question of punishment, it should be remembered that punishment is only one aspect of legitimate law enforcement.

[23] Grotius, *De Jure Belli Ac Pacis.*

[24] Walzer, *Just and Unjust Wars*, 59.

[25] Locke, J., *Two Treatises of Government*, Cambridge: Cambridge University Press, 1960, bk. II; Nozick, R., *Anarchy, State, and Utopia*, Oxford: Blackwell, 1974, esp. ch. 5 and at 137–42.

reason for entering a commonwealth.[26] But the sovereign and his citizens have entered into no social contract with the sovereign and citizens of foreign states. Therefore, they retain all the rights of the state of nature with respect to them—including the right to punish them for breaches of the natural law.[27]

Locke's natural law account of the right to punish may be felt to have affinities with the account of self-defense which I developed in Part I. In my account, the liberty to harm an aggressor in self-defense is grounded in the fact that, through his aggressive conduct, he forfeits certain of his rights against being harmed. This sounds somewhat similar to the Lockean natural right account of punishment. Indeed, it may seem that on my account the two conceptions of self-defense and punishment must be intimately connected, or even that my account of self-defense must covertly presuppose a theory of private punishment. We must, therefore, take seriously the possibility that the justice of defensive wars is grounded not in a theory of defensive rights, as such, but in an account of law enforcement and punishment.

I do not believe that this supposition is correct. Indeed, in my view, it is extremely important to clearly distinguish self-defense from punishment. The best way to do this and to demonstrate that wars between states do not have a proper punitive function is through an investigation of the concept of 'authority' to punish. It is often thought that there is a difficult moral problem about the justification of punishment. There has been much debate about whether punishment is justified as retribution, reform, deterrence, or a combination of these considerations, and there are characteristic difficulties with each of these views.[28] However, the notion of authority provides a different way of approaching the question of the justification of punishment. If we can give an account of what constitutes and explains the authority to punish then we will have shown how there can be a right to punish, and to show this is to show how punishment can sometimes be justified.[29]

---

[26] Locke, *Two Treatises of Government*, bk. II, para. 90.

[27] ibid., para. 91.

[28] See Honderich, T., *Punishment the Supposed Justifications*, Cambridge: Polity Press, 1989.

[29] A. J. Simmons makes a similar point in, 'Locke and the Right to Punish', *Philosophy and Public Affairs*, 1991: 311–49, at 314.

According to Locke and Nozick, the exclusive concentration of authority to punish in the agents of the state is nothing more than an artificial product of the social contract. I want to take seriously the contention that it is more than this, and indeed reflects basic precepts of justice itself. Even in the state of nature, not everyone may rightly punish the guilty, for punishment requires the special kind of inequality, or superiority in the agent of punishment which we call authority. But if we reject the notion of a natural right to punish then we must provide an explanation of what authority is and how it arises. I will suggest that we possess two very basic ways of thinking about the genesis of authority, each of which sees it as arising naturally from characteristic patterns of human interaction without presupposing a natural executive right.

Our first way of thinking about authority can be explained with the help of a very simple form of the social contract model. Imagine two persons who are in a disagreement (they may, but need not, be in a state of nature). The first claims that he has been wronged by the second. If the first person inflicts harm on the second, we are disinclined to call this punishment precisely because we feel that he would not have the authority to punish. But suppose now that there was a third person who was in a position of neutrality between the two, and to whose decision each disputant freely consented to submit themselves. It seems clear that this person would have authority to settle the dispute and administer punishment. This suggests a model of authority with two constitutive elements, two features by which a person may be raised from the private sphere to become competent to administer justice and dispense punishment; namely, impartiality and consensual submission. Each of these ideas will require further explanation.

The requirement that administrators of justice be impartial seems to stem directly from the nature of justice itself. Indeed, justice is often defined in opposition to the partisan and the partial. Those who administer justice must be neutral, which is to say they must, so far as is possible, have no reasons for acting in the case other than reasons of justice itself. This is why it is always unjust for a participant in a dispute to administer or determine punishment in his own case, and why we insist that judges or committee members stand down from a case if their personal interests are involved. While it is not inconceivable that such persons will act impartially, it is far from likely and cannot be relied upon. More importantly, their involvement in the dispute alters the character of their action, giving it the quality of revenge or reprisal rather than punishment.[30] The idea of impartiality is, therefore, internal to the idea of punishment itself (considered as an aspect of justice). What this would seem to suggest is that the meting out of 'punishment' to wrongdoers by private persons in the state of nature is not simply 'inconvenient', as Locke and Nozick argue—rather it may not count as punishment at all, for the necessary requirement of impartiality could well be absent.

The idea that consensual submission is a requirement for the authority to punish may seem less persuasive, for it would seem that punishment is precisely the infliction of a penalty on a wrong-doer against his will. But a system of law, if it is to be legitimate, must express a community's conception of justice and the members of that community must recognize the validity of the rules and processes to which they are subject. The requirement of consent is therefore linked to the requirement of impartiality. A community's consent is constituted by its recognition of the fairness of the system of law to which it is subject. This observation also helps us understand the limit of consent to a system of punishment and when consent may be rightly withdrawn. If a person wishes to live in a community then he must consent to its rules and thereby to the punishment which will be exacted if he violates them. It is not, therefore, open to a criminal to disavow the authority of the court as he is dragged from the stand (in the absence of some genuine procedural impropriety). But if an individual, a minority, or a group start to withdraw their consent from a system of rules because they believe, on reasonable grounds, that an administrator of justice or the system of rules as a whole is partisan, then those judgements cease to be punishment and become a simple mechanism of domination. There is an important sense in which such people are not being punished, they are being fought against. This contrast between punishing someone and fighting them would seem to identify a substantive moral distinction to which we will return below.

This simple contractarian conception seems to identify one very basic way we have of thinking about the authority to punish. But we have another quite different model of authority which is based on

---

[30] There are theories of punishment in which revenge is seen as an appropriate function of punishment. But even on such a conception it is still possible to draw a distinction between private revenge and legitimate punishment.

the rights of punishment possessed by parents over their children.[31] Parents' authority to punish their children does not derive from the child's consent, but seems to stem from three features of the relationship between parent and child, two of which are natural and one of which is normative. The first feature of the relationship is the fact that the parent is naturally superior to the child in knowledge, wisdom, and power. The second is that the parent has a natural attitude of love and care towards the child. The third feature, which is in part derived from the first two, is that the relationship is characterized by reciprocal duties: obedience on the part of the child, care and protection on the part of the parent. This conception of authority is very different to the contract model. For the notion of impartiality, so central to that model, is of peripheral importance to the parental model. The parents' principal responsibility is not to ensure that their administration of punishment is impartial and just, but rather that it is beneficial to the overall welfare and development of the child; impartiality enters only as an instrumental value to this broader end. For this reason the notion of punishment explicated by the parental model should perhaps not be seen as part of an account of *justice* at all. In contrast, in the contract model the emphasis is on justice and it seems less crucial that the punishment be beneficial to the offender.

These two models of authority, the contract and parental models, arise quite naturally out of familiar moral experience and provide two basic frameworks for thinking about the problems of punishment and authority. How do these considerations relate to the possibility of punitive war? If a body were to fight wars which were just by reason of punishment, it would need to possess proper authority to punish. We have seen that this can arise in two ways, either from neutrality and the prior consensual submission of the offender, or from a relationship with the offender which is parent-like. Does the state at war fulfil either of these characteristics?

Let us start with the parental model. The difficulty with this conception of authority is that, as we have seen, it is based on a set of natural and normative inequalities. The punishing authority has a natural superiority in knowledge, wisdom, and power as well as having the best interest of the punished at heart. Now perhaps this *is* how some hegemonic states conceive themselves in their foreign

---

[31] Cf. Locke, *Second Treatise of Government*, ch. VI and ch. VII, para. 86.

policy. But it is clearly not a persuasive description of any state's action in war. More fundamentally, the model could not provide an explanation of the right of one state to punish another because a fundamental assumption of the international legal order and the Just War Theory is the sovereign equality of states. The parental model seems to be a non-starter in international relations, because it conflicts with this basic assumption of the Just War Theory itself. Moreover, it is difficult to see how the infliction of punishment unto death could ever be justified on a parental model of punishment, which, as we have seen, is directed most fundamentally towards the benefit and development of the agent punished.

What about the consent model? This fares little better. A state at war is neither in a position of neutrality and impartiality with respect to the dispute, nor does it have the recognition and consensual submission of the state it purports to punish. As I suggested above, there would seem to be a deep moral distinction between punishing someone and fighting against them. States cannot be said to punish those against whom they fight, for they are rather participants in a dispute in which the question of justice is precisely one of the issues between them. Kant, in his tract *Perpetual Peace*, which we will consider in greater detail below, is emphatic on this point: 'The concept of international right becomes meaningless if interpreted as a right to go to war. For this would make it a right to determine what is lawful not by means of universally valid external laws, but by means of one-sided maxims backed up by physical force'.[32]

The argument for a universal state

The prospect of employing the notion of punishment or law enforcement as a justification for wars of national-defense fought by sovereign states, would seem to be remote indeed. But our results here need not be wholly negative. The considerations which demonstrate the illegitimacy of law enforcement by individual states serve also to reveal how genuine and legitimate international law enforcement may be possible. If there were a body which was genuinely impartial and which had a recognized authority to resolve disputes

[32] Kant I., *Perpetual Peace: A Philosophical Sketch*, in Reiss, H. (ed), *Kant's Political Philosophy*, Cambridge: Cambridge University Press, 1970: 105.

and enforce the law, then its prosecution of military action against international aggressors could be justified. Such a body might, for instance, take action to prevent the invasion of one state by another and could also use force to punish those responsible for aggression. In what follows I will sketch out some of the considerations relating to and consequences of the development of such a positive account. My remarks will be necessarily schematic but, I hope, usefully point towards fruitful future work in this area.

The first important point to make is that if one accepts my argument against exempting soldiers of personal responsibility for their participation in unjust wars, then this has the effect of overcoming the problem posed by the two levels of war. It provides us with a way of understanding why the aggressive soldiers understood as persons, and not simply their state, may be appropriate objects of force. This result would seem to be a necessary precondition for any account of the legitimacy of using military force, be it one grounded in law enforcement, punishment, or national-defense. For without such an account we would seem to be in the unjustifiable position of killing the innocent (the state's soldiers) in order to punish or enforce the law against the guilty (the aggressive state).

Does there currently exist any body with legitimate authority to use military force to enforce the international law? Wars fought under the auspices of the United Nations (for example, interventions conducted under Chapter VII of the UN Charter) seem to fulfil the criteria. The United Nations is a trans-national organization embodying a consensual agreement between legally equal states, each of which binds itself to a regime of law and explicitly consents to the legal repercussions of breaking that law.

Yet there are difficulties in viewing the UN as a genuine authority capable of administering legitimate punishment. The five permanent members of the Security Council each have a veto right on decisions pertaining to the use of force and they therefore possess the power to exempt themselves and their clients from legal sanctions. The permanent members routinely utilize their power to shape UN decisions so as to accord with their own national interest. Because of this the United Nations is not a truly impartial authority and it is difficult to view the military expeditions it authorizes as legitimate forms of punishment or law enforcement. None the less, Chapter VII interventions and UN-authorized wars clearly do have a greater legitimacy than most wars fought by independent states or groups of states acting without UN authorization. A genuine form of justification is clearly operative here even if it is not perfectly realized. It is conceivable that one day the UN may be strengthened and reformed in such a way that it becomes an organ capable of impartially enforcing a genuine international law.

But it also seems clear that such a reformed United Nations would in many ways resemble a universal sovereign state in that it would have the power and authority to enforce the law against particular states and their citizens. In Chapter 7, I suggested that there is a prima-facie Hobbesian argument for the legitimacy of a universal state. We now seem to have reached the tentative conclusion that some organization functioning as a form of universal sovereign, enforcing a genuine rule of law against aggressive states and their soldiers may be required to justify the employment of military force against international aggressors. It is time to consider the question of a universal state in greater detail.

The idea of a universal state has been the subject of fierce attacks from numerous quarters. Amongst philosophers, the positions of Hobbes and Kant are particularly interesting and worthy of consideration. Both philosophers develop arguments which prima facie suggest a universal political community governed by a single sovereign power, yet each repudiates this conclusion; Kant in favour of a federation of free states;[33] Hobbes in favour of a plurality of sovereign states existing in an international state of nature.[34]

Why did Hobbes and Kant shrink from the idea of a universal sovereign? Moreover, if, as I have suggested, there is a valid Hobbesian argument for a universal state, why haven't we got one already? If states exist in a state of nature, as Hobbes asserts, why haven't sovereigns found themselves compelled to covenant together to form a universal commonwealth in the same way that individuals in the state of nature do?

One answer to this question, phrased in terms of Hobbes's own argument, is that unlike persons in the state of nature, sovereigns (considered as natural persons) have little to fear from the existence of an international state of nature. The sovereign's life is generally not endangered by wars with other states. The fighting occurs at the borders and he can always come to terms with the enemy before a

---

[33] Kant, *Perpetual Peace*, Second Definitive Article of Perpetual Peace, pp. 102–5.
[34] Hobbes, *Leviathan*, ch. XIII.

situation arises in which his own life is endangered. Because the sovereign's life is threatened by international war only in the most exceptional of circumstances, he does not personally experience the terrible fear which drives men to abandon their liberty and enter a commonwealth. For this reason the Hobbes-based argument for the universal state would seem to fail.

Yet, this response is too quick. For the sovereign does not exist only as a natural person; the sovereign is also, and more importantly, an artificial person. Understood in this way, the sovereign is defined by the power with which it guarantees the civil laws in the commonwealth. This power, which constitutes the existence of the sovereign state, may be endangered by international war because the incursion of foreign states can weaken or destroy its ability to enforce the law in a given area. The sovereign as an artificial person does not experience the natural fear of death, but it is subject to what we might call 'artificial fear' concerning the diminution of its power. This fear compels the state always to maintain its own security, that is, its ability to ensure its continued existence and independence as a sovereign power.

The explanation of state action appealed to here makes reference not to the psychological motivations of individual leaders or statesmen, but to the impersonal rationality of states understood as systems of power with an inherent interest in their own survival. It is this form of explanation which is explored by international relations theory in its Realist form. Thus if a state fears for its security then it may rationally surrender some of its independence by seeking an alliance with a more powerful state, preferring a partial diminution of its independence to the risk of total destruction. If the international state of nature resulted in a war of all against all in which no state could guarantee its own security, then each state would have a reason to surrender part of its sovereign autonomy to a universal authority capable of guaranteeing its continued existence.[35]

---

[35] Timo Airakson discusses this issue in a stimulating article: 'The Whiteness of the Whale: Thomas Hobbes and a Paradox of War and Fear', in Bertman, M. A. (ed.), *Hobbes: War among Nations*, Aldershot: Avebury Press, 1989. Airakson's reading of these considerations differs, however, from mine. He sees the artificial fear experienced by the sovereign as leading inexorably to war as sovereigns assume 'a proudly threatening posture against all other sovereigns' (see at 58–62). As I explain below, I think that, given the right historical conditions, the sovereign's artificial fear may lead instead towards the establishment of a universal commonwealth.

Yet this form of argument also seems to fail, for states do seem to be able to preserve their security to a tolerable degree even within the state of nature. As Hume observed, while persons require a stable law-governed association to prevent a disastrous war of all against all: 'nations can subsist without intercourse. They may even subsist, in some degree, under a general war. The observance of justice, though useful among them, is not guarded by so strong a necessity as among individuals'.[36]

Why should this be so? Why should the state of nature, intolerable for men, yet prove tolerable for sovereign states? An answer to this question may be constructed on the basis of Hobbes's explanation of why the state of nature between individual persons leads inevitably to a war of all against all. One of the assumptions to which he appeals in support of this conclusion is the approximate equality in power between persons in the state of nature: 'For as to strength of body the weakest has strength enough to kill the strongest, either by secret machination, or by confederacy with others, that are in the same danger with himself'.[37] Given this, each man has a roughly equal basis for hope of attaining goods and riches and yet he must constantly be in fear that others will kill him for the goods he has already acquired.

In contrast to this, states generally display a much greater disparity in power. The international system is most frequently dominated by one or several great powers who are able to control a network of client states and maintain a (relatively) stable balance of power with their enemies. Such states are able to ensure their own security and to make use of the unfettered liberty of the state of nature for their own enrichment. They thus have little incentive to enter into a commonwealth with other states. The lesser powers are unable to compel the great states to submit to the rule of law and so must seek their security as best they can as vassals and clients of the hegemonic powers. Thus the international state of nature never generates a period in which all states are in mutual fear for their security, which is the basis of the social contract. When a state is ascendant, it thinks only of exploiting the state of nature for its own power. When its power wanes and it would wish to seek the protection of

---

[36] Hume, *Concerning the Principles of Morals*, quoted in Luard, E., *Basic Texts in International Relations*, London: Macmillan, 1992: 48.

[37] Hobbes, *Leviathan*, ch. 13: 60.

law, it is no longer able to compel the rising states to submit themselves to it.

This argument proposes a Realist response to the argument for a universal state; the universal state is impossible because it is not in the interests of individual states as they currently exist to allow it to be realized. But, even in purely Realist terms there may be reason to doubt this argument, particularly in light of recent developments in military technology which dramatically alter the balance of security considerations. Nuclear weapons may be possessed by even very small states, such as Israel and North Korea, and provide their owners with the capacity to inflict unacceptable damage upon even great powers. The security of the great powers is already compromised by international terrorism, and guerrilla warfare restricts the ability of great powers to assert their power and influence. Both terrorism and guerrilla warfare have been the subject of an extraordinary development in range and effectiveness throughout the last century. Each enables small and relatively weak groups to inflict disproportionate harm on greatly superior forces and may be likened to the 'secret machinations' which Hobbes identifies as a source of fear amongst persons in the state of nature.

Another powerful consideration is that nuclear weapons have brought about a situation in which the costs of fighting a war are potentially so great as to result in the destruction of the states involved—indeed of all states. Thus, for the first time in history, the means of war are potentially destructive of the very end for which they are employed, namely, the security of the state. For these reasons, it is conceivable (though perhaps no more than conceivable) that a time may arise when states conclude that it is rational for them to surrender their absolute independence to a universal authority in order to preserve their security and survival. Thus even in Realist terms it may be possible to construct a Hobbesian argument for a universal state operative solely at the level of existing sovereign entities considered as participants in a system of power driven by a need for security.

I now want to suggest, however, that in an important respect this argument fundamentally misrepresents the nature of the moral case for a universal state. Kant, in his pamphlet *Perpetual Peace* distinguishes between three possible forms of legal constitution. It is, he says, a necessary classification with respect to all persons who can in any way influence each other and who are not in a state of nature:

(1) a constitution based on the *civil right* of individuals within a nation (*ius civitatis*)

(2) a constitution based on the *international right* of states in their relationships with one another (*ius gentium*).

(3) a constitution based on *cosmopolitan right*, in so far as individuals and states, coexisting in an external relationship of mutual influences, may be regarded as citizens of a universal state of mankind (*ius cosmopoliticum*).[38]

What Kant's distinction immediately enables us to see is that the above discussion of the Hobbesian argument is premised on a misconstrual of the contractarian basis of international morality. This is because it restricts itself to consideration of the rights and interests of sovereign states in respect of one another—that is, Kant's second form of constitution, the *ius gentium*. This level of analysis is inadequate because it fails to recognize that, on a contractarian conception, the fundamental normative function of the state is to further the interests and security of its citizens. When seeking to understand the basis of international morality, therefore, the relevant contractarian question is not whether the security of sovereigns (understood either as natural or as artificial persons) is best served by binding themselves to a universal system of law, but rather whether the security of the individuals who participate in these states is served by having them so bound. Put in the language of the state of nature (or the original position), the question we must ask is whether the original contractors have greater reason to place themselves within a sovereign commonwealth existing in an international state of nature, or within a non-sovereign political society which is subject to the law of a universal sovereign.[39]

Having identified this as the relevant level of enquiry for a conception of international justice, it would seem that there is a clear prima-facie case for thinking that the original contractors would choose a universal state rather than a system of states existing in international anarchy. For, though the international state of nature may not fundamentally challenge the security of states, it certainly

---

[38] Kant, *Perpetual Peace*, 98 n.

[39] This is the error made by Rawls in his analysis of international morality. He envisions the law of nations as determined by decisions made within the original position, not by persons, but by the sovereign *states* (or their representative). But this procedure fails to recognize that justice between states is not necessarily the same as justice between persons. For though the commonwealth is generated to serve the interests of its citizens, once established it possesses an interest in its own continued existence which may be in conflict with those of its citizens. Rawls, J., *A Theory of Justice*, Oxford: Clarendon Press, 1972: 377–9.

does threaten the security of citizens who must risk their lives in combat when hostilities inevitably erupt between states.

None the less it may be that there are good reasons why persons in the state of nature should prefer to institute a plurality of independent states rather than a universal state, despite the fact that, as I suggested in Chapter 7, such a regime only imperfectly removes them from the state of nature. Why might this be so? Kant claims that a universal state would quickly descend into a 'soulless despotism', and, 'after crushing the germs of goodness, will finally lapse into anarchy'.[40] If this were the case then persons might rationally prefer the risks of international war over the risk of an unstable tyranny.

Yet it is difficult to see how this argument is supposed to work. The risk of despotism is implicit in any form of political organization or sovereign power; why should it be greater in a universal state than in sovereign powers existing in a pluralist world system? It cannot simply be a matter of the greater size and power of the universal state, for we would then be in the absurd position of having to argue that the United States has a greater propensity to tyranny than Myanmar because it is many times larger and more powerful. Perhaps the thought is rather that a universal state would tend towards corruption because it possesses untrammelled power, and is not balanced by any external power capable of checking its ambitions. Yet this argument is not borne out by empirical observation; Iraq has historically been balanced by Iran and China is balanced by Russia, yet this has not prevented the development of repressive regimes in these states. Indeed, the opposite effect is often evident—the presence of an external threat provides a useful pretext for despots to assert and justify a highly repressive internal regime. Even states with a long history of liberal democracy and respect for individual rights enforce draconian measures when they are at war, or feel threatened by a foreign power. A final explanation might be that if the universal state did develop despotic tendencies it would be extremely difficult to organize an effective resistance. For the universal state would have at its disposal immense resources and there would be no foreign powers capable of providing diplomatic and financial support for rebels, or a safe refuge for dissidents.

There is clearly some truth in this observation, but there are two points that should be borne in mind. First, the international state of

---

[40] Kant, *Perpetual Peace*, 113.

nature could be brought to an end by an extremely minimal form of sovereign power. It may, for instance, consist solely in the establishment of a world monopoly of military force together with a minimal judicial mechanism for the resolution of international and internal disputes. We might call this the idea of an ultra-minimal universal state to distinguish it from a substantive conception of world government with a broader administrative mandate. Understood in this way, the idea of a universal state need not in principle be excessively frightening, though it would clearly constitute a momentous transformation of the international system as we now know it.

Secondly, if the moral desirability of an ultra-minimal universal state is in theory recognized, then we can proceed with the task of working out a substantive set of principles of political subsidiarity under which such a state might operate. These principles would seek to balance the rights and interests of the diverse interlocking communities to which I made reference at the end of the last chapter—nations, states, regions, cities, as well as the global community of mankind. Indeed, Kant's conception of cosmopolitan right can be understood as a contribution to precisely this project. It is important to realize that for Kant, the final instantiation of international *recht* is effective at each of the three possible levels of lawful constitution.[41] It establishes a just regime of law, first, between persons considered as citizens within a political community; secondly, between states in an international system; and finally between persons and states coexisting in a cosmopolitan community. It is a magisterial, inclusive conception of international right which holds the tantalizing prospect of transcending the divide between individualist and communitarian conceptions of justice.[42]

It is not suggested that the development of these principles will be a simple task. But it is a project to which Kant has already made a significant contribution. It was Kant's revolutionary proposal that the rights of states in the international system and the rights of citizens within the state are linked. For Kant, the only form of legitimate civil constitution is a 'republic', by which he means a representative government which guarantees for all citizens freedom, equality, and due process before the law, in other words what today

[41] See Brown, C., *International Relations Theory*, New York: Harvester Wheatsheaf, 1992: 36.

[42] Indeed, Kant's tripartite conception seems almost to suggest the form of a Hegelian dialectic.

we would call a liberal democracy.[43] Authors such as Fernando Tesón have argued that the claim has both an empirical and a normative component. The empirical claim is that republican states have a natural propensity for peace and the respect for international law. The normative claim is that a state only has legitimacy within the international system and therefore a claim to recognition by other states if it protects and does not violate the rights of its citizens.[44] In this way, a nascent conceptual mechanism for balancing and restraining the rights of states as against the human rights of their citizens may be developed.

The argument that I have sketched in this chapter is at best germinal and will require much elaboration and development. However, its intent has been to show that the failure of the analogical argument for national-defense need not leave us at a moral dead end with respect to the problems of aggression and communal violence. These problems do demand an effective response from moral theory. Although, as I have argued, we are unlikely to find an effective grounding for a right of national-defense, it is possible to construct a justification for military action against aggression on the basis of a conception of law enforcement. The conditions which could make such a form of justification effective are not yet realized in the world, for there is no impartial international body capable of enforcing a genuine international law. None the less, I have suggested that there are good grounds for believing that a valid contractarian argument for the justice of such a body could be constructed. If this were the case, then the project of bringing such a body into existence would identify a significant and pressing moral goal.

[43] Kant, *Perpetual Peace*, First Definitive Article of Perpetual Peace, 99 ff.

[44] Tesón, F., 'The Kantian Theory of International Law', *Columbia Law Review*, 92 (1996), 53–102, at 70–4; id., *A Philosophy of International Law*, Boulder, Colo.: Westview Press, 1997, ch. 1. See also Luban, D., 'Just War and Human Rights', *Philosophy and Public Affairs*, 9 (1980), 160–81.

9

Conclusion: Morality and Realism

Any moral philosophy must take cognizance of the fact that it is promulgated in a political world, and of the possibilities and limitations that this implies. To its great credit, the Just War Theory has always recognized this fact. It is an attempt—an heroic attempt—to combine moral principles with a pragmatic sense of political realism; to forge a middle path between an introverted moral withdrawal from the political realm, and a Realist abandonment of all moral restraint. It insists, as Grotius says, that: 'Men may not believe either that nothing is allowed, or that everything is allowed'.[1]

It is largely due to this daring conception that the Just War Theory owes its enduring power. It is indeed one of the few basic fixtures of medieval philosophy to remain substantially unchallenged in the modern world. It has seemed to many theorists and practitioners that the system of concepts developed by the Just War Theory provides the best, and perhaps the only, hope for the effective moral regulation of war. Yet I want to suggest in this final chapter that the Just War Theory has largely betrayed this promise. It has failed to provide a robust set of principles for effective operation in the political realm. Yet the collapse of the national-defense paradigm leaves us with a difficult question. If there is no valid justification for wars of national-defense, what personal moral response should we make in the face of international aggression?

The moral conception of self-defense depends, as I argued in Part I, on a very intimate set of normative relationships between the parties involved, and in particular on a moral contrast between the culpability of the aggressor and innocence of the defender. Within international relations, however, this contrast between aggressor and defender becomes subverted in a number of crucial ways. The first way in which this happens stems from the historicity of international conflicts. Disputed territories and rights almost always come with a history which in many cases casts doubt on the picture of an innocent

---

[1] *Prolegomena*, 29. Quoted in Röling, B. V. A., '*Jus Ad Bellum* and the Grotian Heritage', in *International Law and the Grotian Heritage*, The Hague: T. M. C. Asser Instituut, 1985: 115.

victim confronted by a wrongful aggressor. Many settled international borders are the result of previous acts of aggression and continued occupation. The Just War Theory has an answer to this problem. 'The land follows the people', says Walzer, quoting an argument from Sidgwick's, *The Elements of Politics*.[2] If after a period of time, the majority of people in an unlawfully seized territory come to accept the new rulers then their title to the land is made good. But clearly there is something troubling about this idea. Marxist and third world states have long argued that colonial occupation should be viewed as a form of 'ongoing aggression' which justifies defensive action at whatever time and by whomever is able to resist it. What seems true in this claim, once the rhetoric has been stripped away, is that historical understanding of a dispute often subverts the contrast between victimhood and aggression, innocence and guilt which I have argued underlies the basic argument of defensive rights. Britain's war for the Falklands/Malvinas was undeniably a defensive one, but in a deeper sense we cannot but be troubled by the question of whether Britain had a right to be there in the first place.

The second way in which the contrast between victim and aggressor is subverted concerns the background conditions under which international disputes arise. In a memorable passage, Hobbes describes the situation with great acumen:

> ... in all times Kings and Persons of Soveraigne authority, because of their Independency, are in continual jealousies and in the state and posture of Gladiators; having their weapons pointing and their eyes fixed on one another; that is, their Forts, Garrisons, and Guns upon the Frontiers of their Kingdoms; and continual Spies upon their neighbours, which is a posture of war.[3]

The argument for self-defense depends on a certain settled condition of peace against which the unlawfulness of an act of aggression is clearly displayed. But when the background conditions consist in an environment of mutual mistrust and preparedness for conflict, the distinction between aggressor and victim, and between offense and defense can begin to break down irreparably.

This is particularly evident when the background relationship between states consists in a 'balance of power' or a nuclear 'balance

---

[2] Walzer, M., *Just and Unjust Wars*, New York: Basic Books, 1977: 55–6.
[3] Hobbes, T., *Leviathan*, Tuck, R. (ed.), Cambridge: Cambridge University Press, 1991, ch. 13, para. 12.

of terror' between long-standing rivals. For states are most fundamentally concerned with their own security which derives not from absolute military capability, but from comparative strength as measured against potential threats. But the balance of power, and with it a state's real interest in its own security, can be affected by defensive as well as offensive measures. In such an environment, acts of aggression shade plausibly into pre-emptive defense, while apparently defensive acts take on provocative, menacing, and offensive qualities. For example, if one asks whether Khrushchev's decision to deploy missiles on Cuba was an aggressive or defensive act, whether Ronald Regan's proposal to build a missile defense system in the 1980s was offensive or defensive, or whether Athens's decision to assist Corcyra against the Corinthians in the Peloponnesian War[4] constituted aggression or defense, the answers are by no means clear. The reason is that in each of these examples (though most clearly in the last two) a seemingly defensive action by one state has the effect of fundamentally altering a pre-existing balance of power and thereby significantly threatening the security of another in a way that is perceived, with justification, as aggressive.

Thus there is a political and strategic ambiguity between defensive and offensive acts as they occur in the real world.[5] This ambiguity has proved a tremendous source of difficulty for international law. For the entire moral weight of the *jus ad bellum* rests on the determination of a single decisive moment of unlawful aggression. Yet, against the backdrop of simmering antagonism, this is often more weight than such a determination can plausibly bear. As the distinguished lawyer J. Combacau says:

...unless, in an escalating series of acts going from the insignificant local action of a nervous NCO to a full-scale army offensive, we can pick out the one which oversteps the bounds of legality, it will almost always be possible for one State to see in the previous conduct of the other party an antecedent which justifies its own.[6]

---

[4] See Thucydides, *History of the Peloponesian War*, Warner, R. (trans.), Harmondsworth: Penguin Books, 1954, bk. I.

[5] This ambiguity is identified clearly in strategic discussions of war. See Clausewitz C., *On War*, Howard, M., and Paret, P. (eds.), Princeton: Princeton University Press, 1976, bk. 6 sect. 1.

[6] Combacau, J., 'The Exception of Self-Defence in U.N. Practice', in Cassese, A. (ed.), *The Current Legal Regulation of the Use of Force*, Dordrecht: Martinus Nijhoff, 1986: 9–38, at 21.

The task of determining such a point in a substantive and normatively significant way is, he suggests, often a futile one. This has predictably led to two related but contradictory tendencies in international law. The first is that the notions of aggression and defense have grown to occupy increasing importance in law. The second is that the law has become increasingly muddied and indeterminate as states have struggled to assert an interpretation of the law that serves their own interests. This is evident in the continuing uncertainty in numerous areas of international law—most dramatically over the legality of anticipatory defense, but also concerning the legality of military action against states whose territory is used as a base for rebel operations, the legal status of reprisals, and in the fact that fifty years after the drafting of the United Nations Charter there still exists no adequate and universally accepted legal definition of international aggression.

Now these doubts and uncertainties about the concepts of international aggression and defence certainly do not negate their moral intelligibility. There clearly are such things as wholly aggressive wars, ones in which the determination of victim and aggressor can clearly and meaningfully be made. Such a description is often accurate of colonial and imperial wars, and more generally of wars fought between great powers and their smaller neighbours. What is clear, however, is that such conflicts represent an ideal type of interstate relations of a rather uncommon kind. By attempting to make the aggressor/victim model derived from these cases apply to all international conflicts, the Just War Theory gravely distorts our thinking on international ethics.

This can be seen most clearly by considering a very different anatomy of international conflict which centres on the idea of brinkmanship. The phenomenon of brinkmanship is most often observed in the relations between great powers, or between states of roughly equal military capability existing in an unstable balance of power. The characteristic pattern of such relations is that, when a dispute arises, each side escalates a series of threatening actions and responses, gambling that the other side will back down before the brink of conflict is reached (which all parties agree would be the worst outcome for all concerned). Often, of course, adversaries who engage in this form of strategy are unable to control the process and, through arrogance, miscalculation, or stupidity, tumble into catastrophic conflicts. The *locus classicus* of the phenomenon of brinkmanship in the twentieth century is the Cuban missile crisis, but the above is probably also a not unreasonable analysis of the commencement of the First World War.

The notion of brinkmanship provides us with a radically different picture of international relations from that of the national-defense paradigm. It is a view without culpable aggressors and innocent victims, but one in which states gamble with the lives of their own citizens and those of other states for finite political gains. The wars that result from such interactions cannot be described as just on one side and unjust on the other, but are the responsibility of each of the parties which hazard to play at this dangerous game.

Brinkmanship is, of course, an ideal type of interstate relations, just as pure aggression is. The two forms of interaction could be placed on the extremes of a continuum and most real life conflicts would fall in the messy spaces in-between. The point is that international law and the just war tradition generally, have become transfixed by the notions of aggression and national-defense and wrongly attempt to treat all interstate conflict within the bounds of this model. Thus international law is committed to the view that, in any conflict, it is in principle possible to determine which side has culpably overstepped the bounds of lawful behaviour, and hence which side possesses a right of lawful response.[7]

There are certainly reasons for this preoccupation. International aggression is an appalling thing and it is natural that we should be concerned to curtail it. What is more, the national-defense model has an appealing moral simplicity and elegance which the quagmire of brinkmanship and *realpolitik* manifestly lacks. But the tendency to view all conflict through the lens of aggression and defense is at once morally misleading and dangerous. It is misleading because, to the extent that conflicts are infected by the politics of brinkmanship, the application of the categories of aggression and defense is often nothing more than an exercise in moral bad faith.

It is dangerous for several interrelated reasons. First, it may actually encourage participation in the dangerous game of brinkmanship. The national-defense paradigm encourages states to push at the boundary of lawful action, employing all the measures of intimidation and coercion open to them short of the line of legality (a line which I have already argued is ambiguously defined and poorly

---

[7] See above, p. 107.

understood). This is because forcing one's opponent to overstep that boundary brings with it the substantial benefit of having one's military action legally endorsed as *justum bellum*. Competition to grasp this title, and the legal benefits it brings, explains why, in the majority of conflicts in the last hundred years, the right of national-defense has been claimed by both belligerents. What is more, the politics of brinkmanship has learned to appropriate the moral vocabulary of the national-defense paradigm, and indeed this vocabulary has become a central source of the ongoing legitimacy of brinkmanship. For forty-four years the grubby politicking of the cold war was fuelled and legitimated by the rhetoric of national-defense while the world waited nervously under the shadow of a potential nuclear cataclysm.

The second way in which the preoccupation with national-defense is dangerous, is that it entirely fails to address the problems of civil war and internal oppression. Because it concentrates exclusively on sovereignty and the rights of states, the national-defense paradigm fails to provide, and indeed obstructs, legal regulation of the recourse to internal military conflict. The failure of Just War Theory in this respect is perhaps most evident in Walzer's argument that civil war must be recognized as a form of legitimate collective self-determination and protected from outside intervention on this basis.[8] In other words, while international aggression is seen as the ultimate crime against peace, justifying immediate defensive and punitive military action, initiating an internal or 'civil' conflict is enshrined as a basic right of every political community. That this argument could be made at a time when the majority, and certainly the most protracted and consistently brutal, of the world's conflicts are civil wars is nothing short of astonishing.

But Walzer's argument is true to the intellectual commitments of the modern Just War Theory. Though he claims that his interest is in protecting the rights of persons through protection of the integrity of the state, Walzer's arguments belie a thoroughgoing subordination of the rights and interests of individuals to the rights and interests of states. In this he is following a dominant strand of Liberal theory which has, at least since the time of Mill, attributed rights of equality and autonomy in the international sphere, first

---

[8] See Walzer, *Just and Unjust Wars*, ch. 6; id., 'The Moral Standing of States: A Response to Four Critiques', *Philosophy and Public Affairs* (1980), 209–29.

and foremost to sovereign states rather than to individual persons. Thus in *A Theory of Justice* Rawls argues that the principles of international justice are determined by a contract made from behind the veil of ignorance, not, as might be expected by individual persons, but by the representatives of the different states.[9] The fundamental assumption driving this argument is that international justice is justice among states, not justice among persons. As I have suggested at various points, this position leads to unacceptable results when we are faced with states which terrorize and oppress their own people. If states are viewed as unitary moral agents, analogous to individual persons, then internal genocide (the killing by a state of its own population) is most naturally treated as the international equivalent of suicide.[10] On familiar assumptions concerning the liberty of agents, suicide has been a form of activity which liberal law and morality has been reluctant to regulate. It is sobering to contemplate this thought in light of the international community's failure to prevent the genocide which occurred in Rwanda in 1994.[11]

The traditional just war categories of aggression and defense are failing us. They are mute or even obstructive over the problems of civil war and domestic oppression. In the international arena the distinction between aggressor and defender is often impossible to determine because of the cynical way in which states manipulate these categories. If the distinction can be made, it may have little or no moral significance in a particular case because the war is fundamentally one of brinkmanship.

It is tempting to think that the issues raised here are simply those of moral hypocrisy; the old problem that, as Gentili says: 'Each man declares his own war a holy one. Each one insists that his enemies are godless men. Each names his own cause righteous. Every one has upon his lips the words "sacred" and "pious".'[12] To read the situation in this way simply invites more zealous and careful application of the moral concepts involved. But what I have been suggesting in

---

[9] Rawls, J., *A Theory of Justice*, Oxford: Clarendon Press, 1972: 377–9.

[10] I am indebted to Gerry Simpson of the ANU law faculty for this observation.

[11] Walzer does in fact allow an exception to the norm of non-intervention to prevent massacre and human rights abuses which 'shock the conscience of mankind' (Walzer, *Just and Unjust Wars*, 107), but this is an ad hoc amendment which sits uncomfortably with his deeper theoretical commitments.

[12] Gentili, A., *De Jure Belli Libri Tres*, New York: Classics of International Law, 1964: I, ix.

the course of this book is the more fundamental critique that our moral concepts are terminally ill-fitted to their subject matter. Moralists sometimes talk about the 'homage vice pays to virtue' as if this were a vindication of the concepts they employ. In fact, when moral concepts are systematically prone to abuse, it is a symptom of their fatigue and failure. What it shows is that morality has failed to take proper cognizance of politics and its astonishing capacity to subvert, abuse, and manipulate moral categories.[13]

Thus we are led back, this time by a Realist route, to the central negative conclusion of this book, which is that the conception of a moral right of national-defense cannot, in the final analysis, be substantiated. This negative conclusion contrasts sharply with the central positive result which has been the development of a justificatory account of the right of personal self-defense. Though this project was beset by its own distinctive difficulties and problems, our central conclusion was that an account of self-defense as a legitimate right could be formulated. Our account located self-defense within a broader conception of general defensive rights which in turn arose naturally out of basic conceptions of interpersonal moral obligation. The account connected with and was able to explain many moral intuitions concerning proportionality, necessity, the rights of innocents, and the reciprocity of rights against aggression.

The analogical argument from self-defense to national-defense seeks to build on this robust moral conception. The moral principle that it invokes is beguilingly simple and intuitively appealing: a valid conception of international justice can be generated by treating states as unitary moral agents and ascribing to them (with appropriate modifications) a system of rights and responsibilities generated in the context of interpersonal relations. But the fundamental problem with this procedure is that states may not only be considered as unitary moral agents, but must also be considered as collections of individual persons each possessing their own rights and interests. Thus a dual level is set up in the normative phenomenon of war,

---

[13] It is for this reason that Kant calls Grotius, Pufendorf, and Vattel 'sorry comforters', for their texts are duly cited in justification of aggression, yet 'there is no instance of a state ever having been moved to desist from its purpose by arguments supported by the testimonies of such notable men'. This probably overstates the case, but it is easy to sympathize with the sentiment (Kant, I., *Perpetual Peace: A Philosophical Sketch*, in Reiss, H. (ed), *Kant's Political Philosophy*, Cambridge: Cambridge University Press, 1970: 103).

which frustrates the simple conception of the analogical argument. Given this, the analogical argument must resolve into one of two strategies, either the right of national-defense must be explained as a right constructed out of the defensive rights of the individual citizens (a strategy of normative reduction), or national-defense must be seen as a state right analogous to personal defence. But as I have attempted to show, both the strategies of reduction and analogy fail. The model of defensive rights, derived in Part I, which generates a valid justification for interpersonal self-defense, fails to do so for national-defense.

But what are we to make of these conclusions? The right of national-defense is the most salient feature of our intuitive moral framework of war. What sense can we make of its repudiation as a legitimate moral category? My view on these matters is similar to that of the renowned English student of international relations, Martin Wight, of whom it was said: 'His outlook on the world was the combination of a starkly realistic perception of the nature of international relations and a sense of personal moral revulsion from it'.[14] In other words there is a deeply moral response to international conflict which does not seek to contradict the Realist perception that the current mechanisms of international politics are irredeemably devoid of morality, but rather grows out of it. The necessity of a moral critique of international relations derives from an appreciation of the inadequacy, ineffectiveness, poverty, and hypocrisy of the standard conceptions of international morality.

From such a position it would seem that there are two possible ways to proceed. The first is a personal retreat from politics, the most characteristic form of which is a pacifism of conscience (Wight himself was a Christian pacifist). The second is the route which I have recommended in the last chapter. It is to consider a moral transformation in the system of political relations itself. Thus the negative result of displaying the inadequacy of our current moral concepts leads to an urgent positive programme of moral reform. This programme is partly conceptual; it requires the rethinking of our moral categories of warfare, but it is also, and importantly, political.

---

[14] Bull, H., Introduction to Wight, M., *Systems of States*, Leicester: Leicester University Press, 1977: 5.

This may sound like a messianic conclusion, but as Kant has shown it can in fact lead to a very practical and pragmatic programme for action. In *Perpetual Peace* Kant distinguishes between the 'Definitive Articles of Perpetual Peace' which are the measures required for the final institution of an enduring peace, and the 'Preliminary Articles' which are measures which can and ought to be taken in the interim.[15] These measures are designed to reduce the likelihood of war in the current imperfect international system, and prepare the way for the final achievement of law-governed international relations. Thus, although Kant calls for a revolution in the international system, he does not expect it to occur quickly or to be achieved all at once. It will, he says, be a slow, difficult, arduous process, with many set-backs and uncertainties. Kant's approach is essentially gradualist in character and it suggests a two-tier moral strategy. The first seeks to mitigate and moderate the evils of war in the world as it currently is; the second represents the attempt to develop a measured realistic programme for the achievement of a just system of international relations within which a genuine international rule of law can be realised. The need to develop such a programme is the ultimate practical recommendation of my argument.

Yet this still seems to leave a difficult question unanswered. For, suppose one accepts that there is no way to understand the fighting of defensive wars as morally justified, and that the only justifiable response to aggression would be in the context of a genuine framework of international law presided over by a truly impartial sovereign power. Nevertheless, no such framework now exists, and the pressing question is: what are we to do in the meantime?

Aggression faces us with an immediate personal challenge; we must either fight or submit, and many will find the conclusion that one may not fight against an international aggressor morally unacceptable. This conviction may stem from a consequentialist concern for the costs of not resisting aggression, which may be appallingly high especially if the aggressive regime is as repugnant as Nazi Germany or Stalinist Russia. It may arise from the feeling that to fail to resist aggression is to somehow acquiesce morally to it in an unacceptable way. In either case, one may come to the conclusion that in the absence of a genuine framework of law, one simply must fight, that there is 'no choice'.

[15] Kant, *Perpetual Peace*.

I must acknowledge that I feel the force of these reservations. The need to find an effective moral response to the immediate problem of aggression poses a difficult problem for my position. For if one accepts the argument of this book, then aggression, occurring in the world as it currently is, could only face us with a terrible dilemma. My argument shows that fighting a war of national-defense is deeply problematic, while at the same time leaving open the possibility that failing to resist aggression may have unacceptable moral costs.

None the less, we must recognize that such a dilemma is not peculiar to my negative account of the ethics of war. It is a very characteristic human problem which arises in many spheres of moral life. Indeed, establishing that the problem of aggression faces us with such a dilemma is itself a useful and important result. For, at the very least, it serves to remind us to maintain a certain moral modesty in our action. Even for those who are impressed by the thought that there are some forms of aggression which we 'must' fight, my arguments remind us that, if we do so, our action cannot be conceived in terms of right and justice. For, military action, even in national-defense, remains morally problematic in a profound and troubling way.

On a purely practical level, detailed analysis of the concepts of self-defense and national-defense is useful because it can help us to identify and prevent the abuse of these concepts by statesmen and politicians. Moreover, by locating the conditions which could potentially justify military action, we can identify those forms of military action which are, if not perfectly justified, then closer to being just than others.

But the basic lesson we should take from the present argument is that our traditional conceptions of international law and international ethics need to be fundamentally rethought. There is a great scope for real and substantial progress to be made in this area. We need a framework of international ethics which gives greater recognition and protection to the rights of individuals as against states, which can address the problems of civil war and internal oppression, and which is able to more effectively restrain international aggression. By exposing the inadequacy of the traditional paradigm of national-defense, I hope to have gone some small way towards advancing this project.

Bibliography

Airakson, T., 'The Whiteness of the Whale: Thomas Hobbes and a Paradox of War and Fear', in Bertman, M. A. (ed.), *Hobbes: War among Nations*, Aldershot: Avebury Press, 1989.

Alexandrov, S., *Self-Defence against the Use of Force in International Law*, The Hague: Kluwer Law International, 1996.

Anscombe, G. E. M., 'War and Murder', in Rachels, J. (ed), *Moral Problems*, New York: Harper Collins, 1979.

—— *The Collected Philosophical Papers of G. E. M. Anscombe*, vol. iii, 'Mr Truman's Degree', in *Ethics, Religion and Politics*, Oxford: Basil Blackwell, 1981.

Aquinas, St Thomas, *Summa Theologica*, trans. fathers of the English Dominican Province, vol. ii, London: Burns and Oates, 1947.

Aristotle, *Politics*, trans. J. A. Sinclair, Harmondsworth: Penguin, 1962.

—— *Nicomachean Ethics*, trans. Ross, W. D. in *The Complete Works of Aristotle*, vol. ii, Barnes, J. (ed.), Princeton: Princeton University Press, 1984.

Augustine, *De Libero Arbitrio [On Free Will]*, trans. Russel, R. P., in *Saint Augustine*, Fathers of the Church, vol. lix, Washington DC: Catholic University Press, 1968.

—— *Contra Faustus Manichaeum* [Against Faustus the Manichaeum], trans. Stothart, R., in Schaff P. (ed), *Nicene and Post-Nicene Fathers*, 1st series, vol. iv, Grand Rapids, Mich.: Eerdmans, 1974.

—— *De Civitate Dei* [The City of God], trans. Dods, M., in Schaff, P. (ed), *Nicene and Post-Nicene Fathers*, 1st series, vol. ii, Grand Rapids, Mich.: Eerdmans, 1974.

Austin, J. L., 'A Plea For Excuses', *Proceedings of the Aristotelian Society*, 57 (1956), 1–30.

Baradat, L., *Political Ideologies*, New Jersey: Prentice Hall, 1994.

Barnes, J., 'The Just War', in Kretzmann, N., Kenny, A. and Pinborg, J. (eds.), *Cambridge History of Later Medieval Philosophy*, Cambridge: Cambridge University Press, 1988.

Black, E., 'Hegel on War', *Monist*, 57 (1973), 570–83.

Blainey, G., *The Causes of War*, London: Macmillan Press, 1988.

Bowett, D. W., *Self-Defence in International Law*, Manchester: Manchester University Press, 1958.

—— 'The Use of Force for the Protection of Nationals Abroad', in Cassese, A. (ed.), *The Current Legal Regulation of the Use of Force*, Dordrecht: Martinus Nijhoff, 1986.

Brogan, P., *World Conflicts*, London: Bloomsbury, 1989.

Brown, B. S., 'Humanitarian Intervention at the Crossroads', *William and Mary Law Review*, 41 (2000), 1683–741.

Brown, C., *International Relations Theory, New Normative Approaches*, New York: Harvester Wheatsheaf, 1992.

Brownlie, I., *International Law and the Use of Force by States*, Oxford: Clarendon Press, 1963.

—— *Principles of Public International Law*, Oxford: Clarendon Press, 1966.

—— 'The U.N. Charter and the Use of Force, 1945–1985', in Cassese, A. (ed.), *The Current Legal Regulation of the Use of Force*, Dordrecht: Martinus Nijhoff, 1986.

Bull, H., 'Grotian Conceptions of International Society', in Butterfield, H., and Wight, M. (eds.), *Diplomatic Investigations*, London: Allen and Unwin, 1966.

—— 'Society and Anarchy in International Relations', in Butterfield, H., and Wight, M. (eds.), *Diplomatic Investigations*, London: Allen and Unwin, 1966.

—— *The Anarchical Society*, New York: Columbia University Press, 1977.

Cassese, A., 'Return to Westphalia? Considerations on the Gradual Erosion of the Charter System', in Cassese, A. (ed.), *The Current Legal Regulation of the Use of Force*, Dordrecht: Martinus Nijhoff, 1986.

—— *Violence and Law in the Modern Age*, Cambridge: Polity Press, 1986.

—— '*Ex iniuria ius oritur*: Are we Moving towards International Legitimation of Forcible Humanitarian Countermeasures in the World Community?' *European Journal of International Law*, 10/1 (1999), 22–30.

—— 'A Follow-Up: Forcible Humanitarian Countermeasures and *Opinio Necessitates*', *European Journal of International Law*, 10/4 (1999), 791–9.

Caws, P., *The Causes of Conflict, Essays on Peace, War and Thomas Hobbes*, Boston: Beacon Press, 1989.

Ceadel, M., *Thinking about Peace and War*, Oxford: Oxford University Press, 1987.

Christopher, R. L., 'Unknowing Justification and the Logical Necessity of the Dadson Principle in Self-Defence', *Oxford Journal of Legal Studies*, 15 (1995), 229–51.

Clark, I., *Waging War: A Philosophical Introduction*, Oxford: Clarendon Press, 1990.

Clausewitz, C., *On War*, Howard, M., and Paret, P. (eds.), Princeton: Princeton University Press, 1976.

Combacau, J., 'The Exception of Self-Defence in U.N. Practice', in Cassese, A. (ed.), *The Current Legal Regulation of the Use of Force*, Dordrecht: Martinus Nijhoff, 1986.

Coussens, E. M., 'Self-Defence as a Justification for the Use of Force between States 1945–1989', D.Phil. thesis, University of Oxford, 1995.

D'Arcy, E., *Human Acts*, Oxford: Clarendon Press, 1963.

Davis, N., 'Abortion and Self-Defense', *Philosophy and Public Affairs*, 13 (1984), 175–207.

Davison, G., and Neale, J., *Abnormal Psychology*, New York: John Wiley and Sons, 1974.

D'Entrèves, A. P., *The Notion of the State, an Introduction to Political Theory*, Oxford: Clarendon Press, 1967.

De Roose, F., 'Self-Defence and National Defence', *Journal of Applied Philosophy*, 7/2 (1990), 159–68.

Dickinson, E. D., 'The Analogy between Natural Persons and International Persons in the Law of Nations', *Yale Law Journal*, 26 (1917), 564–91.

Dinstein, Y., *War, Aggression and Self-Defence*, Cambridge: Grotius Publications, 1988.

Doppelt, G., 'Walzer's Theory of Morality in International Relations', *Philosophy and Public Affairs*, 8 (1978), 3–26.

—— 'Statism without Foundations', *Philosophy and Public Affairs* (1980), 398–403.

Draper, G. I. A. D., 'Grotius' Place in the Development of Legal Ideas about War', in Bull, H., Kingsbury, B., and Roberts, A. (eds.), *Hugo Grotius and International Relations*, Oxford: Clarendon Press, 1992.

Dworkin, R., *Taking Rights Seriously*, Bristol: Duckworth, 1977.

—— 'Rights as Trumps', in Waldron, J. (ed.), *Theories of Rights*, Oxford: Oxford University Press, 1984.

Eddy, W. H. C., *Understanding Marxism*, Oxford: Basil Blackwell, 1979.

Ewin, R. E., 'What is Wrong with Killing People?' *The Philosophical Quarterly*, 22 (1972), 126–39.

Feinberg, J., *Rights, Justice, and the Bounds of Liberty*, Princeton: Princeton University Press, 1980.

Finnis, J., *Natural Law and Natural Rights*, Oxford: Clarendon Press, 1980.

—— *Fundamentals of Ethics*, Oxford: Oxford University Press, 1983.

—— Boyle, J. M., and Grisez, G., *Nuclear Deterrence, Morality, and Realism*, Oxford: Clarendon Press, 1987.

Fletcher, G., 'Proportionality and the Psychotic Aggressor: A Vignette in Comparative Criminal Theory', *Israel Law Review*, 8 (1973), 367–90.

—— *Rethinking Criminal Law*, Boston: Little Brown, 1978.

—— 'The Right to Life', *Monist*, 63 (1980), 135–55.

—— *A Crime of Self-Defense*, New York: The Free Press, 1988.

—— *Basic Concepts of Criminal Law*, Oxford: Oxford University Press, 1998.

Foot, P., 'The Problem of Abortion and the Doctrine of the Double Effect', repr. in *Virtues and Vices and other Essays in Moral Philosophy*, Oxford: Basil Blackwell, 1978.

Franck, T., 'Clan and Superclan: Loyalty, Identity and Community in Law and Practice', *American Journal of International Law*, 90 (1996), 359–83.

Gallie, W. B., *Philosophers of Peace and War*, Cambridge: Cambridge University Press, 1977.

—— *Understanding War*, London: Routledge, 1991.

Gardam, J. G., 'Proportionality and Force in International Law', *American Journal of International Law*, 87 (1993), 391–413.

Gentili, A., *De Jure Belli Libri Tres* [The Three Books on the Law of War], trans. Rolfe, J. C., New York: Classics of International Law, 1964.

Gewirth, A., *Reason and Morality*, Chicago: Chicago University Press, 1978.

—— 'Are There Any Absolute Rights?' *Philosophical Quarterly*, 31 (1981), 1–16; repr. in Waldron, J. (ed.), *Theories of Rights*, Oxford: Oxford University Press, 1984.

Glover, J., *Responsibility*, London: Routledge and Kegan Paul, 1970.

—— *Causing Death and Saving Lives*, New York: Penguin Books, 1977.

Goldman, A. H., 'The Moral Significance of National Boundaries', *Midwest Studies in Philosophy Volume VII*, French, A., Uehling, T. E., and Wettstein, H. K. (eds.), Minneapolis: University of Minnesota Press, 1982.

Gorr, M. 'Private Defence', *Law and Philosophy*, 9 (1990), 241–68.

Gough, J. W., *The Social Contract*, Oxford: Oxford University Press, 1967.

Grotius, H., *De Jure Belli Ac Pacis* [The Law of War and Peace], trans. Kelsey, F., New York: Classics of International Law, 1964.

Guicherd, C., 'International Law and the War in Kosovo', *Survival*, 41/2 (1999), 19–34.

Hanser, M., 'Why are Killing and Letting Die Wrong?' *Philosophy and Public Affairs*, 24 (1995), 175–201.

Hart, H. L. A., *Punishment and Responsibility*, Oxford: Oxford University Press, 1968.

—— *Essays on Bentham*, Oxford: Oxford University Press, 1982.

—— 'Are There Any Natural Rights?' in Waldron, J. (ed.), *Theories of Rights*, Oxford: Oxford University Press, 1984.

Hauerwas, S., *Should War be Eliminated?* Milwaukee: Marquette University Press, 1984.

Hinsley, F. H., *Sovereignty*, Cambridge: Cambridge University Press, 1986.

Hobbes, T., *Leviathan*, Tuck, R. (ed.), Cambridge: Cambridge University Press, 1991.

Hobsbawm, E., *The Age of Extremes, the Short Twentieth Century 1914–1991*, London: Michael Joseph, 1994.

Hohfeld, W. N., *Fundamental Legal Conceptions as Applied in Judicial Reasoning*, Cook, W. W. (ed.), New Haven: Yale University Press, 1919.

Honderich, T., *Punishment, the Supposed Justifications*, Cambridge: Polity Press, 1989 (1st pub., Hutchinson, 1969).

Horowitz, I. L., *War and Peace in Contemporary Social and Philosophical Theory*, London: Souvenir Press, 1973.

Human Rights Watch, *Human Rights Watch World Report*, New York, 2001.

James, W., 'The Moral Equivalent of War', in Wasserstrom, R. A. (ed.), *War and Morality*, Belmont, Calif.: Wadsworth, 1970.

Jenkins, I., 'The Conditions of Peace', *The Monist*, 57 (1973), 507–26.

Johnson, J. T., 'Toward a Reconstruction of The *Jus Ad Belum*', *The Monist*, 57 (1973), 461–88.

Kadish, S. H., 'Respect for Life and Regard for Rights in the Criminal Law', *California Law Review*, 64/4 (1976), 871–901.

Kant, I., *Groundwork of the Metaphysics of Morals*, trans. Paton, H. J., London: Routledge, 1948.

—— *Perpetual Peace: A Philosophical Sketch*, in Reiss, H. (ed.), *Kant's Political Philosophy*, Cambridge: Cambridge University Press, 1970.

Kenny, A., *The Logic of Deterrence*, London: Firethorn, 1985.

Lackey, D., *The Ethics of War and Peace*, Englewood Cliffs, NJ: Prentice Hall, 1989.

Langen, S. J., 'The Elements of St. Augustine's Just War Theory', in Babcock, W. S. (ed.), *The Ethics of St Augustine*, Atlanta: Scholars Press, 1991.

Lauterpacht, H., *International Law and Human Rights*, London: Stevens, 1950.

Levine, S., 'The Moral Permissibility of Killing a "Material Aggressor" in Self-Defence', *Philosophical Studies*, 45 (1984), 69–78.

Locke, J., *Two Treatises of Government*, Cambridge: Cambridge University Press, 1960.

Luard, E., *Basic Texts in International Relations*, London: Macmillan, 1992.

Luban, D., 'Just War and Human Rights', *Philosophy and Public Affairs*, 9 (1980), 160–81.

—— 'The Romance of the Nation State', *Philosophy and Public Affairs*, 9 (1980), 392–403.

Lucas, J. L., *The Principles of Politics*, Oxford: Oxford University Press, 1966.

—— *Responsibility*, Oxford: Oxford University Press, 1991.

Machiavelli, N., *The Art of War*, New York: Da Capo, 1965.

Mill, J. S., 'A Few Words on Non-Intervention', in *Dissertations and Discussions Vol. III*, London: Longman Green Reader and Dyer, 1875.

—— *Utilitarianism*, London: Dent, 1972.

Montague, P., 'Self-Defense and Choosing between Lives', *Philosophical Studies*, 40 (1981), 207–19.

—— 'The Morality of Self-Defense: A Reply to Wasserman', *Philosophy and Public Affairs*, 18 (1989), 81–97.

Montesquieu, *The Spirit of the Laws*, trans. Nugent T., Berkeley: University of California Press, 1977.

Mullerson, R., 'Self-Defense in the Contemporary World', in Damrosch, L. and Scheffer, D. (eds.), *Law and Force in the New International Order*, Boulder, Colo.: Westview Press, 1991.

Murphy, J., 'The Killing of the Innocent', *Monist*, 57 (1973), 527–50.

Nagel, T., 'War and Massacre', *Mortal Questions*, Cambridge: Cambridge University Press, 1979.

Noble, C., 'Realism, Morality, and Just War', *Monist* (1994), 595–606.

Norman, R., 'The Case for Pacifism', *Journal of Applied Philosophy*, 5/2 (1988).

—— *Ethics, Killing and War*, Cambridge: Cambridge University Press, 1995.

Nozick, R., *Anarchy, State, and Utopia*, Oxford: Blackwell, 1974.

Nussbaum, M., *The Fragility of Goodness*, Cambridge: Cambridge University Press, 1986.

Oppenheim, L. F. L., *International Law*, 8th edn., vol. i, ed. H. Lauterpacht, London: Longmans, Green and Co., 1955.

Otsuka, M., 'Killing the Innocent in Self-Defense', *Philosophy and Public Affairs*, 23 (1994), 74–94.

Paskins, B., and Dockrill, M., *The Ethics of War*, London: Duckworth, 1979.

Plato, *The Apology of Socrates*, in *Plato: The Collected Dialogues*, Princeton: Princeton University Press, 1963.

—— *The Republic*, in *Plato: The Collected Dialogues*, Princeton: Princeton University Press, 1963.

Rachels, J., *The End of Life*, Oxford: Oxford University Press, 1986.

Rawls, J., *A Theory of Justice*, Oxford: Clarendon Press, 1972.

Raz, J., 'On the Nature of Rights', *Mind*, 93 (1984), 194–214.

—— 'Right-Based Moralities', in Waldron, J. (ed.), *Theories of Rights*, Oxford: Oxford University Press, 1984.

Roberts, A., 'Intervention and Human Rights', *International Affairs*, 69/I (1993), 429–49.

—— 'NATO's "Humanitarian War" over Kosovo', *Survival*, 41/3 (1999), 102–23.

Robinson, P., 'A Theory of Justification: Societal Harm as a Prerequisite for Criminal Liability', *UCLA Law Review*, 23/1 (1975), 266–92.

Röling, B. V. A., 'The Ban on The Use of Force and The U.N. Charter', in Cassese, A. (ed.), *The Current Legal Regulation of the Use of Force*, Dordrecht: Martinus Nijhoff, 1986.

Russell, B., *The Basic Writings of Bertrand Russell*, London: Allen and Unwin, 1961.

Ryan, C., 'Self-Defense, Pacifism, and the Possibility of Killing', *Ethics*, 93 (1983), 508–24.

Sabine, G. H., *A History of Political Theory*, Hinsdale, Ill.: Dryden Press, 1973.

Scanlon, T. M., 'Rights, Goals and Fairness', in Waldron, J. (ed.), *Theories of Rights*, Oxford: Oxford University Press, 1984.

Schachter, O., 'The Right of States to Use Armed Force', *Michigan Law Review* 82 (1984).

Simester, A., and Sullivan, G., *Criminal Law, Theory and Practice*, Oxford: Hart Publishing, 2000.

Simma, B., 'NATO, the UN and the Use of Force: Legal Aspects', *European Journal of International Law,* 10/1 (1999), 1–22.

Simmons, A. J., 'Locke and the Right to Punish', *Philosophy and Public Affairs* (1991), 311–49.

Smith, J. C., *Justification and Excuse in Criminal Law,* London: Stevens, 1989.

—— and Hogan, B., *Criminal Law,* London: Butterworths, 1992.

Stoessinger, J. G., *Why Nations Go to War,* New York: St Martins Press, 1990.

Stone, R., *Offences against the Person,* London: Cavendish, 1999.

Sumner, L. W., *The Moral Foundation of Rights,* Oxford: Oxford University Press, 1987.

Teichman, J., *Pacifism and the Just War,* Oxford: Basil Blackwell, 1986.

Tesón, F., 'The Kantian Theory of International Law', *Columbia Law Review,* 92 (1996), 53–102.

—— *Humanitarian Intervention, an Inquiry into Law and Morality,* New York: Transnational Publishers Inc., 1997.

—— *A Philosophy of International Law,* Boulder, Colo.: Westview Press, 1997.

Thomson, J. J., 'A Defense of Abortion', *Philosophy and Public Affairs,* 1 (1971), 47–66.

—— 'Self-Defense and Rights', *The Lindley Lecture,* Lawrence, Kan.: Lawrence University of Kansas Publications, 1976.

—— 'Self-Defense', *Philosophy and Public Affairs,* 20 (1991), 283–311.

Thucydides, *History of the Peloponnesian War,* trans. Warner, R., Harmondsworth: Penguin Books, 1954.

Tolstoy, L., *War and Peace,* New York: Norton Critical Edition, 1966.

Tooke, J. D., *The Just War in Aquinas and Grotius,* London: S P C K., 1965.

Uniacke, S., *Permissible Killing, The Self-Defence Justification of Homicide,* Cambridge: Cambridge University Press, 1994.

Vattel, E., *The Law of Nations,* Philadelphia: T. & J. W. Johnson, 1863.

Vitoria, F., *De Indis Relectio Posterior, Sive de Jure Belle* [On the Law of War], in *Vitoria: Political Writings,* Pagden, A., and Lawrence, J. (eds.), Cambridge: Cambridge University Press, 1991.

Waldron, J. (ed.), *Theories of Rights,* Oxford: Oxford University Press, 1984.

—— *Liberal Rights,* Cambridge: Cambridge University Press, 1993.

Walzer, M., *Obligation: Essays on Disobedience, War and Citizenship,* Cambridge, Mass.: Harvard University Press, 1970.

—— 'World War II, Why Was This War Different?' in Cohen, M., Nagel, T., and Scanlon, T. (eds.), *War and Moral Responsibility,* Princeton: Princeton University Press, 1974.

—— *Just and Unjust Wars,* New York: Basic Books, 1977.

—— 'The Moral Standing of States: A Response to Four Critiques', *Philosophy and Public Affairs* (1980), 209–29.

—— 'The Politics of Rescue', *Dissent* (winter 1995), 35–41.

Wasserman, D., 'Justifying Self-Defense', *Philosophy and Public Affairs*, 16 (1987), 356–78.

Wasserstrom, P., *War and Morality*, Belmont: Wadsworth, 1970.

Weisburd, A. M., *Use of Force, the Practice of States since World War II*, Pennsylvania: The Pennsylvania State University Press, 1997.

Wight, M., *Systems of States*, Leicester: Leicester University Press, 1977.

—— *Power Politics*, Harmondsworth: Pelican Books, 1979.

Williams, B., *Ethics and the Limits of Philosophy*, London: Fontana Press, 1985.

Williams, G., 'The Theory of Excuses', *The Criminal Law Review* (1982), 732–42.

Index